T. S. ELIOT   BETWEEN TWO WORLDS

T. S. ELIOT
BETWEEN TWO WORLDS

A READING OF T. S. ELIOT'S POETRY AND PLAYS

DAVID WARD

ROUTLEDGE & KEGAN PAUL
LONDON AND BOSTON

First published in 1973
by Routledge & Kegan Paul Ltd
Broadway House, 68–74 Carter Lane,
London EC4V 5EL and
9 Park Street,
Boston, Mass. 02108, U.S.A.
Printed in Great Britain by
W & J Mackay Limited, Chatham
© David Ward 1973

ISBN 0 7100 7638 X

Library of Congress Catalog Card 73–82371

TO ISABEL

'To you I dedicate this book, to return as best I can
With words a little part of what you have given me.'

CONTENTS

ACKNOWLEDGMENTS

Excerpts from the poetry and plays of T. S. Eliot are reprinted by permission of Faber & Faber and Harcourt Brace Jovanovich. Many people have helped me in many ways in the writing of this book. Professor Jay L. Halio and Dr David Parker have read much of it in earlier versions, and will, I trust, recognize how much the final version owes to them. My students at the University of Malaya and the University of Warwick have taught me far more than I could teach them, not only about Eliot; in particular I must thank Yap Kun Bek for the stimulus her work on Hopkins gave me. Dr Syed Mohammed Naguib al Attas introduced me to Persian poetry; Joyce Hicks and Nancy Bangs hunted 'That Mysterious Rag' to earth. Ann Beaney, Joan Johnson and Marlene Roberts have all had a hand in the typing. My special thanks are due to Ann Clare for preparing the final version with such care and precision.

Parts of this book are based upon articles which originally appeared in *Essays in Criticism*.

ABBREVIATIONS

KE	T. S. Eliot, *Knowledge and Experience in the Philosophy of F. H. Bradley*, London, 1964.
SE	T. S. Eliot, *Selected Essays*, 3rd enlarged edn, London, 1951.
OPP	T. S. Eliot, *On Poetry and Poets*, London, 1957.
TCC	T. S. Eliot, *To Criticize the Critic, and other writings*, London, 1965.
CP	T. S. Eliot, *Collected Plays*, London, 1962.
UPUC	T. S. Eliot, *The Use of Poetry and the Use of Criticism. Studies in the Relation of Criticism to Poetry in England*, London, 1933.
FT	T. S. Eliot, *The Waste Land: a Facsimile and Transcript of the Original Drafts Including the Annotations of Ezra Pound*, edited by Valerie Eliot, London, 1971.
BN	'Burnt Norton'
EC	'East Coker'
DS	'The Dry Salvages'
LG	'Little Gidding'

CHAPTER ONE

'LET US GO THEN, YOU AND I'
POETRY, PHILOSOPHY
AND PRUFROCK

History, perhaps, is a way of explaining the world we experience now; and the explanation is a part of that experience. So, as we construct an account of our history, we tend to project our own most deeply felt present concerns upon an idea of history. From whatever point of view we look at it, history shapes itself to our needs, our fears and our hopes; and we seize upon certain parts of the past as moments which are peculiarly significant to our present, and see them as landmarks: points at which our world, in this or that way, began to be, or at which an old world, which we may regret or deplore, ceased to be.

For most of us, the two decades which culminated in the First World War form such a moment. They are the years in which T. S. Eliot came to maturity, read for his first degree, became deeply involved in the strange world of a 'quaintly antiquated' philosophy, and wrote his first poems. They are the years, too, in which one of those new philosophies which call all in doubt began to subvert old ways of thinking. A man of extraordinary energy and clarity of mind, Bertrand Russell, whose impatience with muddled thinking enabled him to cut through much that was silly, pompous and unnecessarily contorted, at once reduced and extended the range of philosophy to the cut of his own mind. As time goes on we discern more clearly the limitations of Russell's own mind, and the degree to which he was dependent on what we see as the limitations of the world in which he lived. But there was no doubt that he changed the language of philosophy, and he who changes a language changes what the language can say.

Eliot's mind wasn't a clear one in the sense that Russell's was;

part of the antiquatedness of the philosophical discourse in his doctoral thesis, *Knowledge and Experience in the Philosophy of F. H. Bradley*, is his love of pursuing the problems implicit in the vocabulary of philosophy to the point where the vocabulary, indeed the language itself, is close to breaking down. Russell's language is always hard and clear; he is always master of it, in the way a mathematician is master of his symbols. Eliot is led away by language to explore and multiply, rather than to solve, its paradoxes. Eliot's 'academic philosophizing' ended as the First World War ended, and the kind of philosophy which engaged Eliot's interest ended, for all practical purposes, at about that time too. Its most distinguished proponent, Bradley, had begun to sound the retreat already in 1910 in the face of Russell's *Principia Mathematica*, when, in attempting to argue the inconsistency of Russell's views, he had admitted, 'I am ignorant of mathematics, not willingly but through radical incapacity; and again (it is perhaps the same defect) I cannot follow any train of reasoning which is highly abstract',[1] and continued to apologize for the one-sidedness of his criticism of ideas which he could 'only partially comprehend.' Later, Eliot praised Bradley, in somewhat double-edged terms: 'He has the melancholy grace, the languid mastery, of the late product. He has expounded one type of philosophy with such consummate ability that it will probably not survive him' (*KE*, 207). But it was neither because of Bradley, nor, in the end, because of Russell, that the old philosophy died. It died because it was no longer wanted; no longer wanted, that is, in a public world, though its puzzles and problems continue to trouble innumerable private worlds.

What this really means is that, in the course of changing conventions of behaviour, problems such as those which exercised philosophers like Bradley, Bosanquet and Eliot, no longer found their appropriate expression in academic philosophy; no means could be found to justify the continued debate on that level, since formal philosophy had been propelled irresistibly to new conventions of statement and debate, and no formula could immediately be discovered to fit the old questions into the new conventional structure. When this kind of thing happens, and it has happened a number of times in the history of human thought, what had been considered respectable material for speculative and ratiocinative debate tends, again and again, to seek its expression in art, and particularly in poetry.

Russell's method of logical analysis excluded metaphysics. Bradley and Eliot, on the other hand, thrived upon metaphysics as the only means of stating any essential truth about our experience. But Bradleian idealism implies a far more cautious and sceptical approach to metaphysics than those of the traditional metaphysicians who lie behind Donne, Coleridge or Hopkins. Bradley shared this, at least, with philosophers of the schools of Locke and Hume, and for that matter Russell: that he confined his enquiry within what seemed the limits of human understanding. The starting point of knowledge was, for him, 'immediate experience', that is, experience unmediated by the processes of mind which develop experiences into distinctions and relations, subject and object, time, space and causality. This 'immediate experience' thus proposed is by its very nature beyond human understanding, because it is only through the mediation of the distinction and relation making process that we can be said to understand. 'Immediate experience' is therefore merely a projection from what we know: it cannot be known.

And if Bradley is prepared, in a kind of wholly earnest play, to leave the door open to an imagined phase of being in which experience becomes immediate and only immediate, absolute and beyond understanding, to a kind of being which involves 'the suicide of thought',[2] Eliot, in his researching days, was only too anxious to close it again for him, even though as a poet he was to search for the lost key for the rest of his life. In one way Bradley was as thoroughgoing a sceptic as Russell, but constantly, behind his destructive reasoning, one can hear 'the music from a farther room': his ontology, more by implication than by statement, is mystical in quality.

If Bradley was a late product of a philosophical school, Eliot himself was so much later that he only just arrived in time, as it were, to hear the announcement of closure. Bradley had gone just about as far as man could go in a sceptical critique of thought and of language without abandoning thought and language altogether and entering into a mystical silence. While Russell rang the bell, Eliot, with the lively and faithful curiosity of a disciple, tried pushing a few terms here and there a little further, and drew back alarmed and troubled by the apparent consequences.

After he completed his work for his thesis, Eliot discovered that Bradley's world is unified only by an act of faith: 'The Absolute', Eliot writes in 1916, 'responds only to an imaginary demand of feeling. Pretending to be something which makes finite centres cohere, it turns out to be merely the assertion that they do' (*KE*, 202). Eliot's solution to the problem is at this stage somewhat unformed, but there are hints at a new pattern of investigation which was no less a matter of assertion of faith, but which was to lead him far away from the confines of an academic philosophy. The new philosophy declared the problem not to exist. Bradley, for all his elegance and skill, had no finally satisfying answer to the question how we may break out of the windowless shell of our private world; how I may meet you.[3] The puzzle continued to engage Eliot's troubled attention for many years.

In the chapter on solipsism Eliot gestures towards the problem, achieving a rather frigid and incomplete re-statement of Donne's 'No man is an island':

> we are able to intend one world because our points of view are essentially akin. For it is not as if the isolated individuals had contributed each a share and entered into partnership to provide a public world. The selves, on the contrary, find themselves from the start in common dependence on one indifferent Nature. . . . My mind, that is, I must treat as both absolute and derived . . .
>
> (*KE*, 144)

The statement, sceptically cautious as it is about the possibility of communication, asserts without proving it a kind of human community of being, and implies a looking away from the strict rules of philosophical discourse to those speculations about psychology, anthropology, religious and cultural history, which were to fascinate Eliot so much in his later work.

In the conclusion to his thesis, Eliot hints, briefly, at another kind of investigation, akin to the one just mentioned, which is related to an essential theme of his poetry; and hints, too, at the reasons why the arts are the proper way in which the investigation might be carried on. The self as subject is a construction of the metaphysical imagination. But, metaphysically considered, it is not part of that which we know; and metaphysically speaking, there can be no relation between the knower and what is known. The argument is a difficult one, and one which depends upon conventions of meaning and reason which no longer seem relevant. But Eliot allows himself to freewheel sufficiently to admit that this is merely a theoretical standpoint. We can think of self in two different ways; as subject, unknown and unrelated, and as object, in felt continuity with the body, and capable of relating to other objects. The one point of view is valid metaphysically, the other needed epistemologically and, indeed, needed for our survival. And fine arts, perhaps, have developed in this way. The activity of art begins, perhaps, as simply a behavioural pattern—what we might loosely call self-expression. But as we become self-conscious, as we think of self as object, and relate self as object to other objects, we become aware of aesthetic reactions to objects. Art, then, cannot exist without self-consciousness; and self-consciousness implies duality: ourselves observing ourselves, ourselves as subject and ourselves as object.

Thus, though both Eliot and Bradley would deny the ultimate validity of distinctions between subject and object, real and ideal, both recognize the essential duality of human thought. Immediate reality cannot be known; what can be known is known by a doubling of the world and thus, to speak somewhat loosely, a doubling of the self.

In the development of Eliot's thought, these ideas must have seemed in some sense continuous or parallel with certain other ideas which, though they too belong to that same crucial moment of time, will not seem quite so distant to a modern reader. Eliot went to Harvard in 1906, and there fell under the influence of Irving Babbitt, one of the most important educational theorists in America at that time, though his theory was largely, in the literal sense, reactionary. American universities and colleges were at this time moving decisively towards the elective system. Babbitt balked at what he felt to be the extreme libertarianism that this produced in education; he distrusted the tendency towards 'doing as one likes' as much as that other great humanist, Matthew Arnold, whom he resembles in some important ways. Civilization, he felt, and therefore education for civilization, should depend as much upon restraint as upon expansive energy; the *frein vital* is at least as important in education, indeed in the whole scheme of life, as *élan vital*.

He traced the self-destructive obsession of society with freedom, freedom at the expense of self-restraint, back to the beginnings of Romanticism in Jean-Jacques Rousseau, and in his championing of the unpopular virtue of self-control identified humanism with Classicism; the inner curb upon licence and will was, he declared, a necessary condition for being human.

Nowadays Babbitt is very little read. Readers of Eliot will know something of his name and ideas from two essays in *Selected Essays*:

[5]

'The Humanism of Irving Babbitt' and 'Second Thoughts about Humanism.' The essays are hostile, and understandably so in view of the fact that Eliot had just been converted to Anglicanism in 1927, one year before the appearance of the first essay. Eliot takes Babbitt to task for attempting to offer humanism as an alternative to religion, and interprets this as meaning that humanism can be and should be a *substitute* for religion. In *Democracy and Leadership*, Babbitt makes a distinction between humanism and humanitarianism; between a civilized discipline of self-control and a general feeling of benevolence towards humanity, derived from humanism, but without its inner logic and strength. Eliot asks if humanism doesn't bear the same relationship to religion as humanitarianism does to humanism, whether it isn't 'a derivative of religion which will work only for a short time in history, and only for a few highly cultivated people like Mr. Babbitt—whose ancestral traditions, furthermore, are Christian, and who is, like many people, at the distance of a generation or so from definite Christian belief. Is it, in other words, durable beyond one or two generations?' (*SE*, 472).

Elsewhere, however, Eliot has other things to say about Babbitt. In 1937, writing in the *Princeton Alumni Weekly*, he says of Babbitt and of Paul Elmer More, Babbitt's humanist colleague who had later, like Eliot, taken the road to Anglicanism 'these seem to me the two *wisest* men that I have known.' And it does seem significant that Eliot, so shortly after his conversion, should have chosen to write on *Democracy and Leadership*, which had after all been in print for four years, in the 1928 essay, 'The Humanism of Irving Babbitt.' It is as if, as part of his declaration of a radically new position, he had to declare his stand against the most powerful and appealing arguments, the arguments which tempted him most, on the other side.

It will be worthwhile, then, to look a little more deeply into Babbitt's humanism, and to set it into the context of its time. The context of Babbitt's thought was in many important ways similar to the context of Bradley's thought. Babbitt was by no means a professional philosopher like Bradley; he was a critic, cultural historian, and a student of society. But like Bradley he was faced by the perennial Platonic problem of the one and the many. Neither man found it possible to accept traditional solutions to the problem without alteration. Their own solutions differ, but resemble each other's in certain ways.

Briefly and simply stated, the problem is this. Our daily experience offers us a plurality of objects. We think of these as separate from each other, but at the same time we think of them as part of a total single pattern of relationships which is ultimately one. If we push one of these modes of thinking to its conclusion we can become pluralists, and think of the universe as a collection of diverse and separate objects, each of which is essentially itself and not part of a whole. If we push the other mode of thinking to its conclusion we become monists, and see the universe as a single substance, and each object as an aspect of the whole. Bradley, with an agility and subtlety which is incomparable and perhaps also absurd, took the monist stance; but as we have already seen, he allowed that, though reality is ultimately one, human understanding is necessarily dual in character, dividing all reality into subjects and objects, reals and ideals, in order to make sense of the universe. Babbitt and More took a different position, and one can see in that position the truth of Eliot's charge that humanism of the Babbitt variety, is, as it were, parasitic upon the Christian tradition. Their position was that the world exists simultaneously upon two levels: the level of the flesh and of matter, and the level of mind and spirit. The task of the humanist, the task of being human, is to achieve the correct relationship between the two worlds. More wrote a series of books called *The Greek Tradition*, developing this point in its historical perspective, and seeing a continuity between the Platonic tradition and the Christian precisely in the stress they place upon the duality of man. 'Our purpose', he writes, is 'to show that the Incarnation . . . is, as it claims to be, the one essential dogma of Christianity, that the philosophy underlying it conforms to our deepest spiritual experience, that it is the mythological expression (using the word "mythological" in no derogatory sense) of the Platonic dualism, and thus forms a proper consummation of the Greek tradition.'[4]

In the article cited earlier from the *Princeton Alumni Weekly*, Eliot expresses his deep interest in these volumes, saying how he came to find in them 'an auxiliary to my own progress of thought', and the kind of help which the English theologians, born and brought up in a secure tradition of Christian thought and feeling, could not give him. 'It was of the greatest importance, then, to have at hand the work of a man who had come by somewhat the same route, to almost the same conclusions, at almost the same time.'

The similarities in the two men's careers are, indeed, striking in many ways. Both More and Eliot began their intellectual life with a study of the Classics at a time when classical humanist education was beginning to decline in importance as universities began to concern themselves more and more with the immediate practicalities of science, technology, and modern humanist studies. Eliot went on from his undergraduate courses in Greek literature and prose composition, the history of ancient art and ancient philosophy, Latin poetry and the Roman novel, to take as a graduate a course which More had taken seventeen years before, Lanman's course in Indic philology, a course which led them both to a lifelong interest in Vedic and Buddhist religion. But most striking of all was the way in which they moved from Babbitt's humanism, with its stress upon the fundamental dualism of the human experience and upon the importance of the European tradition, to the Anglican faith as the only vital remaining vehicle of that tradition of dualism.

More and Eliot, and Babbitt also, found the origin of this dualistic philosophy in ancient Indian religion, and saw it as the essential bond between the great religions of the world and humanism:[5]

> This idea that man needs to submit his ordinary self to a higher or divine will is essential not merely to Christianity, but to all genuine religion. . . . In India, though the same preoccupation with the will has prevailed, the will to which man subordinates his ordinary self is often conceived, not as a divinity that transcends him, but as his own higher self. Buddha eliminates many things that are accounted essential in other faiths, including Christianity, but this opposition between man's higher or ethical will and his natural self or expansive desires he does not eliminate. On the contrary, more than any other religious teacher, he plants himself on the naked psychological fact of this opposition; so that Buddhism, in its original form, is the most critical or, if one prefer, the least mythological of religions.

In his criticisms of humanism, Eliot attacks Babbitt and Norman Foerster with their own weapons, suggesting that the dialectic of their humanism rests far too much on the ambiguities of the word human. When they use the word 'human' in opposition to 'natural', he implies, they must really mean 'supernatural', and they are thus smuggling into their discourse of argument a concept that they deny strenuously elsewhere. 'For I am convinced', says Eliot, 'that if this "supernatural" is suppressed (I avoid the word "spiritual" because it can mean almost anything), the *dualism* of man and nature collapses at once' (*SE*, 485).

In other words, in whatever ways Eliot is opposed to Babbitt's humanism, there is a real continuity between his later Christianity and his earlier humanism. Though he rejects Babbitt's dogmatic position, he accepts completely his stress upon certain guiding concepts: tradition, the need for restraint, the superiority of the Classical over the Romantic temper, and above all the dualism of human existence. He simply finds that these concepts, necessary as they are for the survival of the truly human, cannot have meaning in an individualistic ethic such as Protestantism, or a humanism such as Babbitt's which appears to grow from the decay of Protestantism.

Both Eliot and Babbitt stressed the need for tradition, and both in some sense or other felt that tradition is the embodiment of that same ultimate kinship of man, a more positive community of spirit than the dependence on an indifferent nature of which Eliot spoke in his thesis. Both accepted that tradition, and more important, true humanity, depended upon some kind of ascetic programme; the submission of natural desire and will to something more complete and comprehensive, something above the natural. But where Babbitt spoke of a higher self, Eliot looks for the consummation of man in something which cannot be called self; in a community of spirit which shall have its positive embodiment, not merely in idea, but in act; not merely in tradition, but in myth, ritual and creed.

This leads us to a curious, and very important, problem. Babbitt's dualist stance led him into a clear and strong rejection of any monist position: 'Monism is merely a fine name that man has invented for his own indolence and unwillingness to mediate between the diverse and conflicting aspects of reality.'[6] More carried this doctrine and this attitude over into his Christianity. The reason why he chose to enter the Anglican rather than the Roman communion was that Anglicanism seemed to him to preserve the essential Graeco-Christian tradition of dualism, and that Roman Catholicism tended to abandon it for a monistic heresy. Paul, Augustine, and the English divines of the seventeenth century kept the true faith and the true tradition; while Aquinas, Dante and the Jesuits seemed to More, possibly because he didn't entirely understand them, to be a huge and disastrous diversion away from responsibility to the ultimate problem: 'The central truth of dualism'—and, More would add, the essential starting point for Christian understanding—'is a recognition of the absolute distinction between the two elements of our conscious being and an admission of the impossibility of finding any rationally positive explanation of the mutual interaction of these two elements.'[7]

More accuses Eliot of failing to grasp this point in a lively exchange of letters which followed when Eliot sent his essay on Dante to More in 1930. More expressed his detestation of Dante's mediaeval heartlessness and cruelty. Eliot accused More of being merely a humanitarian. More returns to the attack by accusing Eliot of the heresy of monism, and adds: 'your deity is not the Jehovah of the Psalmist nor the [*sic*] of Christ, but an abortion sprung of the unholy coupling of the Aristotelian Absolute and the Phoenician Moloch; you are a Mohammedan or Calvinist, no Catholic. . . . Evidently the *fons et origo* of all this mischief is a form of that damnable sin of the reason called monism. For you the universe is God, or God is the ultimate unique course of the universe, which two are about the same thing.'[8]

The exchange gives us a way of characterizing the difference between the two men. More's dogma of dualism is a way of converting his generalized humanitarian instincts into a religious programme: his thought moves from the one pole to the other. The two poles of Eliot's thought were a humanistic dualism and an ontological monism—whereas More sought to escape from vague benevolence by accepting the terrible paradox of dualism, Eliot sought some final assurance that this doubleness was not all. So that, while both More and Eliot traced with fascination the Graeco-Christian and the Hindu-Buddhist traditions to discover traditional support for their account of the double nature of natural man, More's concern in this was simply to establish the wisdom of a dualistic philosophy, while Eliot sought for a solution to the dilemma.

I shall argue, then, that from the early 'Prufrock': 'Let us go then, you and I', to the late 'Little Gidding': 'So I assumed a double part', the consciousness of dualism is there, but so is the 'overwhelming question', and it is characteristic that his last great poem should end with the assertion of faith in the ultimate atonement:

> And all shall be well and
> All manner of thing shall be well
> When the tongues of flame are in-folded
> Into the crowned knot of fire
> And the fire and the rose are one.

(*LG*, V)

—the search to find this singleness and harmony was, more than anything else, the urgent force behind Eliot's creative impulse.

We can now begin to see what attracted Eliot to the study of Bradley's monism, and also what he found to be ultimately unsatisfactory in it: 'Bradley's universe, actual only in finite centres, is only by an act of faith unified' (*KE*, 202), but yet the faith is insecure and unexplained. Eliot's own version of the dogma in the essay on Leibniz and Bradley is no more satisfactory in this respect:

> The concepts of centre, of soul, and of self and personality must be kept distinct. The point of view from which each soul is a world in itself must not be confused with the point of view from which each soul is only the function of a physical organism, a unity perhaps only partial, capable of alteration, development, having a history and a structure, a beginning and apparently an end. And yet these two souls are the same. And if the two points of view are irreconcilable, yet on the other hand neither would exist without the other, and they melt into each other by a process which we cannot grasp.
>
> (*KE*, 205–6)

But if we cannot grasp the process by which the two are made one, how is it that we know that they are one? From Russell onwards the question becomes meaningless in philosophy, but the problem remains the instinctive impulse behind metaphysical enquiry; and metaphysical speculation is, for good or ill, so deep-seated a human habit that it is bound to survive the philosophers' abolition of those terms which make the paradox possible. It will even survive religion. The only thing that it could not survive, perhaps, is the death of art.

For Bradley, metaphysical thought aims constantly at 'the suicide of thought'. Thought, he says, cannot transcend the dualism of the 'that' and the 'what', and yet constantly aims to transcend it. Suppose for a moment that thought achieves this aim: thought would have destroyed itself. It would become absorbed in a fuller experience:[9]

> It will, in short, be an existence which is not mere truth. Thus, in reaching a whole which can contain every aspect within it, thought must absorb what divides it from feeling and will. But when these all have come together, then, since none of

[11]

them can perish, they must be merged in a whole in which they are harmonious. But that whole assuredly is not simply *one* of its aspects. And the question is *not* whether the universe is in any sense intelligible. The question is whether, if you thought it and understood it, there would be no difference left between your thought and the thing.

If one were to wish to state a theme which unites the whole of Eliot's major work, it is this theme of a divided sensibility seeking for unity; and each of the poems, and in a rather different manner the plays, can be seen as moments in the search. But we must be clear on this point: it is better to see the unifying theme as sentiment rather than philosophical thesis. Various philosophical or quasi-philosophical forms which the sentiment takes in the work of Eliot and his teachers have been touched upon, but, much though these various statements have in common in their stress upon patterns of dualism, there are many differences between them, and Eliot's poetic argument does not, precisely, follow any of them. Philosophical argument may help to form a mind, and if the mind is that of a poet, the poems he writes will be affected, profoundly perhaps, by the philosophy. But to place the philosophy first and the poetry after is a mistake; there is no priority, but constant interchange, and in Eliot, in whom the poetic imagination is far more effective than the philosophical, poetic skills and habits distort the philosophical imagination until it is almost unrecognizable. This is true even in the overtly philosophic discourse, where the occasional literary critical *dicta* spring to life in the midst of an infuriatingly obsolete and irrelevant pattern of philosophical argument.

The 'I' and the 'you', then, which seek to be 'we' or 'one' in the poetic argument are not to be identified simply with any of the opposed couplet terms in the philosophic discourse. The various puzzles proposed by the philosopher return in radically changed ways in the poetry, but it would be nonsense to treat them as philosophy poeticized, as one might, for instance, treat Lucretius or Pope's *Essay on Man*. There are places in Eliot where philosophy and poetry are organized, as they are sometimes in Dante, so that poetry and philosophy depend on each other, are each other. But at these points the philosophy is as new as the poetry. For the most part philosophical ideas merely provide structures or symbols as philosophic myth, and disappear into the poetry.

[12]

Many critics have rightly directed the attention of the reader of 'The Love Song of J. Alfred Prufrock' to the epigraph:

If I believed that my reply would be to someone who ever would return to the world, this flame would wag no more. But because, if what I hear be true, no one ever does return alive from this depth, I reply to you without fear of infamy.

The speaker is in hell, and gives as his reason for speaking freely without fear of scandal his belief that nobody who listens to him could ever possibly return from hell to a real world. The reader is claimed as a companion in suffering—challenged, as he is by the quotation from Baudelaire in *The Waste Land*, 'You—hypocrite lecteur, mon semblable, mon frère', as a companion in suffering and in hypocrisy. We can, I believe, take this epigraph together with the general epigraph to the whole volume: 'Can you understand, then, how much love warms me towards you when I forgot our vanity, treating the shadows as a solid thing.'

The Love Song's epigraph (appropriately since it is spoken by Guido, a man condemned to hell for his continued attachment to the world), treats the world as a reality which is desirable, but never can be achieved again.

The general epigraph to the volume makes the world itself a place of shadows in contrast to another, more real world. It reminds us irresistibly of a tradition of feeling and thought, of which Bradley, with his distinction between appearance and reality, is but a late example. Plato had man standing with his back to the bright light of reality looking at a world of shadows dancing on the cave wall in front of him, and treating the shadows as solid things. And the preacher in *Ecclesiastes* 12, speaking of the moment when dust shall return to the earth, and the spirit return to God, says 'Vanity of vanities, all is vanity.'

'The Love Song of J. Alfred Prufrock', then, should be seen as an essay of the soul which takes place in a world of illusion, suffering, and hypocritical self-deception, a world which we, as readers, are expected to recognize as like the world we ordinarily call real. But illusion implies a reality; and reality lies behind the shadow world of illusion and deceit in both epigraphs and the poem.

The poem is a love song, and we can take the hint of the general epigraph and see the love which the song expresses as love in a world of shadows, a shadow itself of a 'real' love, possible only in a world which is not shadow, a world (to accept the Platonic image) of light. In a world of shadows, then 'you and I' begin a journey. In so far as the poem addresses the reader, the 'you' of 'you and I' is the reader; but the reader is claimed as part of the action, as he is in: 'hypocrite lecteur, mon semblable, mon frère.' The reader is drawn into the persona by insidious invitation, not only as a fellow conspirator, but as part of a unit—'you and I'.

It is impossible to tell exactly how much Eliot knew of Bradley when he wrote this poem. It seems to have been written during the year before he began formal work for his doctorate, so it is at least very likely that he knew *Appearance and Reality* well. But this matters little. The instincts which led him to concern himself with Bradleian problems express themselves in his verse already: his work on Bradley isn't so much a discovery of the paradox of point of view as an attempt to settle it somehow. And at the core of the paradox, as we have seen, is the problem of subject and object. In *Knowledge and Experience* Eliot quotes Bradley with approval: 'At every moment my state, whatever else it is, is a whole of which I am immediately aware. It is an experienced non-relational unity of many in one.'[10] It follows from this that the division between subject and object is in no way essential to feeling. The distinction is, however, necessary to thought: immediate experience may be a unity, but thought depends upon a duality of subject and object. That which is thought of as object is so interpreted because of 'its felt continuity with other feelings which fall outside of the finite centre, and the subject becomes a subject by its felt continuity with a core of feeling which is not related to the object' (*KE*, 21).

Thus, in a simple sentence like 'I love you', 'I hate you' or equally 'I hit you' or 'I see you', the 'you' of the sentence might be said to be an aspect of 'my' feeling or experience. From another point of view, 'I' might be thought of as a kind of fiction, a device which signals the focusing of all that is the experience of loving, hating, hitting and seeing, you, she, he and it, into a single centre of feeling. The puzzle, modern philosophers would argue, is meaningless. It's sufficient that the reader should grasp that the subject 'I' and the object, as well as time and space, are here thought of as tools which the mind uses for understanding and shaping immediate experience, 'a timeless unity which is not as such present either any*where* or to any*one*.' It is by these mediating processes, Eliot remarks, that 'we find ourselves as conscious souls in a world of objects' (*KE*, 24). We can see some part of this process in the development of a child; record the points at which its actions show that it recognizes moving and static objects, colours, shapes, space and time, as it learns to use the methods of discrimination which are integral to thought. But if the human mind discriminates in order to think, there's another process at work at the same time; the instinct for metaphor, for bringing together again the diverse objects which judgment tells us must be kept separate. This process is as much at the heart of Eliot's poetry as it is at the heart of Donne's, or Pope's or Wordsworth's:

> Let us go then, you and I,
> When the evening is spread out against the sky
> Like a patient etherised upon a table.

The image was considered daring, indeed rather shocking, when it first appeared. The reader of poetry in 1915, and indeed most readers today, would feel safer if the sunset were compared to a woman's smile, or a rose in full bloom. And yet there's nothing more daring in comparing a sunset to a patient in an operating theatre than there would be in comparing it to Miss Jones's lips, or the Ena Harkness rose she has just pricked her lovely fingers on. What did Burns mean, for instance, when he said 'My love is like a red red rose'? Clearly not that her stem is covered in thorns and she lives in a plant pot. The simile describes a relationship, not so much between woman and rose, but between two other relationships, two other sets of subject and object, poet and woman, poet and rose. What is ultimately described is neither woman nor rose but a state of feeling in which the distinction between subject and object is blurred, and what one might more normally describe as an emotion of the subject is transferred on to the object. The simple process is essentially the same in 'Prufrock' as it is in Burns. It does not describe evening or patient primarily, but the 'I' who is the subject of the poem, a state of feeling that is passive, and mimics death.

The poem is a love song sung in a world of shadows; a song not of fulfilment, but of desire. Desire for what? We are asked not to ask: it is the overwhelming question, but 'do not ask, "What is it?"/Let us go and make our visit.' Since the question is never asked in the poem, the answer is never given, only an answer that is feared: 'That is not what I meant at all./That is not it, at all,' and the fear tells us nothing exact about the question. It does, however, as part of the extended metaphor of the poem, tell us something about the experience and the feeling which lie behind the unasked question.

This is compounded of fear and of desire; the fear of that which is desired. The condition of desire for the unattainable, a condition combined with fear of the consummation of that desire, is a psychological state that has long been recognized. It even has a name, 'nympholepsy' (possession by nymphs). Irving Babbitt has a long passage in *Rousseau and Romanticism* in which he discusses the phenomenon as one of the central phenomena of Romanticism.[11] Babbitt characterizes Dante as a nympholept with religious overtones, Shelley and Chateaubriand as secular nympholepts. Novalis's equivalent to Dante's Beatrice was Sophie von Kühn, and for Novalis, as for Dante, the nympholeptic obsession is complicated by religious longings. In his devotional songs the blue flower resolves into a beautiful female face, that of Sophie, which escapes the rapt lover, always receding as he approaches, so that it can never be overtaken. And Shelley, who habitually employs the imagery of divine longing for his secular nympholeptic yearnings, adapts a passage from St Augustine's *Confessions* (which curiously appears directly after the passage 'To Carthage then I came' which Eliot uses in *The Waste Land*) as epigraph for *Alastor: Nondum amabam, et amare amabam, quaerebam quid amarem, amans amare*, 'I did not love yet, yet I longed to love, I searched for something to love, in love with love.'[12]

This theme of romantic longing is clearly there in 'Prufrock', as it is elsewhere in Eliot. For instance, in a comment on Stendhal and Flaubert written not very long after 'Prufrock' was published, he remarks that the greatness of these two novelists lies largely in the way that they 'suggest unmistakably the awful separation between potential passion and any actualization possible in life.' He adds, linking the observation with another that recalls an obsessional puzzle that we have met before, 'They indicate also the indestructible barriers between one human being and another.'[13]

A double soul, then, sings a song of unattainable desire, and of fear at what will result when desire should be consummated. The song is one in which, as in Dante, Novalis and Shelley, the religious metaphor lies side by side with the erotic; and the juxtapositions seem to be there not merely for the shock effect of the contrast. On the contrary, the hinted preparations for seduction in

> Should I, after tea and cakes and ices
> Have the strength to force the moment to its crisis?

merge with surprising ease, first into the language of religious mourning, and then into Prufrock's burlesque comparison of himself with
St John the Baptist:

> But though I have wept and fasted, wept and prayed,
> Though I have seen my head (grown slightly bald),
> > brought in upon a platter;
> I am no prophet—and here's no great matter.

And later, when Prufrock wonders

> Would it have been worth while
> To have bitten off the matter with a smile,
> To have squeezed the universe into a ball
> To roll it towards some overwhelming question

—mimicking Marvell's lover in his erotic determination to cheat time
for the sake of love—the transition is easy into the religious metaphor:

> To say: 'I am Lazarus, come from the dead,
> Come back to tell you all, I shall tell you all'.

Here 'I', imagining fearfully what it would be like to return like
Dante from the ultimate experience of Hell and Heaven, once more is
betrayed into the habit of dualism; 'I' would tell 'you' all. The
doubleness remains, and remains above all in the fear of what 'one'
would say, the fear that one-ness, expressed in the erotic metaphor
of the unattainable someone disappointing the sexual experiment,
would somehow deceive, or defeat, or not be what was expected. So
Prufrock stands at the door of life listening to the music from a farther
room, and the eternal footman snickers both at his presumption and
at his fear.

If thought's suicide could be attained, says Bradley, the mind
would no longer move in its accustomed pattern of dialectic between
existence and characteristic: it would experience reality, immediate
reality, 'a harmonious system of ideal contents united by relations,
and reflecting itself in a self-conscious harmony.'[14] It would be
impossible to achieve this end without thought changing its character
entirely, because thought as we know it depends on distinction, relation and duality. The end, if we could achieve it would be:[15]

An immediate, self-dependent, all-inclusive individual. But in reaching this perfection, and in the act of reaching it, thought would lose its own character. Thought does desire such individuality, that is precisely what it aims at. But individuality, on the other hand, cannot be gained while we are confined to relations.

In short, if our humanity consists in our being able to think, and if thought constantly aims at attaining individuality (an end to the duality of experience), then our humanity constantly aims at destruction of itself. 'Prufrock' is a poem which dramatizes our humanity precisely in this respect, and 'you and I' are dramatizations of the single human experience in its necessary duality, seeking, yet fearing, its consummation in a singleness which is at the other end of thought.

At one point Prufrock wishes for a state *below* that of humanity:

> I should have been a pair of ragged claws
> Scuttling across the floors of silent seas.

At others he dramatizes the way in which his mind trembles upon the edge of single consciousness, vacillating between visions and revisions, and self-consciously mocking himself for the portentousness of his half-known desires by returning to the idle rituals of time, or turning back from the moment when he might challenge the universe with utter annihilation of time and self with a wry remark about his balding hair:

> Time for you and time for me
> And time yet for a hundred indecisions,
> And for a hundred visions and revisions,
> Before the taking of a toast and tea.
>
> In the room the women come and go
> Talking of Michelangelo.
>
> And indeed there will be time
> To wonder, 'Do I dare' and 'Do I dare?'
> Time to turn back and descend the stair
> With a bald spot in the middle of my hair.

The question really is an overwhelming one, because its answer is 'annihilation and utter night' (*KE*, 31), the entire destruction of consciousness as we understand it. Constantly Prufrock is pulled back by the world of objects, sunsets and dooryards and sprinkled streets, novels and teacups and skirts that trail along the floor. He is like Shelley's parody of Wordsworth in Peter Bell the Third, who longed to lift the hem of nature's shift and drew back in prudish fear: and his name, Pru-frock, suggests the prudish and yet prudent delicacy of the flirtation.

Metaphysical fear and metaphysical longing may be a motive for the poet just as much as they may be for the philosopher. For the poet, though, they combine with other fears and other longings. In Donne, or St John of the Cross, Dante or Novalis, they merge into the language of sexual desire and sexual defeat, and in the greatest of all love songs, the Song of Solomon, the interpenetration of religious and sexual *motifs* has produced a whole literature of exegesis which is sometimes, perhaps, absurd in its anxiety to suppress the erotic as merely metaphor for the divine; just as Freudian criticism, some-times, becomes absurd in its anxiety to suppress the divine in favour of the erotic significances of religious feeling. 'Prufrock' deals with both erotic and metaphysical desires; each desire is an image for the other, and twines in with its counterpart in an entirely natural way.

Both point to the same thing, a soul divided against itself. There is an 'I' who longs, but does not dare; who is bored with the dreary routine, but depends upon it entirely; who dreams of prophecy and decisive, world shattering action, but knows his limitations; who loves the sensuous detail of the world, but is disgusted by it; who is sickly self-conscious, obsessed by questions of behaviour and appear-ance, but mocks himself for it; who is capable of visionary perception, but shrugs it off, deflates it with a mild quip. And there is a 'you' who is much less active and melodramatic; a 'you' who is concealed under all the flamboyant self-dramatization. It is 'you' who would be faced with the overwhelming question, but must be warned not to ask it; who would be told all, if 'I' could bring himself, like Hercules, Christ, Lazarus or Dante, to return from death with the secret of reality; it is 'you' that is besieged throughout the dreary monotony of time with hands that drop a question on your plate and faces that must be avoided by the elaborate masks of pretence.

'I' is the player within one, the 'attendant lord' who struts and frets his hour upon the stage, but in him action is evasion: he is torn between sensation and dream. 'You' is more potentiality than act or dream; capable of a different kind of knowledge, not simply hearing 'the music from a farther room', but, as it were, capable of being it; not sharing the fear and self-consciousness of 'I', but cheated by it of the knowledge that 'I' as Lazarus, might acquire through death, cheated of the 'Absolute Zero' of self-destruction in an impersonal reality.

The debate is not precisely between body and soul. It is a debate within the soul, if you like; though the word 'soul' itself would be open to critical enquiry from Eliot's philosophical position. It is a dramatisation of a conflict in points of view. In order to explain our knowledge of objects we construct the notion of a self which relates to the objects around us, which exists in a world of objects and is itself an object: 'the function of a physical organism, a unity perhaps only partial, capable of alteration, development, having a history and a structure, a beginning and apparently an end' (*KE*, 206). We may call this the personality, and in 'Prufrock' it is dramatized as 'I'. But from another point of view, the point of view from which we search for metaphysical reality, the soul is a world in itself, and incapable of relating to objects in the world around us. 'You' dramatizes this other point of view, soul as impersonal, unfeeling, and without relationships.

Prufrock evades the question, remains divided, is incorrigibly human, and in the conclusion to the poem his cowardice and his humanity are dramatized in the language of Romantic nympholepsy. The cue here is in part Eliot's old teacher Babbitt, in part a line from Gérard de Nerval's 'El Desdichado':

> J'ai rêvé dans la grotte où nage la sirène
> (I dreamed in the cave where the siren swims).

Despite the characteristic switch from a tone of self-conscious buffoonery to the language of romantic longing, the ending is very beautiful in a romantic way. The rapid change of tone is disturbing, but possible, in a way that wouldn't have been possible in the nineteenth century, because Eliot is writing what is strictly speaking a metaphysical poem, and the co-existence of romantic longing and the flippancy of the buffoon is as consistent here as it is in Nabokov's *Lolita*, which deals with a somewhat similar state of consciousness.

> I shall wear white flannel trousers, and walk upon the beach.
> I have heard the mermaids singing, each to each.
>
> I do not think that they will sing to me.

I have seen them riding seaward on the waves
Combing the white hair of the waves blown back
When the wind blows the water white and black.

We have lingered in the chambers of the sea
By sea-girls wreathed with seaweed red and brown
Till human voices wake us, and we drown.

Throughout, the state of unsatisfied longing, indecision and inaction has been expressed in a series of interlinked images of passivity
and unreality: the evening like an anaesthetized patient gives way to
the shifting cat-like fog which falls asleep around the cityscape and
muffles all. This gives way at last to the monotony of 'time' repeated
with rhetorical urgency until it flows into all experience with the in-
vasive subtlety of the fog. Now at the end the sea takes the place of
time and fog as the image of the all-embracing atmosphere of the
world of 'you and I'. There is some memory of Odysseus and the
islands of Circe and the Lotos eaters; perhaps too of Plato's myth of
the world in the *Phaedo*:

> For our earth, and the stones, and the entire region which sur-
> rounds us, are spoilt and corroded, as in the sea all things are
> corroded by the brine, neither is there any noble or perfect
> growth, but caverns only, and sand, and an endless slough of
> mud.
>
> (*Phaedo*, 110D)

But it has the beauty of a dream world; its sinister and destructive
character is only revealed when a soul caught by sea-nymphs is
awakened from its nympholeptic longing to the discovery of its
divisive human condition.

All this leads us to another question, not quite so overwhelming
as Prufrock's, perhaps, but important enough for all who care for
literature, and see it not merely as an accidental by-product of human
thought or feeling, but the activity, above all, in which man's most
deep engagement with life and reality is expressed in the most subtle
and powerful ways. Eliot's dictum, 'genuine poetry can communicate
before it is understood', is a way of stating the proper precedences in
our response to poetry, though it begs a number of questions;
'Prufrock', it is certainly true, 'communicates' a good deal before we
enter into the sorting and defining processes we have just been

[21]

through, and even so we will not 'understand' it unless it has, to begin with, 'communicated'. This doesn't make it unnecessary or undesirable, though, to take the further step and seek understanding: as Eliot says of Dante,

> you cannot afford to *ignore* Dante's philosophical and religious beliefs, or to skip the passages which express them most clearly . . . on the other hand you are not called upon to believe them yourself. . . . The vital matter is that Dante's poem is a whole; you must in the end come to understand every part in order to understand any part.
>
> (*SE*, 257-8)

'Prufrock' isn't the *Divina Commedia*, and if one uses the word 'belief' about the ideas that go into it, one must use the word in a slightly different way: 'Prufrock' isn't an *assertion* in the way that Dante's poem is; it's a series of questions, and a state of mind that is shaped like a question mark. 'Belief' then, is almost off the mark; there is, however, a way in which it is applicable—even the most sceptical question begins with certain assumptions, and one of the assumptions is that certain questions are worth asking.

The whole structure of the poem, from the hesitant, looping syntax of the first paragraph to the end, renders the state of indecision and doubt primarily by methods other than statement. One could make a precis of the opening thus:

> Let us go then, you and I,
> . . . through certain half-deserted streets
> which lead you to an overwhelming question
> . . . Oh, do not ask, 'What is it?'
> Let us go and make our visit.

All the rest is, in one way, unnecessary, except that it delivers to us a personality, a special state of mind, shuffling, indirect, irrelevant, evasive of purpose. For the time being we do not need translations of epigraphs; we don't really need to puzzle about you and I, taking this simply, perhaps, as an invitation to ourselves to join the expedition. And we respect, for the time being, the injunction not to ask questions, recognizing this, again, as characteristic of the fearful wincing state of consciousness the poem invites us to experience.

We have already been warned that we are not to expect a compact unified discourse; now we are switched away prematurely from the

[22]

direction that the opening, with tremblings, hesitations and diversions, has given us. We are cheated of direction; given merely an accidental image of movement and indirection, of somewhat shallow, perhaps, but perhaps also poignantly attractive conversation: an impression which enters as a sensation rather than a thought, into a consciousness which by its unwillingness to state purpose, its sudden transitions once the question of purpose crops up, betrays a shying obsession with purpose or meaning, and a love of hiding from it in the accidental, disconnected image:

> In the room the women come and go
> Talking of Michelangelo.

And then, still indirectly, the mind which we are experiencing wanders into an image of the torpid uncertainty of its emotions, the closeness and warm yet slightly threatening comfort of fog, entering everywhere, not just in a city but in a mind, closing out sight, sound and movement, restricting the consciousness to a narrow sleepy indolence.

The skill and subtlety of this kind of progression is the reason why we read the poem, certainly; not to find out what Eliot thinks about experience. But if the poem communicates before we understand it, it communicates in a different way after we have entered into the puzzle of meaning.

'FROM HAM TO HAM'
POEMS, 1909-1920

The poems of the *Prufrock* volume were not designed as a unity, but they share many of the same themes and concerns. 'Preludes', for instance, echoes, or is echoed by 'Prufrock' in

> His soul stretched tight across the skies
> That fade behind a city block,

and continues, like 'Prufrock', to create and exploit a curious uncertainty about the relationship between the object and the perceiver, creating a world in which souls stretch across skies and streets have consciences:

> The conscience of a blackened street
> Impatient to assume the world.

The carefully involved ambiguities suggested in words like 'conscience' and 'assume' here give way, as they do in 'Prufrock', to a hint at a redemptive vision, which is yet not given any definition other than that of yearning emotion which accompanies it.

> I am moved by fancies that are curled
> Around these images, and cling:
> The notion of some infinitely gentle
> Infinitely suffering thing.

'Preludes' ends with rather too heavily pointed melodrama, which makes the effect of the wistful vision less rather than more intense; in this slight lack of control it resembles 'Rhapsody on a Windy Night', the ending of which is another rather over-dramatized gesture of pain:

'The bed is open; the tooth-brush hangs on the wall,
Put your shoes at the door, sleep, prepare for life.'

The last twist of the knife.

But the melodrama is not the only thing which links it to 'Preludes', or 'Prufrock'. Both 'Prufrock' and 'Preludes' are sceptical about experience; the 'Rhapsody' makes of memory, and of experience as a whole, a shifting and uncertain thing:

Whispering lunar incantations
Dissolve the floors of memory
And all its clear relations,
Its divisions and precisions.

The dissolution of the normal rules of relation, the abandonment of the normal method and sequence of thought is perhaps only so that the poet can allow himself free rein for a modish sequence of 'imagistic' verses. But it foreshadows a more complex kind of investigation which begins from the same point.

A fine early example of this more subtle exploration of memory and experience is 'La Figlia che Piange', a poem which has suffered from being prematurely popular, and popular for the wrong reasons. It is the poem most likely to appeal to a sensibility not yet attuned to Eliot's frequently bizarre language and his characteristically abrupt changes of tone and mood, but for all that it is a very interesting poem indeed. One might be tempted to speak of it in somewhat the same terms as Eliot speaks of Marvell—'a tough reasonableness beneath the slight lyric grace'—to characterize the delicate, almost fragile phrasing and the lyrical control of movement; but tough and reasonable are neither of them words which would apply: the theme is the uncertain paradoxes of memory and experience, the tone tentative and halting, the contrasts in tonality muted and masked; there is none of the direct assuredness of Marvell—that would be something quite foreign to Eliot's poetic personality.

The poem begins with a memory, as it were arrested in a captured image: a pose, a gesture, a movement and an effect of light; all as perfectly grouped as one could wish a memory to be. But there is some doubt about the realness of the memory. It is a memory in some sense formed by desire and will, or by a sense of aesthetic fitness:

So I would have had him leave,
So I would have her stand and grieve

[25]

and the memory is still open to augmentation and change; the imagination still compelled to elaborate the parting into something even more delicate and fitting:

> I should find
> Some way incomparably light and deft,
> Some way we both should understand,
> Simple and faithless as a smile and shake of the hand.

Our memories have curative and aesthetic skills; they will constantly tidy up the past to enable us to live with it, so the past is made through memory a part of the present. And yet another image lies beside the neat but still changing shape remembered—merely as an unformed possibility to trouble and delight the mind, as the 'infinitely gentle, infinitely suffering thing' troubles and delights the imagination of the 'Preludes':

> And I wonder how they should have been together!
> I should have lost a gesture and a pose.

The memory prefers the rôle of *voyeur* to that of friend or lover, and indeed cannot do much else; however unreal the remembered image is, the alternative is a totally different reality world. And like any *voyeur* it prefers fantasy to reality: the gesture, the pose, the movement, the effect of light are 'what I would have', a construct of desire. And the construct of desire is further described and developed by a set of metaphors which take the incident still further away from an actual past into a world of ideas:

> So he would have left
> As the soul leaves the body torn and bruised,
> As the mind deserts the body it has used.

Perhaps, on the other hand, we might say that the image of memory itself, hedged around and qualified by its verbal moods, is more abstract and unreal than the metaphors of soul and body which have at least some directness, even some brutality. The image elaborates itself in memory to describe an experience which is lost in the changes of memory, though one thing remains constant; the experience of loss and change within memory, its poignancy made very beautiful by the romantic elaborations of memory. As any actual past recedes, the objective of remembering becomes the memory itself; in this case the memory of something incomplete, unfinished, yet incomparably beautiful. The poem has something in common with the episodes of the hyacinth girl and the rose garden, in which similar incidents of memory are orchestrated into a more complex pattern of memory and desire, and their organization into a larger whole makes these episodes far more resonant with unstated or half-stated meaning. But, within its limits, 'La Figlia che Piange' is a nearly perfect little poem.

In another way 'La Figlia' resembles 'Portrait of a Lady'. Both poems have as their basic strategies a memory or series of memories, an unequal love, a failure, a parting, and a late reflection upon the parting and the failure. But, of course, 'Portrait of a Lady' is a very different poem. It has, like 'La Figlia che Piange', a fine control of movement, but the contrasts of movement are employed to render a dramatic contrast of sensibility. Consider, for instance, how much the effect of wistfully excessive sensitivity in the Lady's conversation depends upon the syntactical pattern of her speech, how much less clinging and insidiously, foolishly, possessive her friendship would seem if the reduplications and repetitions were removed in phrases like:

> 'But what have I, but what have I, my friend,
> To give you, what can you receive from me?'

or:

> 'Ah, my friend, you do not know, you do not know
> What life is, you who hold it in your hands';
> (Slowly twisting the lilac stalks)
> 'You let it flow from you, you let it flow,
> And youth is cruel, and has no remorse
> And smiles at situations which it cannot see.'

Consider, too, how much the cruelty and embarrassment of the young man's laconic withdrawal is conveyed by the jaunty brevity of line and crude wit of rhyme:

> I smile, of course,
> And go on drinking tea.

The contest between the two is for possession; the poignancy of the Lady's failure to gain possession of the young man's friendship is matched by his anxiety to keep *self*-possession. 'I keep my countenance,/I remain self-possessed', 'My self possession flares up for a second', 'My self-possession gutters; we are really in the dark.' The jaunty cynicism of his meditations rises from desperation and insecurity as deep as hers; when parting finally takes place there is still no security of self-tenure. Her rôle remains as empty, as vulnerable and as repetitive as ever, her sensitivity as much a matter of empty social rituals:

> I shall sit here, serving tea to friends.

But he, for all the confidence of youth that she has assumed in him, remains unassured, incapable of discovering a self to possess, condemned to a feverish succession of rôles; he refuses to be contained by her yearning affections, but he remains unable to be self-contained:

> And I must borrow every changing shape
> To find expression . . . dance, dance
> Like a dancing bear,
> Cry like a parrot, chatter like an ape.
> Let us take the air, in a tobacco trance—

It is clear that in many senses 'Portrait of a Lady', and even 'La Figlia che Piange' are more external dramas than is 'Prufrock', but also that they cannot be read satisfactorily simply as dramatized incidents, as, for instance, some, but not all, of Browning's dramatic monologues can. 'Portrait of a Lady', like 'La Figlia', becomes more and more complex, more difficult to explain simply as dramatic incident, when we seek to establish the relation between episode and the reflecting memory. The last verse paragraph of the poem suggests powerfully a continuance of the past in the present. At this point the Lady, or the memory of her, has become an element of the male persona's self. If she should die, he feels, he will be in some way incomplete, unable to be certain about his own feelings and understanding, unable to judge his own actions or thoughts. This is, perhaps, a possession more complete than that which he has run away from. If she should die, and leave him

> Doubtful for a while
> Not knowing what to feel or if I understand
> Or whether wise or foolish, tardy or too soon . . .
> Would she not have the advantage, after all?

Any actual series of incidents described in the poem would be as little important as the incident, if there was one, which gave rise to

'La Figlia che Piange'; the exchanges between the Lady and the young man, her advances and his withdrawals, seem rather to dramatize a conflict in a single consciousness. The young man chooses to shrug off the importunity of the Lady, yet wonders at last, not 'how they should have been together', but whether they were ever really apart; whether one can reject entirely the importunity of the *anima sensitiva*, and whether a parting from it can really lead to 'self-possession' or will prove to be an amputation of a whole world of feeling which may, in the final ironic turn, prove profoundly necessary for completeness.

A hint at the precise form which this dangerous decision takes is thrown out in the rather gnomic lines at the end of section II:

> I remain self-possessed
> Except when a street-piano, mechanical and tired
> Reiterates some worn-out common song
> With the smell of hyacinths across the garden
> Recalling things that other people have desired.
> Are these ideas right or wrong?

The passage confirms and extends the sense which is present throughout the poem of something held back, something in reserve, a restraint which refuses to commit itself too precisely to meaning or purpose, some very much more profound drama of ideas held in suspension in the trivialities of the surface action. It is not appropriate, at this stage, to ask what 'these ideas' are, though we may notice in passing how the unanswered question resembles the mystery of the overwhelming question in 'Prufrock'. Part of the problem must wait for partial solution until we discuss the patterns of symbol and philosophic myth in the hyacinth garden passage of *The Waste Land*.

The quatrain poems, written between 1917 and 1919, further develop many of the themes which are introduced by the earlier poems. Their edgy comedy is characterized by an almost neurotic love of witty concealment and evasion which makes it difficult, sometimes impossible, to understand completely, but there is no difficulty in seeing that all the quatrain poems deal in one way or another with the double nature of humanity. The ironies are rarely simple: ascetic or religious purism is as often the butt of the satire as gross materialism; Eliot, like Paul Elmer More, pleads in the beginning that humanity can only achieve its fulfilment in the unresolved absurdities of a dual nature. The hippopotamus, enormous and clumsy in its gross fleshliness, resting its belly in the mud and making odd noises at mating time has yet a better chance of heaven than the Church, with its ascetic and unworldly pretensions.

The form of 'The Hippopotamus', like that of 'Mr. Eliot's Sunday Morning Service' is that of a mock sermon, or to be more precise, that of a versified epistle. The epigraph is from the Epistle to the Colossians, in which one of the classic statements of Pauline asceticism occurs:

> Mortify therefore your members which are upon the earth; fornication, uncleanness, inordinate affection, evil concupiscence, and covetousness, which is idolatry . . . Lie not one to another, seeing that ye have put off the old man with his deeds; And have put on the new man, which is renewed in knowledge after the image of him that created him.
>
> (Col. 3: 5–11)

But the salvation of man, his acceptance into the community of Christ, is impossible without his original sin; the muddy grossness of the fleshly hippopotamus precedes his translation by the blood of the Lamb, as St Augustine, the Bishop of Hippo, wallowed in muddiness before his enlightenment.

The True Church, on the other hand, despite being based upon the rock of Peter, and rejoicing in 'being one with God', is seen, with sly irony, as being more concerned with its material dividends than with spiritual realities. The fun with the flat language of the hymnal and the absurd image of the winged hippopotamus accompanied by angels is delightful, but only superficially conceals a serious concern with the promises and paradoxes of Christianity.

'Whispers of Immortality' clearly enough exploits this idea of the divided sensibility of man. Elizabethan and Jacobean poetry and drama was fond of using death as an image for sexual gratification; the habit of language is turned around here and sensual experience is seen as a way of experiencing death and going beyond death or experience:

> Donne, I suppose, was such another
> Who found no substitute for sense,
> To seize and clutch and penetrate;
> Expert beyond experience,
>
> He knew the anguish of the marrow
> The ague of the skeleton.

Both Donne and Webster, in the conceit of Eliot's poem, used the delights and agonies of the body to explore the region beyond physical experience, to seek and express those yearnings which are defeated by the flesh:

> No contact possible to flesh
> Allayed the fever of the bone.

A characteristic pun suggests the nature of the contact denied to the flesh:

> Grishkin is nice: her Russian eye
> Is underlined for emphasis;
> Uncorseted, her friendly bust
> Gives promise of pneumatic bliss.

The teasing polysyllabic humour of the last line is complicated by the pun on pneumatic—*pneumatikos* would mean spiritual in the Greek, and thus the well-endowed Grishkin becomes an image of the interpenetration of the sensual and the spiritual in man's desire. The fleshliness of the hippopotamus is a necessary condition for its absurd ascension to heaven; similarly Webster and Donne were capable of seeing, what 'our lot' no longer see, that the metaphysical imagination will only come to life through sensual experience, not through a chaste ascetic withdrawal from the world of the senses. Flesh and spirit are interdependent, and the ascetic mortification of the one will destroy the promise of the other:

> And even the Abstract Entities
> Circumambulate her charm;
> But our lot crawls between dry ribs
> To keep our metaphysics warm.

'Mr. Eliot's Sunday Morning Service' even more clearly is built upon an ironic conflict between the ordinary sensual life and the life of *askesis*. The underlying debate is, I believe, entirely serious, but it is expressed in this poem, as in all the other quatrain poems, in a game of ideas; the kind of over-clever play which often is the signal of a delicate and very active mind driven close to desperation by unresolved conflicts. The tone is quite different from that of the seventeenth century Metaphysical poets; Eliot's poems are more purely metaphysical in their natures than most of the poems of Donne, Marvell or Herbert, in whom the metaphysics is only one aspect of a very complex blend of idea and feeling, while in Eliot the metaphysical anxiety overrides everything else and controls the whole world of poetic feeling. The quatrain poems express a metaphysical and therefore a personal sickness, whereas poems such as 'To His Coy Mistress' or Donne's 'Third Satire' or Herbert's 'The Collar', for all their troubled concern with time and death, with truth and with faith, point with assurance towards solutions in living; the quatrain poems remain imprisoned in terrible doubt and uncertainty.

The final stanza of 'Sunday Morning Service' introduces Sweeney, a figure who becomes of some importance in the image structure of Eliot's verse. He is the ordinary sensual man, the focus of all metaphysical and theological problems; mortal in flesh, yet the figure without whom the thousands of years of debate about the spirit, the sacrifice of Christ, the elaborate theology of the Trinity, would all be meaningless. He shifts from ham to ham in his bath, mimicking with his fleshly indolence the chop and change of the austere and abstract metaphysical dialectic of the schoolmen, and at the same time parodying the awful significance of the sacrament of baptism. The whole poem focuses upon this absurd forked naked creature, just as does the whole theological and metaphysical tradition which the poem plays with in its teasing and deliberately blasphemous way.

The doctrine of the Trinity has been at the centre of the belief of many millions of men, and yet it is a curious and irrational doctrine (which is perhaps its great strength). Like the doctrine of the Incarnation, with which it is bound in a subtle complex of mysterious paradoxes, it is an attempt to express and explain the impossible by equally impossible means. Belief in the oneness of God is central to the Christian faith, and so is belief in the divinity of Christ. But so also is the belief that Christ, though divine, became human as well; and since the oneness of God implies His freedom of space, time and mortality, the notion of the Divinity of the Christ who submitted to space, time and mortality raises certain insoluble problems of logic. The Gospel of St John complicates the problem by applying the ancient Greek concept of the *logos* to Christ, and insisting on the co-eternality and consubstantiality of Christ the Word and God the Father:

> In the beginning was the Word, and the Word was with God, and the Word was God.
>
> (John 1: 1)

[32]

Christ, therefore, exists in a timeless unity. But through the incarnation He also exists in Time and Space. This duality parallels the duality of man, who through the sacraments is able to become part of the mystical body of Christ while mysteriously remaining in his natural body.

St John is also responsible for the further complication of the Paraclete, or Comforter. He makes Christ promise:

And I will pray the Father, and he shall give you another Comforter, that he may abide with you for ever; Even the Spirit of truth; whom the world cannot receive, because it seeth him not, neither knoweth him: but ye know him; for he dwelleth with you, and shall be in you.

(John 14: 16)

The language of this clearly suggests a division between the Christian and the world, and a unity of a kind between the Christian and God, a suggestion which is strengthened by:

Yet a little while, and the world seeth me no more; but ye see me: because I live, ye shall live also. At that day ye shall know that I am in my Father, and ye in me, and I in you.

(John 14: 19–20)

The Comforter, the Holy Ghost, thus enters as the third person of the Trinity, but paradoxically in a passage which stresses the unity of the Father with the Son, the Christian with Christ, and the unity of the Holy Ghost with all these. The doctrine of the Trinity is therefore in one way an assertion of unity; a unity in which man shares, through the magic of the sacraments.

We have already seen how Eliot, though attracted strongly by the elegant and supple reasoning of Bradley, began to feel dissatisfied with him. The Christian theological tradition offered something much more substantial and much less abstract in terms of philosophic myths embodying the endless puzzles which are involved in the condition of humanity. There remains for Eliot a feeling of the absurdity that these elaborate and beautiful puzzle-games of unreason should be developed for phallic Sweeney in his bath, and delight in the absurdity combines with the fascination of the problem, and the fear of it, in 'Mr. Eliot's Sunday Morning Service'. So:

[33]

In the beginning was the Word.
Superfetation of το ἕν,
And at the mensual turn of time
Produced enervate Origen.

As in many of the other quatrain poems sexual metaphors are used
for spiritual matters. The Word is one with the Father and yet
begotten by Him; therefore by an inescapable blasphemous logic
begotten upon Himself. The Incarnation expresses in worldly form
the creativeness of the Father; the sexual metaphor is carried over to
describe the 'polyprophilogenitive' priests, fecund in proselytes but
barren in body. The tragi-comedy that the propagation of the Word
should be entrusted to those who deny their own sexual creativity is
sharpened by the reference to Origen, who took Paul's injunction to
mortify one's members all too literally and castrated himself in the
service of God. The phrase 'mensual turn of time' is a problem: the
word mensual is not in the English dictionary, though it must mean
monthly, and must carry some association with 'menstrual'. Perhaps
'the mensual turn of time' suggests an onset of barrenness in the
world of time analogous to the female change of life; the magnificent
creativeness of God becomes represented by a Church and priests
who choose sterility as a pledge of dedication.

The painting of the Umbrian school is an icon which compactly
symbolizes the whole pattern of doctrine. The beginning of Christ's
ministry on earth, and thus the opening of all the problems implicit
in the new covenant, was at His baptism. He is represented as half
in, half out of the water; as it were half in, half out of this world and
that. Above Him are the dove of the Holy Ghost and God the Father
enthroned in majesty; pure spirits in a timeless world, but in His
baptism Christ links the timeless world and the waters of time. The
world is a wilderness against which the cloud of light around His
head glows; it is pale and thin like the water through which the
divine feet shine. Baptism is the sacrament which joins man with
Christ. Thus the baptized God represents Christ, and in doing so
represents man in Christ; represents man, and thus represents Christ
in man. So Sweeney, at the end of the poem, in his baptismal bath,
is in a bizarre way the imitation of Christ; hippopotamus that he is,
he is nearer salvation than the neuter worker-bees of the Church.

'The sable presbyters', sombre with all the mournfulness of
Scots dissenting religion, as well as the sombre celibacy of the

Roman dispensation, approach divine truth through ascetic discipline; they are compared to the angels who swarm about the white heavenly rose of sanctified spirits in Canto XXIII of Dante's *Paradiso* like bees around an earthly flower. The celibate priests, like worker bees or like angels in the convention of mediaeval angelology, are neuter, yet busy themselves in the reproductive processes of the spirit, cross fertilizing the male stamen and the female pistil with love. With somewhat cruel satirical humour the priests neutered by their vows are made hairy-bellied bees rather than the angels of Dante, with their faces of living flame and golden wings, and Sweeney, who is no angel, but yet the essential subject of the incredible theological drama, soaks in comfort containing it all.

He appears again in 'Sweeney Among the Nightingales'. The idea of metamorphosis is implicit in the sacrament of baptism; as it also is in the Ovidian myth of Philomel the nightingale, which is referred to in a deleted epigraph from *Raigne of King Edward the Third*: 'Why should I speak of the nightingale? The nightingale sings of adulterous wrong.'

The surviving epigraph, from the *Agamemnon* of Aeschylus, is the cry of Agamemnon when murdered by his wife Clytemnaestra: 'Alas, I have been pierced deeply by a deadly wound.' The combination of the two epigraphs suggests that the dramatic situation is one of death and rebirth in another form. Sweeney is discovered in a bafflingly complicated situation full of images of adulterous sexuality; his sensuality is expressed in terms of animal imagery: 'Apeneck Sweeney', and particoloured contrast: 'zebra stripes' and 'maculate giraffe', in which 'maculate' is a consciously punning antonym of 'immaculate', as in the immaculate conception. Striped and spotted as he is with sensuality, Sweeney, as ordinary sensual man, stands at the entrance to the other world guarding 'the hornèd gate'—the horn gate through which, according to Virgil, the true prophetic dream emerges from the underworld, though even this phrase is not lacking in punning sexual overtones.

The key to the idea of metamorphosis as it occurs in the poem seems to be in the penultimate stanza:

> The host with someone indistinct
> Converses at the door apart,
> The nightingales are singing near
> The Convent of the Sacred Heart.

In 'The Hippopotamus' the metamorphosis of regeneration is expressed in terms of the Ascension; in 'Mr. Eliot's Sunday Morning Service' in terms of baptism and incarnation; here the sacramental mystery referred to in a series of outrageous word-plays seems to be the Eucharist. The communion of man in Christ is re-enacted in the Eucharist by the administration of the 'host', the flesh and the blood of Christ.

The host 'converses' with someone indistinct. The *Oxford English Dictionary* gives the appropriate (now obsolete) meaning for the verb as to have one's being, to live or dwell in or amongst people or places, or, otherwise, to be familiarly associated with. The word 'conversation' may bear a cognate meaning; for instance the Authorised Version translates Philemon 3: 20 as: 'For our conversation is in heaven'. There is also some punning reference to words like 'convert' and 'conversion'.

The host converses with 'someone indistinct'. Communion is the conversion of many into one; through it Christ enters the communicants and the communicants enter Christ, thus becoming one substance, or 'some one', in which the communicants and Christ are no longer distinct, but 'someone indistinct'. In the words of the Anglican service, when we 'spiritually eat the flesh of Christ, and drink his blood; then we dwell in Christ and Christ in us; we are one with Christ, and Christ with us.'

The myth of Philomel the nightingale follows the familiar Ovidian pattern of rape, death and rebirth in a new form; the nightingales singing near 'the Sacred Heart' are thus a composite icon of Christian re-birth. The word 'Convent' punningly enforces this meaning. The first meaning for the word given in the *O.E.D.* is 'an assemblage or gathering of persons; a number met together for some common purpose; an assembly, meeting, convention, congregation.' The ceremony of Communion is thus 'The Convent of the Sacred Heart.'

The last stanza returns us to the Greek world, where the mystery of metamorphosis is at the root of so many religious myths. Sweeney's *alter ego* Agamemnon cries out at his death in the bloody wood, presumably the sacred wood of death and rebirth and oracular prophecy, and is dishonoured by the nightingales defecating upon the discarded body, the body spurned by the triumphant soul in its spiritual metamorphosis.

There is much that is obscure and incomprehensible in this poem, and it may well be felt by the reader that my own interpretation is an over-ingenious reading: it is possibly so, but I know of no other way of establishing a meaning and pattern for the poem which accords so well with the general development of Eliot's habits of thought and expression at this time, and I offer the interpretation, for what it is worth, as a contribution to the understanding of the poem.

In 'Sweeney Erect', the erotic significances are even more overt. The epigraph, from *The Maid's Tragedy*, sets the scene in a kind of Waste Land, the 'wilderness cracked and brown' of the 'Sunday Morning Service'. Aspatia, the speaker in the play, abandoned by her lover, bids her women to weave her story into a tapestry depicting Ariadne's desertion. Aspatia, Ariadne, the nameless epileptic on the bed, become figures cognate with the deserted ladies in 'La Figlia che Piange' and 'Portrait of a Lady', Sweeney a coarsely comic version of the two lovers in those poems. In 'Sweeney among the Nightingales', Sweeney has played Agamemnon; here, in as much as the deserted woman is an Ariadne, he plays a Theseus, another Greek hero whose fate was seemingly unlike any fate appropriate to the farcical and fleshly Sweeney. Theseus was the hero who destroyed the Minotaur with Ariadne's help, defeated the Amazons, and harrowed hell to rescue Proserpine. He is imprisoned by Pluto but at last is rescued by Hercules. But the farcical contrast between Theseus and Sweeney still links them. Sweeney is a potential hero, a man who lives in two worlds, capable of heaven and hell.

Up to 'Sweeney among the Nightingales' the conflict between the relative claims of the ascetic and the sensual life has been to the disadvantage of the ascetic; in 'Sweeney among the Nightingales' and 'Sweeney Erect', the balance begins the swing the other way. The distaste for the body, which is so vividly evoked in the description of the epileptic, is controlled a little by humour, but not so that it disappears altogether. Sweeney (pinkly male and still absurd) may be merely the farcical mirror image of the heroic Theseus, but there is still an ironic suggestion that his laconic failure to be interested in the pain of the body on the bed is fitting, that he, like the lover in 'A Cooking Egg', must go on to some further destiny.

There is a quieter humour in 'A Cooking Egg'. Pipit here plays the rôle of the deserted woman, the sensitive soul. She, and all that is desired on earth, Honour, Capital and Society, are contrasted with the delights of Heaven, and though these are ironically parodied, there is no doubt as to the choice the lover has made in deserting her;

the promise made by Heaven depends upon the choice which Piccarda de Donati has made, in one of the most beautiful descriptions of submission to the love of God ever written:

> E la sua volontate è nostra pace;
> Ella è quel mare, al qual tutto si move
> Ciò ch'ella crea e che natura face

(And His will is our peace; it is that sea towards which everything moves, that which it creates and which nature makes.)

The ironies cut both ways until Piccarda de Donati enters; until then the promise of heaven is gently parodied and Pipit tenderly regretted; but in the last nine lines the rage against the sadness, the corruption and the horror of the world are a total rejection of the city of earth for the City of God:

> But where is the penny world I bought
> To eat with Pipit behind the screen?
> The red-eyed scavengers are creeping
> From Kentish Town and Golder's Green;
>
> Where are the eagles and the trumpets?
>
> Buried beneath some snow-deep Alps.
> Over buttered scones and crumpets
> Weeping, weeping multitudes
> Droop in a hundred A.B.C.'s.

Eliot resurrects the 'ubi sunt' form of mediaeval and Renaissance literature to lament the passing of the pleasures which innocence and immaturity find in the world; 'the penny world', the cheap comic paper of the turn of the century with its wild adventure stories and improbable comedies masking the unpleasant realities; the heroic eagles and trumpets of a boyish imagination shutting out the terror and the boredom of actual life. Pipit, who must be discarded if Piccarda de Donati's promise of peace is to be fulfilled, is unmistakably associated, for all her pathos and attractiveness, with that world. The lover's rejection of her is as brutal in its way as the desertions of the lovers in 'Portrait of a Lady', 'La Figlia che Piange' and 'Sweeney Erect', and satiric doubt about the outcome of the rejection still lingers, but the choice is nevertheless made. The lover approaches a quest which leads him to the desertion of Honour, Wealth and Friendship, of will, desire and sensuous delight, of the sensitive self which cannot live except in this world, of Pipit in fact, to enquire after the peace of submission to 'la sua volontate'.

The woman in 'Burbank with a Baedeker, Bleistein with a Cigar' is no longer the pathetic but attractive bird-like Pipit; but she is a more sinister relative. Her name 'Princess Volupine' suggests in portmanteau form the Latin 'voluptas', 'voluntas' and 'vulpus', voluptuousness, will and wolfishness. Burbank, with a Baedeker in his hand, is a tourist visiting Venice for the first time. The Venice evoked in the composite epigraph is a chaotic city of the world, a compound of emotions ranging from the jealous rage of Othello—'goats and monkeys!', to the sombre Latin *nil nisi divinum stabile est: caetera fumus* (nothing endures except the divine, the rest is smoke). Burbank, the traveller in this at once charming and beastly city of change and decay 'falls' for the delights offered by the worldly princess, and the fall is a kind of death:

> Defunctive music under sea
> Passed seaward with the passing bell
> Slowly: the God Hercules
> Had left him, that had loved him well.

The 'fall'—the term recalls the Christian usage—is a loss of god-like strength, the strength of a Hercules to harrow the otherworld and return in triumph with its secrets; the death drowns poor Burbank in the same sea as Prufrock, the corrosive destroying sea of the *Phaedo*. The implicit reference to Antony, that other hero held back from conquest of the world by *voluptas*:

> 'Tis the god Hercules, whom Antony lov'd
> Now leaves him.
>
> (*Antony and Cleopatra* IV. iii)

prompts the association between the Princess and Cleopatra:

> Her shuttered barge
> Burned on the water all the day.

while the world continues to revolve in the wheel of change and decay, around the turning axletree.

Sweeney has been divided into two in this poem to accent his duality. He is Burbank, the spiritual tourist whose frailty and sensuous self-indulgence cause him to fail in his quest. He is also Bleistein (his name means Lead-stone) who is never in any danger of falling for sensual temptation; his protozoic grossness is too complete for him to know anything but the material, or to fail to fulfil any heroic Herculean destiny as Burbank has failed by the fall. *Nil nisi divinum stabile est; caetera fumus*—Burbank goes up in smoke when he falls for the Princess precisely because he has lost what he possessed of the divine; for Bleistein there is only the 'smoky candle end of time' declining; his protozoic existence has never shared in the Godlike.

'Nothing endures unless divine'; and at the end of the poem we have Burbank, himself withered away by the fall, meditating upon the Venetian lion of St Mark. The city itself has decayed from its ancient grandeur: it has, ultimately, nothing of the divine in it, and the winged lion, symbol of the divine energy of the evangelist, is no longer an appropriate emblem for such a city: its emblem is now a flea-bitten circus lion, tamed and under constant attention to stop it getting into even worse a condition. The voluptuous Princess, herself a symbol of the spirit of this city of earth, is meagre, blue-nailed, phthisic; her new lover is Klein, a little man, and so she too is an image of decay. Burbank is left wondering about the seven laws (whatever they are, with their suggestion of occult inevitability) and 'Time's ruins'. 'All the rest is smoke'—the Princess, Bleistein, and (after his fall into the sensual snare laid by Venice) Burbank, are all creatures of Time, creatures of Venice, a city not of St Mark, but of Time, and because of this they suffer the decay appropriate to all that does not inhabit the timeless universe of the spirit.

The quatrain poems were not, I think, designed as a sequence, but they nevertheless show distinctly a changing attitude to the problems with which they all deal. In 'The Hippopotamus', Eliot champions the cause of absurd, divided man; he continues to do so in the 'Sunday Morning Service'. As the debate continues he becomes more and more critical of the uneasy discordance of flesh and spirit, until at last he abandons for the time being the amiable figure of Sweeney, who manages to live with some humour and poise despite the conflicts of his doubleness, and splits him into the two poles of his nature: the successful materialist and the failed idealist, Bleistein and Burbank.

The process is perhaps something to do with the form. In attempting to achieve the brittle hard *logopoeia* of Gautier, in confining himself to the narrow boundaries of the rhyming quatrain, he is impelled towards epigrammatic statement, to neatness and cleverness where, perhaps, neatness and cleverness are the worst ways to solve the problems, the best ways to heighten the conflicts. It is clear that Eliot felt at this point the need to adopt a more flexible verse medium, one more adapted to exploration and reflection than to hard comic statement, more adapted to self-discovery than to self-defence. He discovers this mode in 'Gerontion', and in doing so arrests to some extent the process of polarization which has been going on in the quatrain poems; instead of exploiting satirically the divisions of the soul he enters the soul at the anxious moment where it searches for the possibilities of a resolution, or at least meditates upon the reasons why there is, as yet, no resolution.

If it is true that 'genuine poetry can communicate before it is understood', then much of the quatrains is not genuine poetry. For the most part neither are these poems, in the best sense, the poetry of wit. Donne or Marvell will fuse disturbingly discrete elements into a richly human unity of argument which convinces not merely because of its brilliance but because of its power to alter the reader's world in many more ways than statement. They surprise because they unite many kinds of experience unexpectedly; in these quatrain poems Eliot too often merely confounds us with his cleverness, and when one has unravelled the ingenious pattern of his argument, there's an end of the interest.

There's a coarseness of sentiment at times in these poems, too. The anti-semitism of 'Burbank' is not entirely to be explained away by talk about the change of values from age to age, or the use of the Jew as a conventional symbol of materialism. There's a melodramatic vagueness about the disgust with the world expressed in, for instance, the last nine lines of 'A Cooking Egg', and a slightly schoolboyish snigger in the elaborate blasphemies of 'Mr. Eliot's Sunday Morning Service'. I am not complaining that Eliot refuses to be serious—I believe he is in deadly earnest in these farcical episodes—but the quality of his seriousness is somewhat debased by the slight but compelling note of hysteria and the defensive neatness and cleverness, and prevented from achieving those resonances and reverberations of meaning beyond the surface values which poetry must have in order to live.

'Gerontion' and *The Waste Land* are by no means perfect in this— there are times when one thinks of both of these as thought out, merely, not thought through and felt through to the uniting of feeling and thought. But nevertheless in their imperfectness they seem to have the power to go on growing in meaning indefinitely as we read them, while the poet of the quatrains after a time becomes a somewhat tired and tiring clown, whose personal problems, though we can see that they have their pathos and urgency, do not engage our interest for very long.

'US HE DEVOURS'
'TRADITION' AND 'GERONTION'

'Tradition and the Individual Talent' is still a puzzling essay, despite the fact that it has been discussed and commented upon far more than any other single critical essay written in the twentieth century. The fact that it has been so influential, indeed, makes it more difficult to see it for what it really is. So many of our critical tools: the idiom of critical debate, the assumptions that we bring to the problem, have been profoundly influenced by this and other essays that Eliot wrote during the next few years that we find it very difficult to stand back from the essay to see it clearly.

One reason for the difficulty is that, while we see the essay as a classic statement, a starting point for the new poetics and the new criticism, Eliot himself wrote it as a kind of interim report on certain processes of thought and feeling:

> The best of my *literary* criticism . . . is a by-product of my private poetry-workshop; or a prolongation of the thinking that went into the formation of my own verse. . . . My criticism has this in common with that of Ezra Pound, that its merits and its limitations can be fully appreciated only when it is considered in relation to the poetry I have written.
>
> (*OPP*, 106)

This is without doubt true of 'Tradition and the Individual Talent': it cannot be understood fully without relating it to Eliot's verse, and particularly without relating it to a poem which seems to have been written at about the same time, 'Gerontion'. On the other hand the manner of the essay is hardly tentative; one of the reasons why it has impressed so many readers is its high judicial manner. One of Eliot's favourite quotations is Rémy de Gourmont's remark that the critic's task was 'ériger en lois ses impressions personelles.'

Eliot never hesitated to do this, and his remark upon Ben Jonson would apply with equal force to himself: 'A writer of power and intelligence, Jonson endeavoured to promulgate, as a formula and programme of reform, what he chose to do himself; and he not unnaturally laid down in abstract theory what is in reality a personal point of view' (*SE*, 156).

Eliot puts part of the case interestingly in a late essay: he says of the great initiators, poet-critics like Dryden, Coleridge and Wordsworth who help to change the taste of a generation, that they are not so much judges as advocates (*OPP*, 26). And these early essays of Eliot, if they often have the exciting virtues of brilliant special pleading, often have the concomitant faults. A sharp suggestiveness of phrase often covers an inconsequential argument; the stimulating generalization turns out, too frequently, to be a hasty, evasive gloss.

The personal point of view is never wholly idiosyncratic: more often than not it is a re-organization of attitudes, observations and latent, unstated assumptions that are characteristic of the age, a reordering of material which for the most part is not new. What is new is the fresh relationships seen by and advocated from a personal viewpoint; the order, the precedence, the arrangement of materials.

The idea of tradition, for instance, can be traced back if you wish, to Confucius, and both Babbitt and Pound thought it worth while to do so. Babbitt writes of Confucius:[1]

> He aspired at most to be the channel through which the moral experience of his race that had accumulated through long centuries and found living embodiment in these sages should be conveyed to the present and the future; in his own words, he was not a creator but a transmitter. A man who looks up to the great traditional models and imitates them, becomes worthy of imitation in his turn. He must be thus rightly imitative if he is to be a true leader.

This kind of spirit was one of the things which drew Pound's interest towards Confucius, but Pound doesn't have the same reservations about the dangers of traditionalism that Babbitt expresses: 'the present seems to be held in perpetual spiritual mortmain by the past. A purely traditional humanism is always in danger of falling into a rut of pseudo-classic formalism.'[2] Babbitt goes on to speak of the 'highly untraditional and individualistic Buddha' as an example of the virtues which must counterweigh the traditionalism of Confucius in a fully developed kind of humanism.

But however much the writers of the early twentieth century might have found confirmation for their ideas about tradition in the distant past—it seems appropriate, after all, that tradition should be a traditional idea—the concept had a particular value and took a particular form in this crucial period before and just after the First World War. Novelty had ceased to be a novelty; change distorted too much too quickly, and it seemed to that generation that art and literature was running into shallow waters by its neglect of the past. In 1906 Yeats was recommending the aristocratic tradition in highly mannered prose:[3]

> Emotion . . . grows intoxicating and delightful after it has been enriched with the memory of old emotions, with all the uncounted flavours of old experience; and it is necessarily some antiquity of thought, emotions that have been deepened by the experiences of many men of genius, that distinguishes the cultivated man. The subject-matter of his meditation and invention is old, and he will disdain a too conscious originality in the arts as in those daily matters of life where, is it not Balzac who says 'we are all conservatives'? He is above all things well-bred, and whether he write or paint will not desire a technique that denies or obtrudes his long and noble descent. Corneille and Racine did not deny their masters, and when Dante spoke of his master Virgil there was no crowing of the cock. In their day imitation was conscious or all but conscious, and because originality was but so much the more a part of the man himself, so much the deeper because unconscious, no quick analysis could unravel their miracle, that needed generations, it may be, for its understanding; but it is our imitation that is unconscious and that waits the certainties of time.

Yeats brings out more clearly than anyone else the aristocratic sentiment which lies behind traditionalism—and by aristocratic sentiment I do not mean anything to do with social class or structures of economic privilege. The sentiment is anti-democratic not necessarily because it is against social justice or rational progress, but because it prefers to judge the health of society by the 'rightness' of its corporate judgments, values and intelligence rather than by the freedom of its individual members to question, to ignore, or to attempt to alter the values of society.

In as much as it is anti-democratic the sentiment tends to be anti-romantic too, and its leaning towards classicism matches the aristocratic feeling. Already in 1896 Babbitt was exhorting the young men of Harvard with essays and addresses like 'The Rational Study of the Classics', in which he urges that the study of the Classics should be much more than the study of long dead men, but an approach to the understanding of a living tradition, a tracing of the culture of the present through all the ramifications of its history to its still vital roots in the past. Here one can see Babbitt beginning to develop the implications of the classical humanism which was to be the burden of his teaching throughout his life. But I believe that for Babbitt as well as for Eliot the decisive encounter which gave characteristic form to the sentiment was the visit of Gilbert Murray to Harvard in 1907 to give the Gardiner Lane Lectures on Homer—a series of lectures which were published in an augmented form in the same year with the title *The Rise of the Greek Epic*.

For the young Eliot one of the most significant things in Murray's lectures must have been Murray's interest in anthropology. Murray takes as his starting point the investigations of scholars like Sir James G. Frazer, Jane Harrison, Thomson and Cook into the inter-relationships between pre-Hellenic social organization and Greek myth, religion, philosophy, law and literature. From this viewpoint he advances a new interpretation of the Homeric problem, and particularly of the *Iliad*. Since the whole movement to which these scholars belonged is of importance to the student of Eliot, it will be as well to say something about them at this stage.

They have this in common, that they approached the study of primitive society through the study of classical literature, and though they are important as early pioneers in the development of anthropology, they did not possess the methodological tools of modern anthropology. They were concerned in the first place with the classical world, and used what they could learn about contemporary primitive societies at second or third hand in their attempt to chart the genesis and the development of European civilization. They were attempting, one might say, to rebuild their understanding of the past in order to come to terms with the present. For this was an age in which European man came to feel less and less secure in the pride of his civilization, and came more and more to realize how deeply it was rooted in patterns of inherited primitive thought and feeling: this realization of the fineness of the distinction between the primitive and the civilized, the flimsiness of the gloss, being most powerfully expressed, perhaps, by Conrad in *Heart of Darkness* (1902). Thus it became urgently necessary to establish and describe the vital continuity between past and present which gives our civilization its special character; to find firm basis for the present by showing that primitive survivals can be survivals of essential ways of feeling and thinking, and not just survivals but still dynamic forces of social integration and survival.

The whole group had an acutely developed sense of history, and, though they tended to find what they wanted to find in the past, and indeed to impose their own ideas upon the past in a way which was often tendentious in the extreme, they impressed Eliot and his generation with their comprehensiveness of vision and their energy, and Eliot has paid tribute to them in, among other essays, 'Euripides and Professor Murray'.

Frazer, Murray, Harrison and the rest shared a common cultural background with Babbitt and Eliot, and indeed with all the other major thinkers of the age, for instance Freud, or Jung, or Bergson; they could all with an ease and confidence which nowadays seems quite extraordinary, draw upon a common stock of shared classical culture, and trust their readers to see the relevance of the reference. Thus their thought, novel and disturbing though it was, was all the more amenable to the young Eliot, critical, like his teacher Babbitt, of the attenuation which the shared culture was suffering, yet anxious to find means by which it could be restored to its proper dignity and force. Yet the wealth of new ideas demanded by the changing needs of the world disturbed old assumptions, and made it increasingly difficult for a satisfying synthesis to be achieved. 'If we are to digest the heavy food of historical and scientific knowledge that we have eaten we must be prepared for much greater exertions. We need a digestion that can assimilate both Homer and Flaubert' (*SE*, 63).

Frazer, Harrison and their followers seemed to offer tools for building the synthesis, and Eliot accepted them enthusiastically. In *Notes towards a Definition of Culture*, for instance, he develops his ideas about specialization and group culture in modern society by alluding to Dyak society in Borneo, New Hebridean tribal culture and the *Antigone* of Sophocles. This kind of broad eclectic sweep of

[47]

reference is something which the modern anthropologist would usually deny himself, but it is essential to Frazerian anthropology, and it is natural that Eliot should allow himself its freedom, breadth and scope in his own commentaries upon society. And a passage like the following, from *After Strange Gods*, shows how closely the methods and discoveries of Frazerian anthropology and the notion of tradition were linked in his mind:

> Tradition is not solely, or even primarily the maintenance of certain dogmatic beliefs; these beliefs have come to take their living form in the course of the formation of a tradition. What I mean by tradition involves all those habitual actions, habits and customs, from the most significant religious rite to our conventional way of greeting a stranger, which represent the blood kinship of 'the same people living in the same place'.
>
> (*After Strange Gods*, 18)

We can trace back the link between anthropological ideas and the notion of tradition as a positive force to Murray, then, and Murray's lectures also contained the germs of a theory of literary function and responsibility which was a clear challenge to some of the central assumptions of Romantic literary theory. The core of Murray's argument was this: that the *Iliad* was 'a Traditional Book, dependent upon a living saga or tradition.'[4] The idea that the epics of Homer grew by a process of accretion and constant revision by many makers throughout the centuries was not an entirely new one in Homeric scholarship; Murray accepts this interpretation and proceeds to describe the relationship between these many anonymous poets, the Homeridae, and the work they jointly created. Their rôle was a self-effacing one in which the individual was content to subordinate himself entirely to the tradition. The poet's rôle was that of '*Logios Anêr*, or Man of Words . . . the man who possessed the Things Said, or traditions which made up the main sum of man's knowledge.'[5] We have seen earlier the way in which the concept of the *Logos* is an important one in Christian and Greek thought and in Eliot's creative thinking, where it often appears later as 'the Word', or sometimes 'speech'. It is interesting and important to notice here how Murray links the concept to human tradition rather than to Christian theology. In Eliot the two meanings are continuous, and blend into each other, and there is no real paradox in this, as we shall see later.

It is worth quoting Murray at some length here:[6]

But now comes a curious observation. We who are accustomed to modern literature always associate this sort of imaginative intensity with something personal. We connect it with an artist's individuality, or with originality in the sense of 'newness'. It seems as though, under modern conditions, an artist usually did not feel or imagine intensely unless he was producing some work which was definitely his own and not another's, work which must bear his personal name and be marked by his personal experience and character. . . . I do not specially wish to attack this modern prejudice, if it is one. I largely share in it: and its excesses will very likely disappear. But I do very greatly wish to point out that artistic feeling in this matter has not always been the same. Artists have not always wished to stamp their work with their personal characteristics or even their personal name. Artists have sometimes been, as it were, Protestant or Iconoclast, unable to worship without asserting themselves against the established ritual of their religion: sometimes, in happier circumstances, they have accepted and loved the ritual as part of the religion, and wrought out their own new works of poetry, not as protests, not as personal outbursts, but as glad and nameless offerings, made in prescribed form to enhance the glory of the spirit whom they served. With some modifications, this seems to have been the case in Greece, in Canaan, in Scandinavia, during the periods when great traditional books were slowly growing up. Each successive poet did not assert himself against the tradition, but gave himself to the tradition, and added to its greatness and beauty all that was in him.

The intensity of imagination which makes the *Iliad* alive is not, it seems to me, the imagination of any one man. It means not that one man of genius created a wonder and passed away. It means that generation after generation of poets, trained in the same schools and a more or less continuous and similar life, steeped themselves to the lips in the spirit of this great poetry.

We must remember that when Gilbert Murray delivered these words to his assembled audience, which without doubt included both the young Eliot and the distinguished Professor Babbitt, Eliot had already been exposed to Babbitt's reasoned critique of individualism; the traditionalist ethic and the Classic temper had already engaged his imagination; he already had reason to distrust the Romantic insistence upon novelty as the necessary mark of genius. The lectures simply took these assumptions and preferences one stage further. Murray gave his audience a fascinating account of the possible relationship between the poet and his tradition, in which the continuum of thought and feeling within which the poet—any poet—must work, becomes the decisive thing, and not the personal being who works within it.

'Tradition and the Individual Talent' was published twelve years after Murray delivered these lectures. But Eliot is still using remarkably similar terms in his account of the tradition, speaking of:

> our tendency to insist, when we praise a poet, upon those aspects of his work in which he least resembles anyone else. In these aspects or parts of his work we pretend to find what is individual, what is the peculiar essence of the man. We dwell with satisfaction upon the poet's difference from his predecessors, especially his immediate predecessors; we endeavour to find something that can be isolated in order to be enjoyed. Whereas if we approach a poet without this prejudice we shall often find that not only the best, but the most individual parts of his work may be those in which the dead poets, his ancestors, assert their immortality most vigorously.
>
> (*SE*, 14)

It would have been very odd indeed if Eliot had taken over Murray's ideas without change, without naturalizing them to his own point of view on history and art, especially since, as we have seen, there is a real sense in which his critical work is part of a creative process whose proper fruition is in the poetry rather than in the criticism. But many of the developments which take place as Eliot shapes his ideas are already implicit in Murray if one accepts a transition from the notion of the Homeric corpus, as that which bound together the anonymous *Homeridae*, to the idea of 'the mind of Europe' as the continuously developing, central core of thought and feeling which makes Homer and Flaubert parts of one whole. The transition is not quite so bold as it may seem. In a very real sense, if one accepts Murray's interpretation of the problem,

'Homer' *was* the mind of Greece, the common stock of wisdom which changes and develops as the race changes and develops, that which creates community within the community by being a shared focus of experience for all. And 'the mind of Europe' would find its natural origins, more than anywhere else, in 'the mind of Greece'.

It follows, then, that the poet who serves the tradition not merely serves it, he re-creates it in however small a way just as each of the *Homeridae* would, in however small a degree, change 'Homer'. Ten words of the *Iliad* cannot stand by themselves even if they are the sole contribution of an inspired maker; but they may make every other word in the corpus have a new meaning. In the same way:

> No poet, no artist of any art, has his complete meaning alone. His significance, his appreciation is the appreciation of his relation to the dead poets and artists. You cannot value him alone; you must set him, for contrast and comparison, among the dead. . . . The necessity that he shall conform, that he shall cohere, is not onesided; what happens when a new work of art is created is something that happens simultaneously to all the works of art which preceded it. The existing monuments form an ideal order among themselves, which is modified by the introduction of the new (the really new) work of art among them. The existing order is complete before the new work arrives; for order to persist after the supervention of novelty, the *whole* existing order must be, if ever so slightly, altered; and so the relations, proportions, values of each work of art toward the whole are readjusted; and this is conformity between the old and the new.
>
> (*SE*, 15)

The notion of 'the mind of Europe' seems on the face of it a rather fanciful kind of metaphor, one which one would hardly expect from a philosopher trained in the logical disciplines of Bradley's method. Eliot's position *can* be reconciled with Bradley's here, but perhaps there begins to be a certain divergence in spirit from Bradley as Eliot strives to express ideas which demand a language less cool and chaste than that of academic philosophy, more rich in wit than in judgment, quicker and more impatient of reason.

Thus, even though the reader of Bradley is no stranger to the notion that 'the suicide of thought', the surrender of 'self', might lead us to a more harmonious system of being, yet there is some other element of longing in Eliot: 'What happens is a continual surrender of himself as he is at the moment to something more valuable. The progress of the artist is a continual self-sacrifice, a continual extinction of personality' (*SE*, 17). Criticism, no less than poetry, can be expression of deeply felt emotion; it is not all, and especially in Eliot is not all, 'comparison and analysis'. 'Prufrock' expresses the fear and loneliness of an individual longing to leave his individuality behind him and experience some imagined reality beyond his loneliness, but terrified of the step he must take out of his isolation. The quatrain poems at once display and conceal in their verbal fireworks the enormous tensions in that same blend of terror and desire. 'Tradition and the Individual Talent' can be read as a courageous attempt, which only in a curiously stretched way could be called impersonal, to erect a theory to satisfy these metaphysical longings and at the same time act as a programme for art. But the language of 'continual surrender of himself as he is' and 'continual self-sacrifice' tends irresistibly towards the language of religion, and particularly of St Paul. And after all, St Paul is part of the tradition; and the religious symbolism which is so central to the tradition, is much more powerful and multi-valued than that of any academic philosopher—so there is nothing to surprise one here.

I have suggested that in his early criticism Eliot is given to an ingenious looseness of argument which often escapes our attention because of the persuasive confidence of manner. Let me give one example of this from 'Tradition and the Individual Talent', in the part where he first raises the whole curious question of impersonality: 'It is in this depersonalization that art may be said to approach the condition of science' (*SE*, 17).

The scientific metaphor, in which the artist seeks to stress the sobriety and fidelity to detail of art, has a long and interesting history which we need not explore here. Normally, in Flaubert and in Zola for instance, the metaphor is used to compare the *activity* of the scientist with that of the artist, and though in its claim to 'objectivity' it is an extremely leaky vessel, the import of the argument is clear enough. Readers of *The Egoist*, Pound's journal in which the essay first appeared, would have been well prepared to accept its anti-romantic implications almost unconsciously. But Eliot, blandly and without warning, misuses the word 'science', and makes it mean, not the activity, or the method, or the philosophy of science, but what happens on the laboratory bench; that is, the most obvious kind of material or evidence with which a scientist has to deal:

> I therefore invite you to consider, as a suggestive analogy, the action which takes place when a bit of finely filiated platinum is introduced into a chamber containing oxygen and sulphur dioxide. . . . the platinum itself is apparently unaffected. . . . The mind of the poet is the shred of platinum.
>
> (*SE*, 17–18)

The word 'science' is useful in passing, as a kind of charm to dispel Georgian emotionalism and the spinelessly decadent Romantic theory which went with it, but it is very difficult indeed to say what it has to do with Eliot's argument, except in so far as it induces in the reader a receptive frame of mind, by helping him to recall other forms of argument which are, in the most general and superficial kind of way, similar. The real argument, if it can be called that, is a much more complex thing than the essay appears to make it, and depends finally upon a process akin to that which Eliot says elsewhere is at work in the creation of a poem: 'A poem may employ several subjects, combining them in a particular way; and it may be meaningless to ask "What is the subject of the poem?" From the union of several subjects there appears, not the subject, but the poem' (*TCC*, 39).—or perhaps a critical essay which clears the way for a poem by experimenting in the association of diverse subjects; the essay, as I have said, is part of the process which accompanied the genesis of 'Gerontion', and it has much of the same involvedness and ambiguity which make that poem such a complex experience.

One of the 'subjects' is tradition, and we have seen some of the ways in which that idea existed before it entered into the process; perhaps we should look now at some of the elements which helped to precipitate the idea of impersonality. We can single out two events as crucial. One was the publication by the Egoist Press in 1917 of *A Portrait of the Artist as a Young Man*. The other was the intensive propaganda campaign which Pound conducted on behalf of Rémy de Gourmont's criticism between 1917 and 1920. A third event lying a little further back in time, but still recent enough to be influential, was the early development of Thomas Mann's aesthetic, particularly in *Tonio Kröger* (1903).

Joyce's (or perhaps we should say Stephen Daedalus's) theory of

[53]

impersonality has much the same kind of relationship to Thomist theology as Eliot's has to Augustine or Aristotle, with just about the same blend of dependence and distance:[7]

> The personality of the artist passes into the narration itself, flowing round and round the persons and the action like a vital sea. . . . The personality of the artist, at first a cry or a cadence or a mood and then a fluid and lambent narrative, finally refines itself out of existence, impersonalizes itself, so to speak. The mystery of aesthetic like that of the material creation is accomplished. The artist, like the God of the creation, remains within or behind or beyond or above his handiwork, invisible, refined out of existence, indifferent, paring his fingernails.

Gourmont, on the other hand, rejects flatly the idea of impersonality: 'To be impersonal is to be personal in a special kind of way: look at Flaubert. It's a kind of jargon people use; the objective is one of the forms of the subjective.'[8] But in *Le Problème du Style*, he develops his case *against* the notion of impersonality in terms which, paradoxically, seem to contribute directly to both Joyce's and Eliot's account of it. Gourmont declares that the modern poet could have nothing to learn from Homer; Homer is the product of a primitive culture which, stylistically, had not passed beyond the stage of simile to that of metaphor. He sets against Homer the distinctively modern genius of Flaubert, and rejects the notion that Flaubert's genius can be called impersonal with the remark that only mediocre works of art can be called impersonal; that Flaubert's genius is in proportion to the degree to which he filled his work with his own personality, draining his own personal life to the lees to do so. Eliot quotes from the passage in his essay on Massinger: 'Flaubert incorporait toute sa sensibilité à ses oeuvres . . . Hors de ses livres, où il se transvasait goutte à goutte, jusqu'à la lie, Flaubert est fort peu intéressant.'[9] The reader may compare this with the opening of the passage from Joyce quoted above, and with an interestingly similar passage from Eliot's essay 'Ben Jonson', which was published in the same month as the second part of 'Tradition and the Individual Talent': 'The creation of a work of art, we will say the creation of a character in a drama, consists in the process of transfusion of the personality; or in a deeper sense, the life, of the author into the character' (*SE*, 157). All this modifies the notion of impersonality radically; it suggests an idea which is *almost* opposite to the idea as it has generally been understood, and something very close indeed to the doctrine which Gourmont urged *against* the idea of impersonality.

I have already quoted Eliot's remark, published only a few months after 'Tradition and the Individual Talent', that 'we need a digestion that can assimilate both Homer and Flaubert.' This surely is, on one level at least, a reply to Gourmont. Gourmont's idea, that the modern has nothing to learn from Homer, is anathema to anyone whose notion of tradition, like Eliot's, entails a living continuity between past and present, so that the whole tradition, 'the mind of Europe', is, as it were, 'Homer' developed and augmented by all that which has occurred between the pre-Hellenic world and our world. From this point of view, Flaubert's notion of impersonality, and the idea as it recurs through Zola to Mann, Joyce and Eliot, is the modern claim to the same rights and responsibilities for the contemporary artist as those enjoyed by the *Homeridae*; the rôle of the artist, in his essential relationship to other artists and his readers, remains unchanged even though the tradition grows richer and more complex every day. For Eliot, then, the methods and discoveries of anthropology enable one to see where precisely the essential continuity lies between artists as different as the ancient anonymous *Homeridae* and Flaubert with his distinctively modern, and incidentally very individual, sensibility.

The theory implies an important claim for poetry: the poet becomes in it a servant of something infinitely more valuable, almost a prophet of profound mysteries like the ancient Sybil who sat at the mouth of the underworld dreaming those dreams which pass through the gates of horn. Indeed, in the structure of the poems and dramas, characters like Sweeney, guarding 'the hornèd gate', Tiresias, foreseeing and foresuffering all, and the 'Guardians' of *The Cocktail Party* play a prophetic rôle just as certainly as the Sybil hanging in her bottle at the entrance to *The Waste Land*. This would seem to be in some ways curiously close to the Romantic theory of inspiration which Eliot was so anxious to avoid; but the context of the idea in Eliot alters it. Eliot had no time at all for positivist views such as those expressed by I. A. Richards, echoing Arnold in *Poetry and Science*. 'Poetry is capable of saving us', says Richards, dressing up poetry as a substitute for religion, in reply to which Eliot comments acidly: 'it is like saying that the wallpaper will save us when the wall has crumbled', and goes on to speak of 'the religious, ritual and magical view of nature upon which poetry has always depended.'[10] But this implies that everything, the wall itself and our shelter against the chaos of wind and weather depends upon the religious, ritual and magical view; and there are many other places where Eliot shows his belief that poetry not only depends upon this view, it is also one of its integral supports. If the structure as a whole decays, then the fragments left behind may only shore up the ruins; poetry is of one flesh with it, no accidental companion. If we cannot comprehend this view of poetry, we can get nowhere with Eliot's poems, especially with those from 'Gerontion' onwards, or with the dramas.

It can be seen from Eliot's comments on Richards that he had moved well away from the cautious scepticism of Bradley's method— the review I have just quoted was written in 1927, the year of Eliot's conversion, but the process was already well under way by the time of 'Tradition and the Individual Talent'. Eliot is moving towards a much earlier pattern of metaphysics and psychology; a pattern deeply rooted in the European mind, in that Graeco-Christian tradition of which Paul Elmer More was later to write. The end product is neither metaphysics nor psychology, nor is it theology; but the use of various often apparently contradictory philosophical and theological ideas and assumptions as the basis for poetic myth; and the principle of unity isn't a philosophical or rational one, but poetic; Eliot strives for an emotional unity.

Thus, in 'Tradition and the Individual Talent', Eliot draws our attention to Aristotelian psychology and metaphysics, by using this tag as epigraph to Section III:

ὁ δὲ νοῦς ἴσως θειότερόν τι καὶ ἀπαθες ἐστιν.

(*De Anima*, 408b, 29)

(the mind is something more godlike and is *apathes*.)

The mind, or νοῦς, says Aristotle, is unable by itself to pity or love or learn or think, feel anger or fear, to remember or desire, but is the instrument by which one does these things. Mind seems to be unmoving and imperishable and independent; it is not affected by the decay of the body or the organs of sense, and therefore it cannot age. When the individual dies memory and love fail, for they were never part of the mind, but of the whole entity which has perished. But the mind is something more godlike and *apathes*. *Apathes* can

[56]

have many nuances of meaning: without feeling, indifferent or un-affected.

Eliot here gives us a reminder of one of the focal points in an ancient philosophical tradition; a statement of what one might describe as a philosophic myth of tremendous power. The psychology of *De Anima* dominated the late mediaeval Christian tradition; Aquinas wrote a commentary on it and developed its ideas in the *Summae*. But it had also profoundly influenced neo-Platonic thought —the *Enneads* I.i. of Plotinus is in effect a commentary on *De Anima* —and by that route entered the Augustinian tradition. And during the many years when Islam was the conduit through which European philosophy flowed, *De Anima* was the greatest source-book for psychological thinkers. The tradition did not begin with Aristotle, however, nor yet with the pre-Socratic thinkers; Eliot, with his interest in anthropology, would have been interested in its con-tinuity with the religious and magical ideas which preceded philo-sophical speculation—the kind of thing which F. M. Cornford deals with in *From Religion to Philosophy* (1912).

There is obviously a close relationship between the content of this philosophic myth and the matters which we have dealt with in our first chapter. Aristotle's νοῦς bears a close relationship to the soul of the metaphysical imagination, the 'you' of Prufrock in its detachment from emotion, sense-perception and the world of objects. Clearly, too, it has a bearing on Eliot's notion in 'Tradition and the Individual Talent' of the poet's mind; the catalyst, inert and un-changing but in some way the instrument by which objects in the world of sensation and feeling combine and relate. In the dualism of 'the man who suffers and the mind which creates' the mind has a rôle which is similar to the 'more godlike' mind of *De Anima*, while 'the man who suffers' is close to the 'I' of 'Prufrock', the sad buffoon who acts his empty rôle in the world of emotion and sensation, that aspect of the whole entity which, Aristotle says, is able to love, pity and learn.

The critical ideas of 'impersonality' and 'tradition' are, considered by themselves, not new ones, as we have seen. What is most new about the way in which Eliot uses them is that he translates the metaphysics of the tradition into the critical theory, thus giving 'impersonality' and 'tradition' a new context. In a way, his dis-claimer, 'This essay proposes to halt at the frontier of metaphysics and mysticism' (*SE*, 21), is a mild but deliberate deception—a clue

[57]

to the importance of the metaphysical—and also the mystical—
extensions of the idea, and to the many ways in which his aesthetic
parallels the metaphysic.

In 'Gerontion' the pattern is developed in a new direction, and
the 'I' and the 'you' of 'Prufrock' appear once more, but the pronominal conceit is considerably changed, in that 'we' takes on a new
function. In 'Prufrock' there is no reason why we should not read
'we' as the natural entity which comprehends 'I' and 'you'—the
whole man in his natural state. In 'Gerontion', 'we' is a different
kind of unity, the metaphysical unity which lies behind and beyond
the world of you and I. 'The universals', 'the mind of Europe' are
replaced by a concept with a richer and more direct symbolic
strength, a myth central to the tradition which comprehends and
transcends them all—the myth (and like Paul Elmer More I would
ask that myth be not taken in a pejorative sense) of Christ:

> Signs are taken for wonders. 'We would see a sign!'
> The word within a word, unable to speak a word,
> Swaddled with darkness. In the juvescence of the year
> Came Christ the tiger
>
> . . .
>
> The tiger springs in the new year. Us he devours. Think at last
> We have not reached conclusion when I
> Stiffen in a rented house.

The religious myth here is threefold: Christ as *Logos*, Christ as
devourer, and Christ as spirit of the year, or to use a term drawn from
Harrison and Cornford, the *eniautos daimon*.

Christ as *eniautos daimon* comes not at the season of Christ's
nativity but at the season of His return to earth, 'depraved May':
Easter day normally occurs in April and the Ascension is traditionally
considered to have occurred forty days later, normally, therefore, in
May. But perhaps more important than this is the strong relationship
between Christ and the *eniautos daimon* of vegetation rituals which
is so often implied by Frazer and his followers; the spirit of the new
year comes with the new spring in these myths—therefore 'in the
juvescence of the year.'

Christ as *Logos* is a theme we have met before in 'Mr. Eliot's
Sunday Morning Service'. The clearest reference, as in the earlier
poem, is to the Gospel of St John: 'In the beginning was the Word,
and the Word was with God, and the Word was God' (1:1). We have

touched very briefly upon the theological history of the concept of the *Logos*; but the concept has a history which goes back long before the Gospel of St John. With his interests in the origins of our most essential philosophical and religious concepts in the myth and ritual of pre-history, Eliot was surely interested in the survival value of the idea, in the way in which its persistence seems to show that it satisfies some deep need. A remark by Cornford shows how the idea in Greek philosophy and mystery religion concentrates much of that desire to see unity and reality in a dual world of illusion: 'To the mysticism of all ages, the visible world is a myth, a tale half true and half false, embodying a *logos*, the truth which is one.'[11] The way in which Christianity employs the word is good evidence of More's thesis that there is an essential continuity between Greek and Christian philosophical and religious thought; that the Christian myth of the God-man is a satisfaction of the ancient Greek, and not merely Greek, but essentially human, puzzle of unity in duality. Christ as Word therefore has an important symbolic position, as philosophic myth, in the puzzles that trouble Eliot's poetic imagination. The Christian doctrine of the second person of the Trinity is the mythological embodiment of a metaphysical longing which is also expressed by the solar hero, priest-king and the ancient theme of death and resurrection. Each deals with the incarnation of eternal, unchanging, one-ness in the flux of time.

Right at the centre of the Christian mythological pattern which expresses this religious belief is the Pauline doctrine of salvation:

> Know ye not, that so many of us as were baptized into Jesus Christ were baptized into his death? Therefore we are buried with him by baptism into death: that like as Christ was raised up from the dead by the glory of the Father, even so we also should walk in newness of life. For if we have been planted together in the likeness of his death, we shall be also in the likeness of his resurrection. Knowing this, that our old man is crucified with him, that the body of sin might be destroyed, that henceforth we should not serve sin.
>
> (Rom. 6: 3–6)

The Christian hope of salvation lies in the death of one's self, as old man, one's rebirth in a new identity, that which is called in the Catholic tradition 'the mystical body of Christ.' Baptism is thus a symbolic crucifixion, and at the same time a symbolic resurrection in which we lose our individual identity and merge into a new corporate identity: 'I' becomes 'we'. The anthropologists who were contemporaries of Eliot would have had no difficulty at all in finding parallels for this in pre-Christian and later pagan practice; tribal identity is commonly expressed in terms of a corporate spirit, whether by totem or by the initiation rituals associated with the *eniautos daimon*, the vegetation God, or the solar hero. In Eliot's analysis of society this corporate identity, of 'the same people living in the same place', became a necessity for the health of the individual, or indeed of the society. At once, in transcending the narrow limitations of one's individuality, one becomes not only part of a unified society, but part of a metaphysical reality. To change from old man into new is to lose doubleness in a new impersonal identity, to solve the problem of human communication and at the same time the problem of metaphysical isolation. The problem which Bradley never answered seemed to have been answered at least in symbolic, ritual form. In 'Gerontion', Eliot is still confronting the problem only as symbol and as prophecy; philosophic myth is a means of poetic organization, a still somewhat fearful exploration of the possibility offered by the tradition; it must be remembered that the formal step of entering the ritual communion was still to be delayed for another eight years, till 1927.

As St Paul uses the term, 'old man' has nothing to do with age— the original Greek makes this quite clear. The title of 'Gerontion' is from the Greek, and means 'little old man' in the sense of old in years; Eliot habitually uses punning references of this kind, and it is quite characteristic of him that he exploits the ambiguity between the two meanings of 'old', retreating a little from simple correspondences in meaning, enriching the texture by allowing the meaning to shift between one and the other. But if we read the poem with the care it demands we can see that 'old man' is consistently used to describe a dual sensibility, 'I' and 'you' unreconciled, while Christ the tiger's second appearance initiates a new phase in the drama— I and you become we; 'Us he devours.' The new man is 'devoured' in the sense that he, or 'we', is consumed by a new unity. This is the tables turned, for earlier Eliot has used the imagery of eating in what seems to be the reverse way:

> In the juvescence of the year
> Came Christ the tiger

In depraved May, dogwood and chestnut, flowering judas,
To be eaten, to be divided, to be drunk
Among whispers;

How can we explain this mystery, that Christ the tiger is first drunk and eaten, and then devours 'us', both in the new year? The mystery is that of the Eucharist; a ritual which again has its many pagan counterparts, particularly in the ancient religions of the near and middle East. The Eucharist is a re-affirmation of the miracle achieved by Baptism; the flesh and blood of Christ is eaten and drunk by the communicant as a ritual expression of his one-ness with Christ. The ritual meal is an expression of unity; by a metaphysical conceit the unity is said to be 'divided' in the ritual, and there follow various images of divided humanity in all its displaced variety:

by Mr. Silvero
With caressing hands, at Limoges
Who walked all night in the next room;
By Hakagawa, bowing among the Titians;
By Madame de Tornquist, in the dark room
Shifting the candles; Fräulein von Kulp
Who turned in the hall, one hand on the door.

Each character is an image of alien restlessness and impermanence, brought to life briefly by a characteristic gesture or a pose in a way which reminds one of the memory in 'La Figlia che Piange'. Their brief existences in the depraved May of human being are caught, not in actuality but in image; they are not real people but inhabitants of an imagination or memory. So, an Italian in France, his hands restless in a continual caressing movement, his feet restless in movement through the night; an oriental importing his own precise cultural rituals into an ancient and very different cultural milieu where they seem unfortunate and misplaced, even absurd; a Swedish woman, perhaps a medium engaged in a curious ritual of her own, an alien in a world of spirits; the German girl, her momentary gesture caught in a fixed cameo of the memory, expressive of impermanence and change. Each is a private world, a gesture, an action, a part in an inconceivably complex drama. Each is a separate identity, a separate 'person', but only as caught in the memory of an 'I' who remembers and imagines, and expresses the impossibility of actual communication

[61]

through the habit of his memory and his own personality. They are the impossibly isolated elements of experience, each caught taking part in separate rituals, but at the same time a common, eucharistic ritual, attending upon the alchemy of an incredible miracle: they are 'vacant shuttles', but they 'weave the wind'.

The mind in which these images occur is an 'I' addressing a 'you' —'An old man in a draughty house' which is the natural body which confines the experience. Within the private world of memory and imagination he summons a world of people to act out a ritual, and the ritual, as acted out, deepens the paradox. The knowledge of isolation and of decay, the knowledge of restlessness and impermanence, the knowledge of incompleteness and indirection are dramatized in the ritual, but so is the daring hope that all this may be transcended:

'After such knowledge, what forgiveness?'

—for that which is promised by the ritual of the Eucharist is a special grace, a gift of forgiveness and of union. But knowledge implies sin, so how can one hope that the ritual may be completed in a new unity; how can such a gift be solicited?

'I', an old man, addresses 'you' (who is yet himself) saying 'Think now': the 'I' who remembers may only 'remember' fragments which are constructed to satisfy the present passion, but perhaps 'you' can do better. As the mind of the poet may be the point of view from which an otherwise lamed and undistinguished personality may catch at and bring into life the wisdom of a race and a culture, so perhaps 'you' may discover the answer, not in any personal memory, but in the corporate memory which is history. Whereas the self, in its sensuous and imaginative mode, may only construct a private world of inchoate images, it may appeal to the mind which creates to look at experience from the point of view in which self recedes, and experience approaches a universal knowledge. But the process is difficult and uncertain; Augustine speaks of the complexity and confusion of such a probing into *nescio qui secreti atque ineffabiles sinus eius*—'the cunning passages and contrived corridors' which frustrate the seemingly endless search for meaning. Vanity and ambition, the squabbling demands of the personal self, divert and distort the search, and when some real discovery is made it is often at the wrong time because of our inattention or faithlessness, or it 'gives too late/ What's not believed in, or is still believed,/In memory only, reconsidered passion.' The intellect may in certain stages or in certain

[62]

ways be an independent agent, but it is still part of a whole; there may be a kind of belief attained, but it still may not be significant, because it immediately becomes part of the inchoate world of accidentals. Belief, in the private world of the personal self's constructs of memory, may become image rather than reality. Or it may be given to a Prufrock: 'Gives too soon/Into weak hands, what's thought can be dispensed with/Till the refusal propagates a fear.' The gift is not given for private virtues—'neither fear nor courage saves us'—and so the workings of this special grace seem bafflingly ambivalent and contradictory:

> Unnatural vices
> Are fathered by our heroism. Virtues
> Are forced upon us by our impudent crimes.

These are the paradoxes of the classic tragedy, the fates forced on Lear, Othello and Coriolanus, whose sins against the natural moral law are products of their heroism, or whose virtues are forced upon them by their crimes. The whole passage recalls not only the paradoxical fates of Elizabethan tragedy but also its sinuous and energetic language, though there is no sense of anachronism. The paradoxes of tragedy are *exempla* of the ambivalent paradoxes of natural man: the *felix culpa* by which Adam gained knowledge at the expense of sin, and gained the possibility of forgiveness by incurring the anger of God, at last results in the drama of the Cross:

> These tears are shaken from the wrath-bearing tree.

The first Adam's tree sheds tears and anger, but implies the atonement offered by Christ, the second Adam. So the search ends, not in any triumph for either 'I' or 'you'—neither for the sensitive self foraging in its memory nor for the questing intellect trying to sort out the involutions of history, but in the special grace extended by the Eucharist, the consummation of the ritual of eating and drinking: 'I' and 'you', now united into transcendent singleness, being 'devoured' by the terrible spirit of Christ:

> The tiger springs in the new year. Us he devours.

The passage which follows depends so much upon the pronominal conceit that it is difficult to see how sense can be made of it in any other way. 'I', the sensitive self, will die, and has only temporary possession of a body, 'a rented house.' But 'we' may survive that death:

> Think at last
> We have not reached conclusion, when I
> Stiffen in a rented house.

'I' is a showman: sensation, image, the 'reconsidered passion' of memory, group themselves and pose like Mr Silvero and his friends in a penny peepshow of the mind. The show is unreal, but not a deliberate deception by malignant spirits; the experience which an uncritical and pathetic sensibility gathers is apparently without meaning but certainly not without purpose. It is a preparation for a simpler and more real state of being:

> Think at last
> I have not made this show purposelessly
> And it is not by any concitation
> Of the backward devils.
> I would meet you upon this honestly.

Eliot was later to deal sensitively with the process of growing up from early childhood to maturity in *Animula*; here the little soul grown into old man looks back over the process now complete. 'I would meet you upon this', but the meeting is difficult now, since the whole process of life has been a progressive dissociation of sensibility: emotion becomes detached from intellect; the mind which creates separates from the man who suffers. The innocent sensuous consciousness of beauty which we as adults suppose to be the gift of children is taken away and fear and doubt take its place as the divided consciousness fails to connect in harmony:

> I that was near your heart was removed therefrom
> To lose beauty in terror, terror in inquisition.

The terrible gap between potential passion and any realization possible in life yawns wider; passion must be compromised, cheapened, mixed with impurities, so passion itself begins to die as it is frustrated of motive and end:

> I have lost my passion: why should I need to keep it
> Since what is kept must be adulterated?

[64]

All the apparatus of sense declines with age as the body dies. The intellective soul, separate as it is from the sensitive apparatus, cannot feel emotion, cannot relate to objects or senses or ideas directly, yet in some way a relationship is achieved, says Aristotle:

> Probably it is better to say, not that the soul grieves, or learns, or thinks, but rather that the soul is the instrument by which man does these things—that is to say that the movement does not take place in the soul, but sometimes penetrates to it and sometimes starts from it.
>
> (*De Anima*, 408b, 14)

The connection is the key mystery of the ancient psychology. In the working model of the pronominal conceit which Eliot uses, the problem is still there: when the body and its sensual organs decay and disappear, can perception continue to relate the elements of a divided sensibility:

> I have lost my sight, smell, hearing, taste and touch:
> How should I use them for your closer contact?

If 'I' and 'you' merge into a more complete unity with the falling away of flesh and sense, will the life that ensues be, in any sense that 'I' can understand, a life at all? An old man, both old in years and old because still unregenerate, marks time waiting for the last spark of an old life to fade, and wondering what in the end can be meant by the promise that self and time and space and decay and corruption will end:

> What will the spider do,
> Suspend its operations, will the weevil
> Delay?

But time has not stopped; these are still 'Tenants of the house'; the rain of spring which brings new life and Christ the tiger are still awaited; and a sign, too, is still awaited.

The contrast between 'Gerontion' and the poems which immediately precede it is remarkable; the freedom of rhythm allows a flexibility of tone and a fine matching of word and tone which is impossible within the smart jaunty metric of the quatrains—Eliot seldom was able to use confining patterns of metre to release a fluid and impassioned energy as Donne or Pope or Yeats did. In this respect, the claim to traditionalism sometimes seems a little odd, but

Eliot's respect for tradition is not of the kind which results in a simple controlling and shaping of the present by the past; indeed it should result in the reconstruction of the past. And that past is not simply the past of verse, or even a literary past; it is a past of religion, magic, myth, philosophy and history; of the whole communal experience of a civilization as it is present in one mind. Traditional feeling, thought, form and action enter into a new relationship controlled by a present experience, as a tiny jolt to a kaleidoscope will cause the same elements to change relationships and therefore change their whole nature within the perceiver's consciousness. Thus, whatever the sacrament of Eucharist, or the Aristotelian doctrine of the soul may mean to St Augustine, Macchiavelli or Mr Gladstone, in this expression of a present personality they enter into a new combination with each other which mutates each element, and mutates an idea of history, and memories of Elizabethan tragedy and a great deal else. There is a sense in which tradition ceases to be tradition if it ceases to mutate in this way; and once the holdings of knowledge and understanding of a culture begin to increase in geometric progression, as they have done in this century, one of the ways by which continued mutation and new relationship is made possible is by a bursting open of the forms which contain the process. In the process a modern tone or accent or mood may mimic one from the past. So we can discover a curious relationship between men widely separated in time and experience, in their worlds as a whole; like that which exists between Eliot and Lancelot Andrewes.

Andrewes's characteristic love of word-play, a witty eloquence in the service of God, is in some ways like Eliot's habit of punning and allusion, though more confident in a more assured and homogeneous tradition. I shall end the chapter with a quotation from Andrewes, not just because it contributes significantly to the imagery of 'Gerontion', but because it demonstrates how a certain type of metaphysical imagination, which Andrewes and Eliot share, will habitually think and feel about the sign or symbol whether in religion or literature, standing aside and looking at it; walking around and sniffing it closely; developing it from every point of view to extract the last drop of its significance before leaving it alone. Andrewes in his way was a prophet, but one suited to the ingenious English listener of the seventeenth century. Eliot's ingenuity—nervously taut and frequently distorted into sickness and incoherence—self-conscious and insecure, adventurous and impatient with life, is more

[66]

suited to the twentieth century, with its desperate uncertainty in questions of value or truth. So here is Andrewes:[12]

> *Signes* are taken for wonders: (*Master we would faine see a Signe*, that is, a *miracle*). And, in this sense, it is a Signe, to wonder at. Indeed, every word (heer) is a wonder: τὸ βρεφος *an infant*; *Verbum infans*, the *Word* without a *word*; the *aeternall Word* not hable to speake a word; 1. A wonder sure. 2. And the σπαργανισμός *Swadled*; that a wonder too. *He*, that (as in the 38 of *Job* he saith) *taketh the vast body of the maine Sea, turnes it to and fro, as a little child, and rolls it about with the swadling bands of darknesse*; He, to come thus into *clouts*, himselfe! 3. But yet, all is well; all children are so: but in praesepi, that is it, there is the wonder: Children lye not there; He doth: There lieth He; the *Lord of glorie*, without all *glorie*. Instead of a *Palace*, a *poore stable*; of a cradle of state a beasts *cratch*; no pillow, but a lock of hay; No hangings, but dust and cobwebs; No attendants, but *in medio animalium* (as the fathers read the third of Abakuk): For, if the *Inne* were full, the *stable* was not empty, we may be sure. A Signe this, (nay three, in one), able to amaze any.

'Tradition and the Individual Talent', says Eliot 'proposes to halt at the frontier of metaphysics or mysticism', but in 'Gerontion' there is a toe, or a whole foot, over the border. The troubled quest for a way through this further kingdom continues in Eliot's next major poem, *The Waste Land*.

[67]

'BETWEEN TWO LIVES'
THE WASTE LAND

No one is likely to dispute that *The Waste Land* is one of the most important poems written in English in the twentieth century. It is something of a mystery that this should be so. In the twenties and the thirties it was felt to be representative of the age; an indictment of the sterility and muddle of the contemporary world: many readers continue to respond to the poem in the same way. In the twenties and thirties many readers felt that the poem explored new modes of poetic statement and structure, that it opened the way to a new kind of poetry more suited to contemporary experience than any poetic mode attempted in the past. The abrupt, elliptical mode of the poem, its withdrawal from clearly articulated narrative or argument, its deliberate discontinuities, seemed to reflect a general disorientation, and at the same time to reflect an anxious search for direction and continuity which was characteristic of the age.

It is not always possible to trust a poet's statements about his own verse, especially when they are made after a long interval: even when such statements are accurate accounts of the writer's experience of his own work, they may be irrelevant to our experience of his writings. But a remark like the following (which Mrs Eliot allows to stand as a kind of epigraph to her edition of the *Facsimiles and Transcripts*) at least shows that Eliot felt in later life that the wrong kind of respect had been accorded to *The Waste Land*:

> Various critics have done me the honour to interpret the poem in terms of criticism of the contemporary world, have considered it, indeed, as an important bit of social criticism. To me it was only the relief of a personal and wholly insignificant grouse against life; it is just a piece of rhythmical grumbling.

(FT, 1)

It is not 'just' a piece of rhythmical grumbling; but to treat it as an objective or detached criticism of the world is to ignore the way in which an eccentric and very *personal* energy informs the whole work; to treat it as an entirely purposeful and carefully designed structure in which every ellipsis, every abrupt shift in tone, every secretive allusion and unexplained symbol is there for precisely such a reason, is to ignore the almost accidental nature of the poem's structure as it is. By accidental I do not simply refer to the history of the poem's gestation and its retrieval by Pound the midwife. The Caesarian section would not have been needed if Eliot had not been in a muddle about the poem; the muddle was, I believe, not quite the purposeful muddle that artists frequently tolerate as they work towards a clear goal, a goal which they grasp, in some way or other, before they actually achieve it. In part, at least, the poem's discontinuities and uncertainties arise from the muddle that Eliot's mind was in as he wrote; the poem is, on one level, the expression of an emotional mess.

Pound put his pencil through a great deal of material which is coarsely inadequate, poor in spirit, sloppy in feeling; and yet the deleted passages are never completely out of keeping with the rest of the poem, as when the draft speaks of the swarming, huddled life of London:

> Knowing neither how to think, nor how to feel,
> But lives in the awareness of the observing eye.
> Phantasmal gnomes, burrowing in brick and stone and steel!
> Some minds, aberrant from the normal equipoise
> (London, your people is bound upon the wheel!)
> Record the motions of these pavement toys
> And trace the cryptogram that may be curled
> Within these faint perceptions of the noise,
> Of the movement, and the lights!
>
> Not here, O Ademantus, but in another world.

(*FT*, 31)

'Not here, O Ademantus' gestures towards the kind of 'aberrant' consciousness needed: as Mrs Eliot reminds us, Adeimantus and Glaucon, Plato's brothers, were two of the interlocutors in *The Republic*. But Plato and his Socrates, even though their ironies often bite sharply, even though they measured the inadequacies of this world against an ideal world of philosophical truth, would not permit themselves the note of arrogance and almost hysterical rage which creeps in here. Truth wasn't a 'cryptogram' for Plato, though indeed the philosopher was a man of special gifts and finely trained in using them; but truth, for Plato, shone through everything if a man loved truth enough. And there is nothing of the philosopher's equipoise in 'pavement toys', or in the painful contempt of the successive phrases which were deleted before Eliot arrived at this last version: 'huddled toys', 'tarnished toys' and 'poor cheap toys'. In *The Waste Land* Eliot assumes something of the prophetic manner; but it is often ill-mannered prophecy, crotchety, grumpy, and wilful, morally insecure and sometimes too clever by half.

It may seem uncalled-for to take Eliot to task for passages which he finally deleted; but it is sometimes necessary to find means of standing back from a familiar work and looking at it from a new vantage point: the passage quoted will serve to bring out the element of railing at the world, at man, at life, which is central to *The Waste Land*.

Yet railing is an almost necessary element of all prophecy, particularly of prophecy in the Hebraic tradition: Isaiah, Ezekiel, Jeremiah, nagged the Hebrews into a sense of purpose. They criticized their own society, however, from the standpoint that it had veered away from the true path and could be brought back to normality, whereas Eliot's somewhat arrogant assumption in this and in later works—for instance in 'Sweeney Agonistes' or *The Family Reunion*—was that only a very special sensibility could discover clarity of spirit. Eliot, perhaps for these reasons, could not achieve the Hebrew note of assured prophetic statement; he is (as Pound suggests in a marginal note to the manuscript) altogether too 'personal'; but it is nevertheless of great importance to see the prophetic ambitions of the poem, and at the same time to see how these ambitions are compromised (and the poem made more interesting) by the erratic individual note of spleen and anguish.

Eliot planned, at one stage, to publish 'Gerontion' as a kind of preface to *The Waste Land*. *The Waste Land* was to be what went on in Gerontion's—the old man's—mind. Pound dissuaded him from doing this, but Eliot finally got round Pound's guard in one of his notes to the poem. 'What Tiresias' (another old man) '*sees*, in fact is the substance of the poem'. Tiresias is blind; what he *sees* is nothing to do with what is ordinarily called sight. The substance of the poem, therefore, is visionary or prophetic experience: in the original draft version Tiresias first appears directly after the deleted passage quoted above: he represents the aberrant consciousness which is capable of reading the cryptogram. And this capacity to *see* has a great deal to do with the comprehensiveness of his experience:

> Just as the one-eyed merchant, seller of currants, melts into the Phoenician Sailor, and the latter is not wholly distinct from Ferdinand Prince of Naples, so all the women are one woman, and the two sexes meet in Tiresias.   (Note to line 218)

The pronominal conceit, which is so prominent a part of 'Prufrock' and 'Gerontion', has a less important part to play in *The Waste Land*. Instead of 'I', 'you' and 'we' (with, sometimes 'one')— that insubstantial elusive cast in Eliot's dramas of the soul—the doubleness of human experience is represented, dramatically, in a series of sexual encounters, and the ambivalent totality of that experience represented in Tiresias. Sexual encounters, or evasions, have provided the structure of several of the earlier poems; in 'Portrait of a Lady', 'La Figlia che Piange' and in several of the quatrain poems there is more to the encounter, or to the parting of the sexes, than narrative or anecdote.

THE EPIGRAPH

We do not know precisely at which stage Eliot decided to preface the poem with an epigraph. It seems to have been at a fairly late stage (but before he showed the poem to Pound) that he hit upon the first choice of an epigraph from Conrad's *Heart of Darkness*:

> Did he live his life again in every detail of desire, temptation, and surrender during that supreme moment of complete knowledge? He cried in a whisper at some image, at some vision—he cried out twice, a cry that was no more than a breath—
> 'The horror! the horror!'

Pound didn't feel Conrad was 'weighty enough to stand the citation'; Eliot protested that the passage 'is much the most appropriate I can find, and somewhat elucidative', but finally accepted Pound's criticisms, and replaced Conrad with the epigraph from Petronius, which, though it is also elucidative, throws light on different things in the poem:

> Nam Sibyllam quidem Cumis ego ipse oculis meis
> vidi in ampulla pendere, et cum illi pueri dicerent:
> Σίβυλλα τί θέλεις; respondebat illa: ἀποθανεῖν θέλω.

The epigraph from Petronius stands; in its indirectness and ambiguity it comments with a certain wit upon the action of the poem, and also contributes to the elliptical, gnomic manner: 'With my own eyes I saw the Sybil hanging in a bottle at Cumae, and when the boys said: "Sybil, what's the matter"; she replied: "I long to die." ' Longing for death seems to go together with certain kinds of philosophical idealism and religious feeling almost inevitably. Plato makes Socrates say in the *Phaedo*: 'Other people are likely not to realize that those who pursue philosophy rightly study nothing but dying and being dead'; St Paul speaks of the death of the old man in the birth of the new; the ancient cults of the dying gods seemed to Eliot and to his anthropologist contemporaries to embody a broadly similar religious and philosophical aspiration. And yet the tenor of the epigraph from Petronius is not simply to indicate a longing for the timeless, ideal beauty of eternity; it is also to suggest the weariness, the burdensome weight of prophetic knowledge; the dissatisfaction and disgust with the world which must be felt by those gifted with the seer's insight.

I think we must inevitably look upon the prophetic cry of Conrad's Kurtz in a rather different way: the Sybil is a prophetess by profession; Kurtz is a prophet only in the sense that he is at last brought to the point, which any or every man might reach, where the whole structure of action and belief collapses in upon itself, and leaves only emptiness, hopelessness, loneliness, a horror which seems to summarize the universe. And yet, in *Heart of Darkness*, Kurtz's experience is mediated by Marlow's narrative: Marlow, in some sense or other, *sees* the horror which Kurtz *sees*, and yet he returns—an alien, but a wise and human one—to the world, with a calm tranquillity which stems from the ultimate experience of horror. All this makes it in certain important ways a more fitting preparation for *The Waste Land* than the epigraph from Petronius; but the most enlightening thing of all about the Conrad, perhaps, is the way in which it speaks of 'complete knowledge' as something which recapitulates and culminates 'desire, temptation and surrender'. In this respect it announces an aspect of the plan of the poem which is in every way more fundamental than the structural patterns drawn from Jessie Weston and Sir James Frazer. Memory and desire, temptation and surrender, occupy the poet's attention throughout, leading to horror, balanced and confined by the longing for completeness of knowledge, teased by the elusive disappearing vision which hovers on the margins of sight, while the world remains full of darkness and death.

'THE BURIAL OF THE DEAD'

This was the first title for the poem which developed into *The Waste Land* (in so far as one can speak in this way of a poem which grew out of so many disparate fragments and false starts). A later title, added above the first: 'He Do the Police in Different Voices' seems to do two things mainly: it suggests the aspect of ventriloquial melodrama in the poem, and reflects Eliot's own trembling self-consciousness in a self-deprecating gesture. It was only, it seems, much later in the development of the poem that Eliot began to incorporate structural symbolism from Jessie Weston's account of the Grail Legend.

The most important stimulus and source of imagery for the first part of the poem is, then, the Order for the Burial of the Dead in the Anglican *Book of Common Prayer*. Eliot's interest in this and in the Christian modulation of the theme of death and resurrection was by no means new. The first text in the burial service, Christ's words to Martha before the raising of Lazarus from the dead, is the starting point for one of a group of three fragments which were among the bundle of miscellaneous pieces which Eliot sent to Quinn together with the original manuscript of *The Waste Land*: 'I am the resurrection and the life: he that believeth in me, though he were dead, yet shall he live', is transmuted into:

> I am the Resurrection and the Life
> I am the things that stay, and those that flow.
> I am the husband and the wife
> And the victim and the sacrificial knife
> I am the fire, and the butter also.

(FT, 111)

[73]

Mrs Eliot suggests that there is here a combination between the language of Christianity and that of the great Hindu scripture, the *Bhagavad Gita,* and the suggestion is entirely plausible, even though the date of this fragment and the other two that belong with it is early, perhaps even before the 1914 war. Eliot's interest in oriental religion at Harvard had surely been stimulated by its preoccupation with the reconciliation of disharmony into unity. This is what makes the image of 'Christ the tiger' come alive for Eliot in 'Gerontion'; it is what prompts him to experiment with the fusing together of words from Augustine and the Buddha in *The Waste Land*; *The Waste Land* carries one stage further the anxious internal moral debate which is at the heart of his poetry from a very early stage. But perhaps the text from the Order for the Burial of the Dead which stimulated Eliot's interest most is the long passage from Paul (I Cor. 15:20) which speaks of the duality of the human personality, and its ultimate resolution into unity, in the evocative imagery of the sowing and harvesting of grain:

> So also is the resurrection of the dead. It is sown in corruption; it is raised in incorruption: It is sown in dishonour; it is raised in glory: It is sown in weakness; it is raised in power: It is sown a natural body; it is raised a spiritual body.

I suppose we will never really know how much St Paul's choice of words was affected here by the prevalence of vegetation-cults in Mediterranean religion; but there is no doubt at all that Eliot was interested by the way that, once again, death and rebirth are spoken of in terms of planting and harvesting: there was, it seemed, a continuity between the ritual experiences of the worshippers of Adonis, Attis and Osiris, and the familiar rituals of the English church:

> we therefore commit his body to the ground; earth to earth, ashes to ashes, dust to dust; in sure and certain hope of the Resurrection to eternal life, through our Lord Jesus Christ; who shall change our vile body, that it may be like unto his glorious body, according to the mighty working, whereby he is able to subdue all things to himself.

The Order for the Burial of the Dead, seen in this light, is a magical ceremony to ensure the re-birth of the dead into a larger community of the spirit; just as the Eucharist may be seen as a magical ritual in which the living partake in the mystical body of Christ.

Nevertheless, for all his interest in the symbolism of the Christian church, it was to be a long time before he could give the assent of belief to it; in the meantime he acted out the paradoxes of his attitudes towards its doctrine and ritual with a strange mixture of awe and irreverence, fear and bullying, longing and bitter disenchantment. Like a complex and strenuously, sinuously developed oath *The Waste Land* plays a cat and mouse game with stubborn vestiges of faith, but ends uncertain which is cat and which is mouse. Oaths and prophecy are closely related, but the mixture of spleen, weariness, arrogance, belief and uncertainty with which Eliot begins and ends is not likely to lead to any of the more familiar modes of prophecy; or to any stable or consistent tone and manner. Instead Eliot deliberately, like Joyce in *Ulysses*, chooses to employ many different 'voices', with the understanding that each is to be taken as representing an aspect, a phase, of the same person; a person split like Tiresias by contending impulses; a multitude of desires, memories and failures, like Gerontion, but sufficiently a prophet ('aberrant from the normal equipoise') to be acquainted with a world beyond this one, and aware of the dreams that enter through 'the hornèd gate'.

So 'He Do the Police in Different Voices'. Now, with the publication of the *Facsimiles and Transcripts* we can read the first voice which Eliot tried. Its deliberately flat, banal and wandering manner is something of a shock; one has come to expect terse ingenuity from the author of the quatrain poems, elliptical rapidity from the author of 'Gerontion'; the slackness of this, it seems, prompted Eliot to delete it before he sent it to Pound. It is the aimless voice of the living dead describing the living death of the world, a world compact of memory and desire and ruled by appetite. Mrs Eliot has shown that some of Eliot's own personal memories went into this deleted section of the poem.

It is no surprise to find such personal memories in *The Waste Land*; it would be impossible to imagine a poem which explores the terrain which Eliot sets out to explore in this poem, the indistinct borderland between memory and appetite on the one hand and an imagined ideal world on the other, which managed to speak of memory entirely impersonally. What *is* somewhat surprising is the way in which, as we read the original drafts, the opening lines of the final published version have a markedly different impact.

[75]

> April is the cruellest month, breeding
> Lilacs out of the dead land, mixing
> Memory and desire, stirring
> Dull roots with spring rain.

In the draft version, 'memory and desire' refer back to an aimless and miscellaneous sequence of memories; when the first fifty-four lines of the draft are deleted, this new beginning acquires a more universal air of general statement. 'Memory and desire', not related as yet to anything specific, are made, by the metaphor, part of a biological process; not a unique process as we each take our own memories to be unique, private, secret and constantly changing in shape and meaning, but a repeated process in the world outside ourselves, subject to impassive natural forces and not to our wills or our creative imaginations. The mind is made a helpless thing, no more able to resist the forces that work upon it than a root can control the response it makes to rain. The image remained an evocative one for Eliot through his life: in 'Burnt Norton' IV, for instance, he transmutes it, creating a very different view of man's nature and potential by a similar analogy with the biology of plant growth.

April, then, the month of spring flowers and Canterbury pilgrims, is, with deliberate paradox, made 'the cruellest month'; and not cruel by default either; cruel in action, 'breeding', 'mixing', 'stirring', an alchemist or wizard working upon the passive earth; by extension ('memory and desire' slipped in among the roots and the rain) an April of the mind, a cyclical renewal of experience, becomes something which is neither willed nor welcomed, a matter of habit and ritual imposed upon us whether we will or no.

It is, therefore, appropriate that the memories which follow the opening—of the Hofgarten and the Archduke's, of a vanished world of middle-European aristocracy before the Great War—should, so very clearly, not be the poet's own private memories. We know now, thanks to Mr G. K. L. Morris and Mrs Eliot, that these are particular memories—the Countess Marie Larisch's memories of her childhood with the Austrian Imperial family—but that kind of knowledge adds little or nothing to our understanding of the poem, and whatever it does add is somewhat irrelevant.[1] They are *instances* of memory—very evocative ones, it is true—instances of the way in which memory nostalgically attempts to recapture a buried life, to re-create the pleasures of the past, but the real pleasure (and the pain) are in the act of recollection. These instances of memory, particular as they are, are offered, almost, as part of a collective memory, or at least as a model of the way we are all betrayed into pleasure and pain by the habit of nostalgia, regret for the passing of childhood, regret for the passing of a world more secure and more pleasurable than the contemporary world (and both kinds of regret have their element of make-believe).

This is the point at which Eliot most unambiguously refers to the language and habit of Hebrew prophecy:

> What are the roots that clutch, what branches grow
> Out of this stony rubbish? Son of man,
> You cannot say, or guess, for you know only
> A heap of broken images

The Hebrew prophets were custodians of the Jewish tradition: it was their function to criticize Hebrew society for its backslidings, to remind it of the imperatives of morality, ritual and social structure laid down by God; but frequently the prophets went beyond a simple re-assertion of the conventional code of behaviour, exploring with some subtlety the secret motives of man's behaviour towards God and towards other men. Certainly Ezekiel (to whom Eliot refers us in a note at this point) is capable of such insights into unacknowledged habits and motives lying beneath the conscious level. This, at least, was how Ezekiel was seen by many of Eliot's contemporaries, who had begun the novel experiment of treating prophetic scripture as psychological insight. Some mention will be made in the next chapter of Jane Harrison's development of a theory of religious behaviour which is partly based upon Jung's work with archetypal images. In an age when Jungian and post-Imagist theories of art were prevalent, and when Joyce was creating his huge modern myths out of re-current allusions to ancient fable, and quasi-mythical images, the Lord's instructions to Ezekiel to prophesy destruction to the cities of Israel—particularly for breaking the commandment not to set up any graven images—must have seemed peculiarly meaningful. But, of course, the particular quality of the modern interest in myth and image distorts and reforms the old prophecy: 'And your altars shall be desolate, and your images shall be broken. . . . In all your dwelling places the cities shall be laid waste, and the high places shall be desolate' (Ezekiel 6:4–6). Broken images, a waste land, fallen cities, and a desolate altar (like the empty chapel in 'What the Thunder Said')—the parallels between Ezekiel and *The Waste Land* could be multiplied much further, but it will be sufficient here to draw attention to one of Ezekiel's most peculiar prophetic episodes, one which has enough eerie complexity of suggestiveness to excite Freudians to compare it with Freud, Jungians to compare it with Jung, Augustinians to compare it with Augustine, and Eliot (who would have had all three somewhere in his mind, though he would not accord an equal respect to each of them) to see, not only great psychological interest, but also fascinating anthropological resonances.

Ezekiel is told to dig into a wall (Ezekiel 8:5–18) and discovers a secret door; fulfilling his prophetic function, like Tiresias, he *sees*: but like Tiresias, what the Hebrew prophet *sees* is a world of inner realities. He sees the Lord's house; but though it has outer and inner courtyards like the temple at Jerusalem, it is rather a dream temple symbolizing the sickness and apostasy of the Hebrew mind than the real temple of rock and stone:

> So I went in and saw; and behold every form of creeping things, and abominable beasts, and all the idols of the house of Israel, portrayed upon the wall round about. . . . Then he said unto me, Son of man, hast thou seen what the ancients of the house of Israel do in the dark, every man in the chambers of his imagery? for they say, the LORD seeth us not. . . . Then he brought me to the door of the gate of the LORD's house which was towards the north; and behold, there sat women weeping for Tammuz.
>
> (Ezek. 8:10–14)

Tammuz (the west Semitic version of the Greek Adonis) is the dying god blasphemously mourned by the women in Ezekiel's Temple, the dying god which, in his many manifestations, is hunted down by Frazer's eager eclectic scholarship in *The Golden Bough*: the Spartan version was Hyakinthos. As we shall see, the mourning of the girl in the hyacinth garden is surrounded by many diverse allusive patterns drawn from more than one culture, but the god Hyakinthos is one of the memories courted by the episode. And, as we shall also see, the image of the Temple as a lumber room of images of nostalgic power but limited value, is one which lies behind the pattern of 'A Game of Chess'.

But this is looking forward: for the meanwhile the reference to Ezekiel is for two reasons—to imply that prophetic knowledge is embodied in the poem (however mixed with failure and uncertainty), and to strengthen the image of the mind as desert: a desert embarrassed by the cruel flowering of memory and desire:

> Only
> There is shadow under this red rock
> (Come in under the shadow of this red rock),
> And I will show you something different from either
> Your shadow at morning striding behind you
> Or your shadow at evening rising to meet you;
> I will show you fear in a handful of dust.

This passage, too, takes its origin from reflections upon a kind of dying god: it is adapted from an earlier poem, 'The death of Saint Narcissus' (1915), a difficult and ambiguous myth of metamorphosis in which an inordinate self-love is consummated in an ironic martyrdom:

> Come under the shadow of this grey rock
> Come under the shadow of this grey rock
> And I will show you a shadow different from either
> Your shadow sprawling over the sand at daybreak, or
> Your shadow leaping behind the fire against the red rock . . .
> (*FT*, 95)

The shadows in both poems are, fairly clearly, shadows in the same sense that shadows are all that the prisoners in Plato's cave can see, chained with their backs to the bright reality. But in 'The death of Saint Narcissus' we are turned from one kind of shadow to a different kind, from one kind of unreality to another; in 'The Burial of the Dead' the prophet's voice (like that of Kurtz looking into the abyss, or the Sybil longing for death) points to something which is *reality*: 'fear in a handful of dust'. If this were a personal statement, simply a report upon experience, it would be disturbing, an account of the terror a man might feel in moral or spiritual anarchy, conviction of the barrenness of life. But it is not presented as this; it is presented as prophetic statement. And the kind of prophetic knowledge claimed is somewhat different from the prophetic knowledge which Marlow brings back from the heart of darkness, where the experience of horror informs a wisdom and dignity, a quiet stability and poise, whereas here the terror manifests itself in evasion, instability and hysteria—not prophetic knowledge, nor even prophetic doubt, but prophetic ignorance of anything but the terror and the failure. At least one can say that this is peculiarly insecure ground for the prophet's criticism of life; one might, and perhaps should, go further and say that the insecurity and negativeness of the experience makes the tone of prophecy illegitimate, even morally despicable.

There is one small, almost indefinable note of qualification in this, and I am not sure how much real significance it has as a way of relieving the irresponsibility ('To me it was only the relief of a personal and wholly insignificant grouse against life') of Eliot's rhetoric. In a careful and deliberate alteration of the words found in 'Saint Narcissus' he makes 'you' into a traveller—and if a traveller's shadow strides behind him in the morning and rises to meet him in the evening, he is travelling eastward, which is the way a pilgrim travels. The sense that one continues to move on through illusion and despair in a steady direction tends to create a certain ambiguity in the prophecy (and oracles thrive on ambiguity). The ambiguity is deepened by the quotation from *Tristan und Isolde* which follows: 'Fresh blows the wind towards the homeland, my Irish child, why do you linger?' Here the sense of a journey towards some conclusion (a direction which remains valid throughout, despite the fear, the anguish, the boredom) is linked with a sense of opportunities lost. All this prepares for the episode of the hyacinth garden, which, whether we take it as a dream of the past, a nostalgia as imperfect as memories of the Hofgarten, or as an ever-present ideal of beauty, beautiful because of its incompleteness, a promise of consummation which always recedes like Novalis's blue flower; whichever way we take it the hyacinth garden is not dust, or fear:

> You gave me hyacinths first a year ago;
> 'They called me the hyacinth girl'.
> —Yet when we came back, late, from the hyacinth garden,
> Your arms full, and your hair wet, I could not
> Speak, and my eyes failed

Eliot continues to speak, throughout his poetry, of an ecstatic experience which is remembered with tender regret, but also with pain, an ecstatic promise which is not consummated (and it is in this imperfectness that the nostalgia, the beauty and the pain lie) which remains held in suspension in the memory to criticize and render barren the world of ordinary emotion. In a finely suggestive essay Leonard Unger relates some of these ecstatic moments—the hyacinth garden, the rose garden of *Four Quartets*, the tale of the shabby waiter in 'Dans le Restaurant'—to Dante's experiences in the *Vita Nuova*.[2] In his essay on Dante (1929) Eliot speaks of Dante's infantile experience of love:

> In the first place, the type of sexual experience which Dante describes as occurring to him at the age of nine years is by no means impossible or unique. My only doubt (in which I found myself confirmed by a distinguished psychologist) is whether it could have taken place so *late* in life.
>
> (*SE*, 273)

Eliot continues to compare the attitudes towards such an experience (an experience which he assumes we all share) which would be characteristic of Dante's time and our own post-Freudian age:

> The attitude of Dante to the fundamental experience of the *Vita Nuova* can only be understood by accustoming ourselves to find meaning in *final causes* rather than in origins. It is not, I believe, meant as a description of what he *consciously* felt on his meeting with Beatrice, but rather as a description of what that meant on mature reflection upon it. The final cause is the attraction towards God.
>
> (*SE*, 274)

The essay on Dante is a kind of manifesto, a defence of Eliot's Catholicism (he had been converted two years before the essay was published) and is therefore provocative and assertive in its preference of an antique psychology to more modern ideas—the *Vita Nuova* is, he says:

> a very sound psychological treatise on something related to what is now called 'sublimation'. There is also a practical sense of realities behind it, which is antiromantic: not to expect more from *life* than it can give or more from *human* beings than they can give; to look to *death* for what life cannot give.
>
> (*SE*, 275)

However, the same emotion, and some of the same sense of its significance (though hedged about with ironies and doubts) are already present before Eliot's conversion—no doubt they were a powerful force in prompting his conversion.

In the context of *The Waste Land*, then, the hyacinth garden refers, in its beauty and in the incompleteness of its experience, to some half-understood notion of 'final causes'. Experience of this kind is central to the tradition in which Eliot places the *Vita Nuova* —Eliot calls it the tradition of 'vision literature'—for instance St John of the Cross calls this kind of incident in the history of the soul 'the divine touch', or 'the touch of a spark', and refers us to the Song of Solomon. I quote from the Douay version, since it follows the Vulgate, the version which would almost always lie behind the tradition of 'vision literature':

> Let my beloved come into his garden, and eat the fruit of his apple-trees. I am come into my garden, O my sister, my spouse. I have gathered my myrrh, with my aromatical spices. . . . I sleep, and my heart watcheth. The voice of my beloved knocking: Open to me, my sister, my love, my dove, my undefiled: for my head is full of dew, and my locks of the drops of the nights. . . . My beloved put his hand through the *key*-hole, and my bowels were moved at his touch. I arose to open to my beloved: . . . but he had turned aside, and was gone. My soul melted when he spoke. I sought him and found him not: I called, and he did not answer me. . . . His cheeks are as beds of aromatical spices set by the perfumers. His lips are as lilies dropping choice myrrh. His hands are turned and as of gold, full of hyacinths.
>
> (Douay, Canticle, 5, 1–6, 13–14)

The strange beauty of the encounter in the hyacinth garden troubled Eliot's imagination for many years, and it would never quite explain the memory, or the desire or (since the image itself is intended as an enactment of feeling in some way independent of personal emotions) the *community* of its effect, to declare yet another allusion in the already congested allusive pattern of *The Waste Land*. Many commentators have spoken of the Lakonian Hyakinthos, yet another version of the myth of the dying god; there's no reason why he should not be remembered at this point. There's no reason, either, why we shouldn't recall a stanza of Catullus:

> talis in vario solet
> divitis domini hortulo
> stare flos hyacinthinus
> sed moraris, abit dies:
> prodeas, nova nupta.

This epithalamium (Poem LXI) was one of Pound's favourite poems, and one would be surprised if Eliot did not know it well. And its tone and theme coincide remarkably with much of *The Waste Land*: in the first place it is a marriage song (like Solomon's song), and the anticipation, or the failure, or the corruption, of a wedding is a structural metaphor which runs right through *The Waste Land,* most obviously in the adoption of a refrain from Spenser's *Prothalamion* as a significant device in 'The Fire Sermon'. In the second place it echoes (or is echoed by) the allusion to *Tristan und Isolde*: 'So, in the gay little garden of a rich lord a hyacinth-like flower is accustomed to stand; but you delay, the day goes by, come forth, new bride.'

If theories of psychology have any validity (and I suppose they have), their validity lies in the assumption that certain mental or psychic episodes, dreams, habits of expression, behaviour, memory or representation, draw together into a knot or focus a great deal of a man's inner experience, his hopes, fears and desires. If imagist, symbolist, and related aesthetic theories have any validity (and I suppose they have), their validity lies in the assumption that an image or a symbol, the meaning of which may not be immediately clear, and which may even resist perfect explanation permanently, can provide a *way in* to forms of experience which otherwise resist expression, but are fundamental in some way or other. If Eliot's theory of tradition has any validity then the image, the symbol, the episode which carries with it the force of myth or dream, may provide a way in, not simply to the personal experience, but to experience which has its significance precisely because it is not limited to the person of the poet. Paradoxically, in this *way in*, the poet seeks to discover a way *out* of the self, just as in religious ritual, or in the ancient dream conventions of poetry, myth has traditionally been the mode by which men attempt to traverse the area of unreason, the peripheries of experience which, in the ritual, magical or religious view of life, are so extraordinarily important. Thus, a complex of images: hyacinths, a garden, a bride, mourning, a moment of ecstasy interrupted, infantile sexual experience as a promise of divine joy, death and rebirth, sowing and reaping, these and many others may occur in different combinations in the course of human experience and may be expressed in many ways in human literature. Each time they are so used will extend the area of discovery (imaginative discovery, if you will) not only of the poet as adventurer, but also of all those who share sensitively in his exploration.

[83]

So it comes about that, in 'Portrait of a Lady', the young man is challenged by a song and the smell of hyacinths: images which insidiously attack 'self-possession'; which disturb the imagination with desires and ideas which are felt not to be of the 'self', but are felt to be of 'other people'—'common':

> I remain self-possessed
> Except when a street piano, mechanical and tired
> Reiterates some worn-out common song
> With the smell of hyacinths across the garden
> Recalling things that other people have desired.
> Are these ideas right or wrong?

Again, in 'Dans le Restaurant', the snobbish diner complains to the shabby waiter: 'De quel droit payes-tu des expériences comme moi?', admitting the communality of the waiter's memory and desire, and the shared experience of failure: 'Mais alors, tu as ton vautour', so that both diner and waiter suffer endless punishment for a Promethean discovery. And the experience which both remember is a dilapidated equivalent of Dante's meeting with Beatrice in the *Vita Nuova* (as Unger shows); or of the encounter of the Shulamite and her Beloved in the Song of Solomon:

> 'Je la chatouillais, pour la faire rire.
> J'éprouvais un instant de puissance et de délire.'

In the Song of Songs the Bride says 'Dilectus meus misit manum per foramen, et venter meus intremuit ad tactum eius'—My Beloved put his hand through the opening, and my belly trembled inwardly at his touch—and in the restaurant the waiter remembers: I tickled her to make her laugh. I felt a moment of power and joy.

The essential pattern of images can be discerned in many shapes in Eliot's poetry, and in tonalities varying from knockabout farce (as in the portrait of Mr Eugenides, or the teasing dialogues of Sweeney and Doris) to tender nostalgia, as in the rose garden and the hyacinth garden. But in each version, the 'final cause', which is 'attraction towards God' is adumbrated, in however reserved or doubtful a way; and in particular there is, in many manifestations of the pattern, some play with images of seeing:

> I could not
> Speak, and my eyes failed, I was neither

> Living nor dead, and I knew nothing,
> Looking into the heart of light, the silence.

If eyes have failed, then 'looking into the heart of light' must be seeing, not of the eyes, but of the soul; 'the heart of light' (a conscious reversal of Conrad) must be nothing to do with the physical properties of light, but everything to do with the ecstatic illumination of the soul; if, by synaesthetic illogic 'the heart of light' is 'silence', and one *looks* into silence, then the experience pointed to is something entirely beyond sense. 'I was neither/Living nor dead, and I knew nothing', then, while it is an impossible paradox, has a real poetic meaning. It points to a re-definition of 'I', by an irrational and negative use of language, but in a case, perhaps, where any other use of language would be inefficient.

This is a curious territory, and one which may only interest those, who, like Eliot, are in rebellion against sense, or accept that poetry may be meaningful still when it deals with non-sense. If one feels the need to react by saying (following the natural punning logic of language) that it is also nonsense, there is very little to argue about, but it is at least a very ancient form of nonsense, and its tricks of speech and its natural metaphors have contributed a great deal to the history of the human mind. For instance, the traditional interpretation of the Canticle of Canticles has changed very little in its essentials from the very earliest Jewish and Christian commentaries. In the middle of the third century Origen wrote 'It seems to me that this little book is an epithalamium, that is to say, a marriage song, which Solomon wrote in the form of a drama or song under the figure of the Bride, about to wed and burning with heavenly love towards her Bridegroom, who is the Word of God. And deeply indeed did she love Him, whether we take her as the soul made in His image, or as the Church.'[3]

In pagan religion, too, as Frazer, Harrison, Cornford, Murray, and other contemporary anthropologists pointed out, the wedding, a wedding which is in some way or other the burial of the dead, is the master-metaphor for a central experience of the religious sensibility. Cornford, in particular, demonstrates the way in which this solemn and significant metaphor may take other forms than the more obviously serious. In *The Origin of Attic Comedy*, a book which Eliot took very seriously, Cornford observes that Aristophanic comedy has a deeply serious religious purpose; and its most profound moment (as well as its most ribald and apparently irreverent moment) is a wedding procession in which the bridegroom, a riotous and ridiculous buffoon, escorts a mute bride to a marriage. Cornford's analysis is probably faulty in many ways, but Eliot followed him in believing this episode to be a celebration of the *daimon* of the year uniting with the earth goddess, a representation of magical ritual intended to restore the fertility of the earth, to make the waste land green again.

It is not surprising, then, that the touching and beautiful incident in the hyacinth garden is immediately followed by farce and buffoonery. As the Greek tragic trilogy is followed by the satyr play, so the clairvoyant joy of the hyacinth girl is followed by the absurd Madame Sosostris.

In one way, of course, the abrupt shift in tone is defensive; with such violent tensions in mood the reader is not entirely sure how to respond, and the poet himself released from some responsibility. In another way the abrupt change is expressive of a state of mind in which memories of beauty may alternate rapidly with moods of rejection and despair, of self-deprecating silliness. There is always an element of the dandy in Eliot, especially when he finds himself confronted by insecure and ambiguous emotions. Madame Sosostris, for instance, performs an important structural task: she prefigures much of the symbolism of the poem; the Tarot forecasts the action in a real way. At the same time Eliot shrinks from exposing too much of the feeling which lies in the experience of the poem; he pretends, in his best dandy pose, that he is only concerned with mannered social satire.

Of course Eliot didn't take the Tarot seriously in the same sense as Yeats (who was wise and silly in different ways from Eliot) or Arthur Waite, a member of the Order of the Golden Dawn (which gave Yeats and its other members the opportunity to indulge their tastes for mumbo-jumbo). But the Tarot is a rich source of imagery: images broken, meaningless, absurd in themselves, no doubt, but richly evocative, suggestive in many ways of the kind of experience, the kind of longing which obsesses Eliot in so much of his poetry. Waite's almost certainly was the version of the Tarot which Eliot had seen; I quote from his comment on that crucial card, the Hanged Man:[4]

The gallows from which he is suspended forms a Tau cross, while the figure—from the position of his legs—forms a fylfot cross. There is a nimbus about the head of the seeming martyr. It should be noted (1) that the tree of sacrifice is living wood, with leaves thereon; (2) that the face expresses deep entrance-ment, not suffering; (3) that the figure, as a whole, suggests life in suspension, but life and not death. . . . I will say very simply on my own part that it expresses the relation, in one of its aspects, between the Divine and the Universe.

He who can understand that the story of his higher nature is embedded in this symbolism will receive intimations concern-ing a great awakening that is possible, and will know that after the sacred Mystery of Death there is a glorious Mystery of Resurrection.

In Eliot's own words 'all the women are one woman': Madame Sosostris is one aspect of the persona whose other aspects are the Sybil and the hyacinth girl, as well as the lady who sits in the Chair in 'A Game of Chess', the garrulous port-and-lemon in the pub scene, and all the ladies of 'The Fire Sermon'. Like the Sybil, she is a prophe-tess, like the hyacinth girl a seer; but it is neither the pathos nor the beauty of prophecy that Eliot stresses here; it is the absurdity with which we grope towards meaning, using the only tools we have.

The Tarot is, after all, a kind of do-it-yourself poetry kit and primer in prophecy; nothing could be more silly, more of an invita-tion to fraud and pomposity ('He who can understand that the story of his higher nature is embedded in this symbolism will receive inti-mations of a great awakening. . . .'); and yet the Tarot is merely an externalization of a process which is entirely essential to human thinking. The Tarot passage is not simply satire on fortune tellers; it is bitter sarcasm about the natural human anxiety for knowledge, the longing to know 'what it all means', laughter at the presumption of the poet and the philosopher as well as the crystal-gazer. And yet the laughter is insecure: the materials which the absurd fortune-teller handles are those which the poet himself uses:

> Here, said she,
> Is your card, the drowned Phoenician Sailor,
> (Those are pearls that were his eyes. Look!)
> Here is Belladonna, the Lady of the Rocks,
> The lady of situations.
> Here is the man with three staves, and here the Wheel,
> And here is the one eyed merchant . . .

[87]

And thus the most important point about Madame Sosostris is what she does *not* see: 'I do not find / The Hanged Man'; though, like Homer's Tiresias summoned from Hell, she can warn the traveller who seeks her oracle to 'Fear death by water', she is less than sure about 'the final cause'. The defensive ambiguity of the passage is even greater in the original draft, where Eliot inserts between lines fifty-six and fifty-seven an allusion to the prophetic voice of St John the Divine '(I John saw these things, and heard them)'. The brackets may possibly have been intended to suggest an ironic aside, critical of Madam Sosostris's pretensions; whether this is true or not, it is a rather uncertain wobble of feeling, as if the poet were learning to ride a bicycle, and had not got the hang of it yet, as if he isn't quite sure whether to trust his skills or deride himself by falling off in too spectacular a manner. But what follows is masterly:

> Unreal City,
> Under the brown fog of a winter dawn
> A crowd flowed over London Bridge, so many,
> I had not thought death had undone so many.
> Sighs, short and infrequent, were exhaled,
> And each man fixed his eyes before his feet.
> Flowed up the hill and down King William Street,
> To where Saint Mary Woolnoth kept the hours
> With a dead sound on the final stroke of nine.

In the original draft this began 'Unreal City, I have sometimes seen and see', which perhaps insists upon the prophetic vision too much. The final version (more reminiscent, curiously, of parts of Dickens than of Baudelaire or Dante) delivers not so much visionary understanding as the terror of alienation, not so much a heightening of knowledge as the nightmare pain of detachment and withdrawal. The hesitant circularity of 'so many, / I had not thought death had undone so many' conveys this in one way, the passive syntax of 'Sighs, short and infrequent, were exhaled', in another: consider how much of the terrifying unreality of this would disappear with a more direct word-order—'They exhaled short and infrequent sighs', or less deliberately impassive vocabulary 'They sighed briefly from time to time.' Consider too, how the absence of subject in 'Flowed up the hill' robs the throng of moving humanity of any warmth, vitality or personality.

All this provides a context for the curious encounter with Stetson, where, in a fresh use of the pronominal conceit, 'I' calls 'you' to ask about corpses planted in the garden.

'You gave me hyacinths first a year ago': the encounter in the hyacinth garden is remembered with tenderness and nostalgia; the aching sense of loss is tempered by hope, the expectation that what happened, first, a year ago, may happen again. The cry to Stetson appears to mock this hope with a facetious parody:

> 'That corpse you planted last year in your garden,
> 'Has it begun to sprout? Will it bloom this year?'

Once again Eliot, with an anxiety born of insecurity and self-doubt, plays an elaborate game with antique symbolism. The incredibly elaborate funerary rites of ancient Middle Eastern religions, the *rites de passage* of pagan African cultures, even the familiar ceremonies for the burial of the dead in the Anglican prayer book, are magical rituals intended to fulfil the hope that a physical death shall become a spiritual re-birth. A complex development of these ancient rites has entered the inner recesses of the European imagination, become so essential to its image making processes that we frequently employ its strategies in more or less oblique or direct ways in our habits of language or thought, without always recognizing what we are doing. When we *do* recognize what we are doing the recognition may often bring with it a shock of surprise, embarrassment, or absurdity. But at the same time the sense of embarrassed disbelief is mixed with awe: we can never, even if we have rejected the dogma of the Christian faith, overcome the awe we feel at the most powerful of all the dramatizations of death and rebirth, the passion of Christ. It is difficult, for instance, to read Psalm 22 (the one which begins 'My God, my God, why hast thou forsaken me?') without being moved deeply by its apparent prophecy of the passion, even if the emotion is nothing to do with dogmatic belief:

> For dogs have encompassed me: the assembly of the wicked
> have inclosed me: they pierced my hands and my feet. I may
> tell all my bones: they look and stare upon me. They part my
> garments among them, and cast lots upon my vesture. But be
> not thou far from me O LORD: O my strength, haste thee to
> help me. Deliver my soul from the sword; my darling from the
> power of the dog.
>
> (Ps. 22: 16–20)

It would be quite hopeless to try to discover when, or why the dog became established as an image of sensuality, of danger to the immortal soul, for the Jews and the inheritors of the Hebrew tradition. Dog-headed Anubis, for instance, was one of the guides to the reborn soul in Egypt, Cerberus the dog guarded the Greek underworld; but in the Hebrew tradition, and in the Muslim and Christian traditions which take so much from the Jews, the dog is unclean, an enemy to spirituality. St John of the Cross, with characteristic, and somewhat wearying eagerness, allegorizes St Matthew:[5]

> . . . for so long as the soul is subjected to the sensual spirit, the spirit which is pure and spiritual cannot enter it. Wherefore our Saviour said through S. Matthew: *Non est bonum sumere panem filiorum, et mittere canibus.* . . . And elsewhere . . . *Nolite sanctum dare canibus.* Which signifies: give not that which is holy unto the dogs. In these passages Our Lord compares those who deny their creature desires, and prepare themselves to receive the spirit of God in purity, to the children of God; and those who would have their desire feed upon the creatures, to dogs.

I don't suppose for a moment that Eliot had the Spanish mystic in mind as he wrote his words to Stetson:

> 'Oh keep the Dog far hence, that's friend to men
> 'Or with his nails he'll dig it up again!'

But he did, like St John of the Cross, have the Psalmist in mind. The passage has much in common with that in 'Dans le Restaurant', where the waiter's childish experiments with joy are interrupted by a dog which mauls him and his childish partner, stopping them half-way in their ecstasy. In 'Dans le Restaurant' the diner reproaches the waiter for sharing *his own* experience. In *The Waste Land* Eliot accuses *the reader* of sharing the guilt and the failure: 'You! hypocrite lecteur! mon semblable,—mon frère!'—and the reference to Baudelaire deepens the sense that in some way it is a communal guilt, a shared human failure, that is being spoken of.

In 'Dans le Restaurant' it is impossible to escape the feeling, common in Eliot's verse, that the two participants are really aspects of each other; and that 'Phlébas, Le Phénicien' is an aspect of both waiter and diner. It is also necessary to think of 'I' and 'you' in 'The Burial of the Dead', the speaker and Stetson, as parts of each other.

In a similar way, 'You! hypocrite lecteur!' is not merely a direct address to the reader, but a claim that the reader is part of the process of guilt and shame, part of the self that the poem expresses. It is astonishing, when one stops to think about this, how simply, without protest, so many readers have accepted this imputation of common guilt and common shame. Astonishing, except that most of *The Waste Land*'s readers are more deeply preoccupied with guilt, an inheritance from one side of the complex Christian tradition, than they will readily admit. 'Those who sharpen the tooth of the dog, meaning/Death', writes Eliot in *Marina*, warping (if only momentarily) a beautiful poem by a harsh puritanical grumbling. But the warping process goes deeper into the fabric of *The Waste Land* than it does in *Marina*. It is as if the challenge of the abrupt, elliptical style, the deliberately difficult manner of the poem, forces the reader on to the defensive, causes the reader to retreat before the brutality of the onslaught, to admit to hypocrisy, to shame, to the bestiality of his instincts, rather than to admit that he does not understand the poem.

Let me repeat; on one level the poem is the expression of an emotional mess, and it is characteristic of certain kinds of emotional muddle that the sufferer projects his own troubles on to everybody else. But, paradoxically, the emotional inadequacies of the poem add to its persuasive power: *The Waste Land* catches at and exploits a self-hatred which too often distorts the human spirit, and did so at a time when, though man was no more prone to bestiality and hypocrisy than before or since, had reason to be more acutely conscious of these failings than at any previous time. In this way, at least, *The Waste Land* richly deserves its classic status, that it expresses a certain kind of civilized morbidity more powerfully than it has ever been expressed. And what is more important, it expresses that morbidity directly, by action in words, not through a series of poses and conventional gestures as, for instance, Byron was apt to express the morbidity of the Romantic temperament.

'A GAME OF CHESS'

'A Game of Chess' grew out of an abandoned poem, 'The Death of the Duchess', which is printed in facsimile in Mrs Eliot's edition. 'The Death of the Duchess', in its turn, is suggested by a scene in Webster's *The Duchess of Malfi*. In Webster's play the widowed Duchess marries her steward, Antonio, secretly, against the wishes of her brother Ferdinand. In Act III scene 2 they are together in the Duchess's bedchamber with Cariola, the Duchess's serving-woman. There is some conversation about marriage, about the judgement of Paris, and other matters, and as the Duchess brushes her hair and talks, compulsively, insecurely, with anxiety at the approach of age and with the slightly desperate sensuality which is characteristic of her, Antonio and Cariola creep away out of the bedchamber to tease her. Her brother enters and eavesdrops.

In 'The Death of the Duchess' Eliot adapts this tense little claustrophobic scene to purposes of his own. The poem begins with rather feeble satire upon the monotonous regularity and drabness of surburban life:

> They know what to think and what to feel
> The inhabitants of Hampstead are bound forever on
> the wheel.

> But what is there for you and me
> For me and you
> What is there for us to do?
> Where the leaves meet in leafy Marylebone? (*FT*, 105)

Once again, we can distinguish the use of the pronominal conceit, little more than an echo of 'Prufrock', with no new sharpness of edge to enliven the tame rhetoric: 'you and me', together, are something different from the inhabitants of Hampstead, something which may perceive a world outside 'the wheel', who can move towards an overwhelming question, perhaps, but have no words to answer it: 'What words have we?' But at the thirty-fourth line, as Eliot enters an imaginative reconstruction of the scene in the Duchess's bedchamber, using the situation as a frame for a dramatic account of anxieties of his own, then the verse takes on a new urgency and strength:

> Under the brush her hair
> Spread out in little fiery points of will
> Glowed into words, then was suddenly still.

(*FT*, 105)

This, of course, in a changed form, became part of 'A Game of Chess'; and after alterations, this too was incorporated:

> And if it rains, the closed carriage at four.
> We should play a game of chess
> The ivory men make company between us
> We should play a game of chess
> Pressing lidless eyes and waiting for a knock upon the door.
>
> *(FT, 106)*

'The Death of the Duchess' returns again and again to questions about love, or more precisely, questions about what might happen after a confession of love; as Pound remarks in several marginal comments, there are cadences and phrases which remind one too much of 'Prufrock', and 'Portrait of a Lady'—and this is no surprise, for all three poems explore the same anxieties of the soul. The male *persona*, retreating like his *alter ego* of 'Portrait of a Lady' into an ironic interior monologue, muses:

> And if I said 'I love you' should we breathe
> Hear music, go a-hunting, as before?
> The hands relax, and the brush proceed?
>
> *(FT, 106)*

The question, like the 'overwhelming question' of 'Prufrock' remains unanswered, but the fear of failure takes a somewhat more specific form; 'That is not what I meant' becomes:

> If it is terrible alone, it is sordid with one more.
>
> *(FT, 106)*

And the mirror image of the fear is expressed as well: if a confession of love is followed by disappointment, is it possible that a rejection of love should achieve precisely the same result?

> If I said 'I do not love you' we should breathe
> The hands relax, and the brush proceed?
> How terrible that it should be the same!
>
> *(FT, 106)*

'The Death of the Duchess' forms a sort of bridge between 'Prufrock' and 'Portrait of a Lady' on the one hand and *The Waste Land* on the other. It cannot be thought of, simply, as an account of a hesitant, unsatisfactory sexual affair. It is the dramatization of an

[93]

inner conflict, the edgy uncertainties of a divided personality wondering whether and how its divisions can be overcome, whether and how an imagined unity, feared and desired at the same time, can *really* be so desirable (or so fearful) as it would seem to be. The game of chess, that very suggestive device borrowed from *Women Beware Women*, is not simply the complex tactics of sexual conquest, but the even more complex strategies of self-conquest, the search for a meditative harmony of the soul.

Another hint from *The Duchess of Malfi* assists the process whereby 'The Death of the Duchess' is transformed into 'A Game of Chess'. Earlier in the bedchamber scene Cariola has declared that she will never marry. Antonio answers her with instances from the *Metamorphoses* of Ovid:[6]

> O, fie upon this single life! Forego it.
> We read how Daphne, for her peevish flight,
> Became a fruitless bay-tree; Syrinx turn'd
> To the pale empty reed; Anaxarete
> Was frozen into marble: whereas those
> Which married, or prov'd kind unto their friends,
> Were by a gracious influence transhap'd
> Into the olive, pomegranate, mulberry,
> Became flowers, precious stones, or eminent stars.

Metamorphosis is a kind of re-birth; the question behind 'The Death of the Duchess' and 'A Game of Chess', like that which lies behind 'Prufrock' is 'Would it have been worth it, after all?'—whether the end of this transformation feared and hoped for with such tremulous uncertainty, will be sterility or a new, richly fertile life? It is quite natural, then, that the Ovidian myth of Philomel and Tereus should play such a prominent part in 'A Game of Chess'.

But there are yet other elements which enter into the processes of change and development which produced 'A Game of Chess'. The allusions to *Women Beware Women* and *The Duchess of Malfi* both recall ambiguous and uncertain marriages; to these allusions others are added, allusions to the opulent, ambiguous and ill-fated unions of Classical history and myth: Cleopatra and Antony, Dido and Aeneas, all of them half-marriages which end in the death of the woman. All the women are rolled into one woman, and her boudoir is described in great detail. In the drafts Vivien Eliot, who, no doubt, knew a good deal of the processes which went into Eliot's

[94]

verse, has written against the description of the boudoir: 'Don't see what you had in mind here' (*FT*, 10).

What Eliot seems to have had in mind is, indeed, somewhat surprising. The Lord's instructions to Moses for the furnishings of the temple in Exodus 25–7 are as detailed as Eliot's account of the Lady's boudoir. Moses is to place a golden chair over the ark which contains the stone tables of the law. On either side of the chair there are to be two golden cherubim. In front of the chair there is to be a table with a seven-branched candelabrum. There are elaborate directions for the proper jewels, incenses, perfumes and unguents:

> The Chair she sat in, like a burnished throne,
> Glowed on the marble, where the glass
> Held up by standards wrought with fruited vines
> From which a golden Cupidon peeped out
> (Another hid his eyes behind his wing)
> Doubled the flames of sevenbranched candelabra
> Reflecting light upon the table as
> The glitter of her jewels rose to meet it . . .

The match between temple and boudoir is not exact—of course not—but close enough to disturb the imagination with awkward questions. Why should Eliot put this woman figure, so rich in associations of sensuality, self-indulgence and hysteria, this amalgam of so many illicit lovers who die for their loves, in such a setting? 'In using the myth, in manipulating a continuous parallel between contemporaneity and antiquity' wrote Eliot, reviewing Joyce's *Ulysses*, Joyce and Yeats are discovering 'a way of controlling, of ordering, of giving a shape and significance to contemporary experience.' What possible mythical significance has the old Temple of Jerusalem; what bearing could it have on contemporary experience? For Jews in the ancient world the significance of the Temple was clear; after the destruction of the temple and during the diaspora, however, the temple became not so much an actual building, more an emblem signifying the one-ness of the race. For Christians the significance of the old temple was different; it was in contradistinction to the temple of the new faith: 'know ye not that your body is the temple of the Holy Ghost which is in you, which ye have of God, and ye are not your own?' writes St Paul, and the author of the Epistle to the Hebrews (traditionally attributed to Paul), spells out in more detail the contrasting significances of temples old and new:

[95]

Now when these things were thus ordained, the priests went always into the first tabernacle, accomplishing the service of God. But into the second went the high priest alone once every year, not without blood, which he offered for himself, and the errors of the people: The Holy Ghost this signifying that the way into the holiest of all was not yet made manifest, while as the first tabernacle was yet standing: Which was a figure for the time then present, in which were offered both gifts and sacrifices, that could not make him that did the service perfect, as pertaining to the conscience: Which stood only in meats and drinks, and diverse washings, and carnal ordinances, imposed upon them till the time of reformation. But Christ being come an high priest of good things to come, by a greater and more perfect tabernacle, not made with hands, that is to say, not of this building.

(Heb. 9:5–11)

The ancient propitiatory ritual is made a prophecy of the new covenant, the old temple into a figure of the new temple of the Christians, which is within the heart and mind of the Christian himself. Possibly the most memorable treatment of this persistent and rather beautiful Christian myth is in Augustine's *Confessions*:

But where in my memory abidest Thou, O Lord, where does Thou there abide? What manner of chamber hast Thou there formed for Thyself? What sort of sanctuary hast Thou erected for Thyself? Thou hast granted this honour to my memory, to take up Thy abode in it, but in what quarter of it Thou abidest, I am considering. For in calling Thee to mind, I soared beyond those parts of it which the beasts also possess, since I found Thee not there amongst the images of corporeal things; and I arrived at those parts where I had committed the affections of my mind, nor there did I find Thee. And I entered into the very seat of my mind, which it has in my memory, since the mind remembers itself also—nor wert Thou there. For as Thou art not a bodily image, nor an affection of a living creature, as when we rejoice, condole, desire, fear, remember, forget, or aught of the kind; so neither art Thou the mind itself . . .

(*Conf.*, X, 25)

There are ways in which Augustine is repellent to the contemporary sensibility; there are other ways in which his sensibility is

[96]

curiously modern. Eliot certainly discovered a kinship in the way Augustine interprets old myths in such a way as to explore, not only the dogmatic commonplaces of tradition, but the inward experience of men, the anxious search for truth and understanding, the urgent quest which drove Conrad's Marlow towards the heart of darkness, and drives Eliot's quester on towards an ambiguous and uncertain conclusion. One way of expressing this *terminus ad quem*; this point beyond which no further investigation is possible, or needed, is the image of the new temple, the sanctuary within. One way of expressing an interim stage, a half-way house which teases the imagination by mimicking conclusions, is the image of the old temple. Eliot puts his male and female personae, his bride and bridegroom, in a mimic temple, a synthetic parody of the inner chamber complete with golden mercy-seat and seven-branched candelabra, but tawdry, cheapened, empty of real significance, full only of the 'broken images' which represent, imperfectly, as through a glass, darkly, the world of reality.

The curious quality of the light, sea wood burning with a sea-coloured light of green and orange, fed by copper, the Cyprian metal of Venus, reveals one such 'broken image', 'withered stump of time'. The dolphin was a symbol of re-birth in early Christian art. In Greek mythology (and in the poetry of Yeats, using the ancient myth) the dolphin carried the souls of the dead to the islands of the blessed. The oracle at Delphi, according to the Greek aetiological myth was founded by Apollo in the guise of a dolphin (the Greek word is *delphis*).

The myth of Philomel, Procne and Tereus (the nightingale, the swallow and the hoopoe) is also suggestive of re-birth. In one of those moments when the rigorous philosophical argument will not serve, and when he is forced into myth as a way of gesturing towards intuited philosophical truths, Plato makes the three birds, and the dying swan, figures for prophetic philosophy:

But men, because of their fear of death, misrepresent the swans and say that they sing for sorrow, in mourning for their own death. They do not consider that no bird sings when it is hungry or cold or has any other trouble; no, not even the nightingale or the swallow or the hoopoe, which are said to sing in lamentation. I do not believe they sing for grief, nor do the swans; but since they are Apollo's birds, I believe they have prophetic vision, and because they have foreknowledge of the blessings in the other world they sing and rejoice on that day more than ever before.

(*Phaedo*, 85A)

The boudoir, with all its furniture and ornaments, is a complex image of death and re-birth, of the purity and calm which results from a spiritual regeneration: but it is merely an image, a complex of images, and this is what gives the setting its claustrophobic intensity. The images, and the troubled, confused state of doubt, fear and mental stagnation which they collectively represent paradoxically work *against* the tenor of the images. Far from creating the harmony and peace of spirit which they seem to promise, they create tension and claustrophobia:

> staring forms
> Leaned out, leaning, hushing the room enclosed.
> Footsteps shuffled on the stair.
> Under the firelight, under the brush, her hair
> Spread out in fiery points
> Glowed into words, then would be savagely still.

Here is a case where revisions have improved the tension of the verse quite remarkably: the original 'Spread out in little fiery points of will', too didactically pointed in its account of the woman's role in the drama, is abbreviated; the commonplace 'suddenly' of 'The Death of the Duchess', becomes 'savagely', a word which conveys with the greatest economy the heavy anxious atmosphere, the static charge which threatens in every one of her words.

The words she speaks are neurotically restless, but they are given a deliberate purpose, a clear direction. She tells the man who is with her to stay with her, to speak, to think, and to interpret a noise. He is asked whether he knows nothing, sees nothing, remembers nothing; at last he is asked 'Are you alive or not? Is there nothing in your head?' In short he is asked to perform all those functions which give human consciousness its peculiar character—thought, memory, speech, sensation.

His replies are curt and surly; it seems that they amount to little: he thinks they are in rat's alley; he hears the wind under the door; he says the wind is doing 'Nothing again nothing'. But the ungracious terseness of his speech hints at knowledge, thought and memory which transcend his surroundings:

[98]

> I remember,
> Those are pearls that were his eyes.

In the drafts, the nature of the memory is made even more specific; the 'sea-change' of *The Tempest* is blended with the memory of the garden:

> I remember
> The hyacinth garden. Those are pearls that were his eyes, yes!

The consciousness of the woman, restless, hungry for action and sensation, a mass of frustrated appetitites and unfulfilled desires, is imprisoned in the claustrophobic temple of the mind with a consciousness of a very different kind; one which dwells upon memories and promises of ecstasy. But even these promises of new life, however tenderly and nostalgically they are preserved, are almost immediately mocked:

> O O O O that Shakespeherian Rag—
> It's so elegant
> So intelligent . . .

'That Mysterious Rag', one of Irving Berlin's earliest successes, was still popular in the early 1920s. Eliot's parody of it pushes the tense little dramatic dialogue over the edge into the hysterical laughter that has been close to the surface throughout. And Berlin's song exploits just that quality of menace mixed with obsessive recurrent memories which Eliot wants to produce at this point:[7]

> Did you hear it? Were you near it?
> If you weren't then you've got to fear it
> Once you've met it, you'll regret it.
> Just because you never will forget it
> If you ever wake up from your dreaming
> A-scheming, Eyes gleaming
> Then if suddenly you take a screaming fit
> That's it! That mysterious rag
> While awake or while you're slumbering
> You're saying, keep playing
> That mysterious rag.

The piece of ragtime is one of the ways in which Eliot strives to manipulate 'a continuous parallel between contemporaneity and antiquity'. He readily accepted Pound's objections to 'the closed carriage' as '1880' and replaced it with a 1920 'closed car'. The long vigil is made to persist into a world of motor cars and demobilization, waiting for a knock at the door. The flat cockney speech of the pub scene, the talk of abortion, the cry of the landlord, are intended to produce a similar result, to bring the criticism of life right up to date. But there is something a little forced and a little arrogant in this sequence, and something more than a little silly in the contrived use of the Landlord's cry 'HURRY UP PLEASE IT'S TIME' to set the reader sorting out the several alternative portentous puns implicit in the words.

'THE FIRE SERMON'

In the original version of *The Waste Land* which Eliot sent to Pound, 'The Fire Sermon' begins with a long pastiche of *The Rape of the Lock*. Later, in 1928, Eliot wrote that Pound 'induced me to destroy what I thought an excellent set of couplets; for, said he, "Pope has done this so well that you cannot do it better; and if you mean this as a burlesque, you had better suppress it, for you cannot parody Pope unless you can write better verse than Pope—and you can't". Indeed, the parody is for the most part nerveless and slack; but it pursues a theme which is central to the poem, a theme in which Eliot found instinctive sympathy for the Augustans and their moral attitudes. Man exists in the middle state, a narrow isthmus between divinity and bestiality; Fresca, the frivolous, slothful, self-indulgent loose-living heroine, propelled into the world of fashion under the patronage of Lady Katzegg, has the potential for sainthood as well as whoredom:

> Fresca! in other time or place had been
> A meek and lowly weeping Magdalene;
> More sinned against than sinning, bruised and marred,
> The lazy laughing Jenny of the bard.
> (The same eternal and consuming itch
> Can make a martyr, or plain simple bitch)
> . . .
> For varying forms, one definition's right:
> Unreal emotions, and real appetite.

(FT, 27)

The last line compactly defines the moral subject of 'The Fire Sermon'. However, accepting Pound's deserved strictures on the pastiche of Pope, Eliot went back to searching for a more oblique way of entering into the moral statement. He chooses, as a starting point, the refrain from Spenser's 'Prothalamion', or song before marriage:

> Against the Brydale day, which is not long
> Sweet *Themmes* runne softly, till I end my song.

In 'Prothalamion' the poet escapes from London, an Unreal City of 'idle hopes, which still do fly away/Like empty shaddowes', to where the river is still clear and its banks pastorally idyllic. He meets 'a Flocke of Nymphes' who celebrate the coming marriage of two white swans, images of bridal chastity. The poem is in honour of the Earl of Worcester's two daughters, whom the swans represent; later the scene of the poem changes to the 'high Towers' of London, where their marriages are to take place.

On the reverse of the deleted opening, then, there is the first sketch of the opening lines as they now appear. However sordid the sexual encounters in 'The Fire Sermon' appear to be, it is important to bear in mind the way in which Eliot introduces the whole movement with a reference to a marriage song. The word 'nymph' itself means 'bride' in Greek: each of the nymphs in 'The Fire Sermon', the picnicking friends of city gentlemen, Mrs Porter, Mr Eugenides' friend, the poor bored typist, Elizabeth, the Thames-daughters, each of them, like Fresca, is, ambiguously, a whore or a martyr. By the same token each of the men is, ambiguously, a lecher or a hero of the soul. And each encounter between male and female is tawdry, loathsome, boring, but at the same time holds, suspended, a promise of spiritual ecstasy. The 'unreal emotions' mimic and distort the 'real' ones; the sequence of sordid amours prepares the way for a hesitant, broken prayer which brings together the Buddha and St Augustine, two men who turned to the ascetic life after a youth more than usually sensually indulgent; who sought freedom in turning away from the satisfactions of sense to a quietly persistent meditative enquiry, turning away from 'appetite' to a search for 'real emotion'.

When this has been said of the contrived pattern, it must also be said that the tone of 'The Fire Sermon' is not the tone of assured understanding; the voice is not that of a man who, like Augustine or the Buddha, has made his way through to detachment and poise. It is the tone of vehement loathing; the voice of a man in panic, who has come to detest his own humanity—in particular, to detest sexuality. It is not the impersonal voice; quite the contrary: it is painfully personal. It offers to escape personality by courting inhumanity; but it is as little inhuman as it is impersonal: it is a desperate cry of human weakness and human pain.

The waste land of the grail legend, as interpreted by Jessie Weston, is the interval between a death and a birth, the winter of the year and the winter of the soul. The ritual of the grail demands a magical wedding, the union of lance and cup, before the world can be re-born. The world which Eliot evokes here seems sterile in a more profound sense than the sterility of winter. The verse is studded with allusions to past worlds of time and belief, earlier and more happy stages in the growth of the European Mind, in which myths embodying the certainty of new life and re-birth had all the authority and strength that could be given to them by a community and assuredness of faith. All these evocative memories are dislocated and set in a tawdry modern setting, the rat-infested world between canal and gashouse, in some cases with deliberately absurd effect, as when the virile Sweeney plays Actaeon to Mrs Porter's Diana; a comedy version of the dying god meeting a farcical earth-goddess.

But there is a whole gamut of tones in the passage, from deliberate farce of this kind to quiet seriousness. 'By the waters of Leman I sat down and wept'—a very personal piece of autobiography; Eliot had recently spent some time in Geneva, by Lac Leman, seeking a cure for his nervous disorders—adapts Psalm 137, 'By the rivers of Babylon, there we sat down, yea, we wept, when we remembered Zion'. This, a song of exile, asks the question 'How shall we sing the LORD's song in a strange land?' The application of the Hebrew lament to a modern world is clear; the life of the waste land is one of exile. The much-abused word 'alienation' has a very precise application to *The Waste Land*; particularly to 'The Fire Sermon', with its anguished sense of separation and unreality. Thus almost every word has several layers of meaning: defensively ironic surface meanings and painfully felt meanings of a more profound nature. 'The nymphs are departed' refers on one level to the good-time girl with her loitering boy-friend; perhaps in a sly, slangy way, to nymphomaniacs. On another level it refers to Spenser's swan-like brides, the nymphs of classical mythology, even to the Bride of Solomon: to the collapse of a world in which such beauty is inviolate, because it is believed in.

There are other, more or less obscure or difficult punning references to more profound myths: it is not only in Christian and Hebrew myth that 'the river' has significance as the source of life, or that 'the wind' carries the word of God. But it is only in nomadic communities like the Hebrew, that tents, or tabernacles, became portable places of worship. Thus 'The river's tent is broken' may become part of a lament that an old way of believing is no longer possible, here, in this alien world.

The tone of the verse is volatile, unstable; it slips into and out of bawdy burlesque, into and out of morbid horror, into and out of chaste images of beauty only slightly stained by their surroundings: so the irreverent farce of Sweeney and Mrs Porter gives way to the line from Verlaine's 'Parsifal', 'Et, O ces voix d'enfants, chantant dans la coupole!', in which the Grail Knight, still pure despite all temptations, hears the pure voices of boys singing in the choir—a tender ambiguity here as in the original, for the boys' voices represent a chaste beauty of experience which remains a possible joy *because* it is not achieved. So, too, the morbid memories of death: 'the king my brother's wreck/And on the king my father's death', hold within them a concealed beauty, recalling as they do 'Those were pearls that were his eyes', the 'sea-change' of new life.

And yet, as a whole, the tone is one of hysterical confusion; ugly laughter and sick nostalgia alternating with feverish imprecation: as in some of the Quatrain poems the sickness and pain is arrogantly declaimed, yet at the same time half-concealed by an insolent ingenuity:

> Unreal City
> Under the brown fog of a winter noon
> Mr. Eugenides, the Smyrna merchant
> Unshaven, with a pocketful of currants
> C.i.f. London: documents at sight
> Asked me in demotic French
> To luncheon at the Cannon Street Hotel
> Followed by a weekend at the Metropole.

As in the induction to the meeting with Stetson in 'The Burial of the Dead', 'Unreal City' is an abbreviation of a more overtly prophetic phrase: 'Unreal City, I have seen and see'. Indeed, Stetson merges into Mr Eugenides, 'just as the one-eyed merchant, seller of currants, melts into the Phoenician Sailor, and the latter is not wholly dis-

tinct from Ferdinand, Prince of Naples', and all these have some relationship to the lover in the Hyacinth Garden. Each one of these
gentlemen is in some way related to death and rebirth: Stetson plants
corpses in the garden and waits to see them bloom; the lover in the
hyacinth garden brings blooms to his loved one, and she is neither
living nor dead. Ferdinand remembers a death which is in some way
better than life, and in a way *is* life; the Phoenician sailor dies, but
his death in some way is a beginning of life. How does this seedy
Levantine with his sordid propositions fit the pattern? The answer is
to be found in a series of outrageous and unlovely puns: the elaborate
ingenuity is characteristic of a mind under the greatest possible stress
seeking to adapt itself to unfamiliar emotions.

Eugenides means well-born, of good family. Clearly this is, at
least partly, ironic: an unshaven Levantine of doubtful sexual habits
is not what we usually think of as 'well-born'. But if we have been
persuaded, as the verse continually suggests us, and as Eliot's notes
somewhat intrusively insist, that Eugenides is in some way like
other men in the poem, like Ferdinand Prince of Naples, the Bridegroom in the Hyacinth Garden or the Phoenician Sailor, then the
irony of 'well-born' becomes somewhat deeper and more complex.
The 'well-born' man appears in a multitude of guises, and on each
occasion his acts are disturbingly ambiguous: he kills to re-create,
dies to be re-born, rapes to make chaste, marries to destroy. In this
incident he follows directly after the song of the nightingale, directly
after the uncompleted name of Philomel's ravisher: 'Tereu'; the last
syllable prompts the first of his name 'Eugenides'. The Eugenides
passage, as it were, translates the nightingale's song into a comic
dialect, but points (with similar ambiguities) to a metamorphosis
which shall follow the rape.

Eugenides, the well-born, is a merchant. The quester, the male
persona who acts out dramatically in so many ways his encounter
with the female figure, is obsessed by a memory: 'Those are pearls
that were his eyes.' 'The kingdom of heaven is like unto a merchant
man, seeking goodly pearls: Who, when he had found one pearl of
great price, went and sold all he had, and bought it' (Matt. 13: 45–6).
The allusion, I hasten to say, is not a *necessary* one: there is no reason
why we *must* accept that Eliot had Matthew's merchant in his mind
as he wrote of Eugenides; but it is a probable enough relationship:
Eugenides, like all the other men in the poem, is searching for something of transcendent value. He trades in something big.

[104]

Eugenides, the merchant, is identified with one of Madame Sosostris's cards:

> And here is the one-eyed merchant, and this card,
> Which is blank, is something he carries on his back,
> Which I am forbidden to see. I do not find
> The Hanged Man.

Eugenides trades in something big; something which the fortune-telling Madame says she is forbidden to see. Eliot's half-serious, half waggish play with the Tarot is somewhat like his injunction in 'Prufrock': 'O do not ask what is it?': it sets us agog to discover the information denied us, and points us firmly in the right direction (disclaiming any responsibility at the same time). His later discouragement of 'wild goose chases after the Tarot' is an extension of this teetering irony: he doesn't wish to be pinned down to the level of Arthur Edward Waite. He didn't need to bother: the Hanged Man, for instance, is as good a conventional image of 'something big' as any other.

The merchant on Madame Sosostris's card has one eye. Here Eliot plays with a conventional image far older than the Tarot. 'Thou hast ravished my heart with one of thine eyes', sings the bridegroom of the Song of Solomon (Song 4, 9) and in the Gospel of St Matthew we find 'The light of thy body is the eye: if therefore thine eye be single, thy whole body shall be full of light' (Matt. 6: 22). Christian mystical writers have taken up this image of the single eye and elaborated its meaning with absorbed intensity: Meister Eckhart and St John of the Cross both used it, and here is the *Theologia Germanica*:[8]

> Now the created soul of man has also two eyes. The one is the power of seeing into time and the creatures. . . . But these two eyes of the soul of man cannot perform their work at once, but if the soul shall see with the right eye into eternity, then the left eye must cease and refrain from all its working, and be as though it were dead.

The chances are that Eliot did not know the *Theologia Germanica*; it is quoted merely to illustrate the convention in a typical form. Of course this is not Eliot's only use of the conceit: there is a great deal of play with the one-eyed Riley and Julia Shuttleworth's broken spectacles in *The Cocktail Party*, and the functions of the Guardians in that play are defined rather more precisely than that of Mr

Eugenides in *The Waste Land*. In that Satyr play the one eye clearly becomes a comic symbol of spiritual far-sightedness.

Eugenides is a Smyrna merchant. Smyrna is a town in Asia Minor where one of the seven churches of Revelation had its meeting place; it is also the Greek word, σμύρνα, for myrrh.

Myrrh is, of course, the resinous gum of an Arabian tree, used in ancient times for embalming the dead, in the hope that they might rise complete in body in the next world. The gift of myrrh to the infant Christ by the three Magi is traditionally associated with the promise of resurrection. The bridegroom of the Canticle is repeatedly associated with myrrh: when the Shulamite bride opens the door to him, her hands 'dropped with myrrh' (Song 5, 5); she says that his lips are 'like lilies, dropping sweet smelling myrrh.' And at one point the bride asks, 'Who is this that cometh out of the wilderness like pillars of smoke, perfumed with myrrh and frankincense, with all the powders of the merchant?' (Song 3, 6). The appearance of myrrh and merchant together here may or may not have interested Eliot; but throughout the Bible, as in Egypt and all the ancient world, myrrh would be one of the means by which one attempted to ensure everlasting life, and by a small metaphoric extension the merchant of myrrh could be thought of as a bringer of re-birth.

Even the currants Eugenides carries seem to be part of the pattern. Though by themselves they would have little significance as emblems or figures, in a context of such complex word play one remembers 'I am the true vine, and my Father is the husbandman' (John 15: 1), and begins to wonder whether, in the context of the controlling metaphor of aridity in *The Waste Land*, dried grapes might mean more than they seem to do. An *uncertain* reaction is the right one; mystification and bewilderment are the weapons which Eliot uses most freely: irony to disengage himself from complete involvement; allusive echoes, not fulfilled to a certainty, to draw the reader further on.

'C.i.f. London: documents at sight' is just such a piece of allusive irony, a piece of sophisticated tomfoolery which is, perhaps, intended to confuse. The c.i.f. contract is one in which the vendor undertakes to pay in full for the cost, insurance and freight of the goods delivered—in this case Smyrna currants—to the specified place. The buyer must repay the merchant in full to complete the contract.

Let us imagine what this contract might be, given the context within which it is mentioned. The place of delivery is London, the Unreal City. The time is winter, yet at the same time dawn; it is difficult to see because of the weak light of winter dawn, and the eye is further baffled by the fog. But the seer is Tiresias, who in any case sees in a peculiar way because he is blind.

Eliot bids us believe that Tiresias is everyone he sees; he is both the vendor and the vendee of the contract; he is both Tereu/Eugenides and the little nightingale. And so the weekend, away from the Unreal City, at the Metropole (μητρόπολις, the chief city, the mother-city) is one which brings together parts of himself, and this may be the point of the contract.

The line of reasoning takes us to the point where it is natural to express extreme caution; to the point where we wish to retrace our steps and try again. We may ask ourselves where, in the complex inheritance of the European tradition, is there a contract which fits the situation? Prompted in this way (and it may be, I concede, *only* when we are prompted in this way that the answer is so clear) we remember the Christian doctrine of the redemption. Christ has paid fully, the buyer redeems the contract in full, and the documents of the Christian canon define the whole transaction in the greatest detail. The contract of exchange is implicit in all the Christian sacraments, in baptism, marriage and the burial of the dead. All are magical ceremonies in which the Christian barters the old man for the new. All involve a communion, a joining together of disparate and dissociated elements.

Which brings us to Tiresias, who comprehends all the persons in the poem, and in whom the two sexes meet:

> I Tiresias, though blind, throbbing between two lives,
> Old man with wrinkled female breasts, can see . . .

In the *Odyssey*, Odysseus is advised by Circe to travel to the land of the Cimmerians to consult Tiresias. After Odysseus has performed the proper libations and sacrifices the shadows of the dead appear, thronging in crowds, and among them Tiresias, who warns Odysseus to find a home far from the sea, and prophesies his death by water. (*Odyssey* XI, 134–6). The encounter is central in importance to the structure of the *Odyssey*.

In his own notes to the poem, Eliot quotes Ovid's version of the myth of Tiresias, stressing its 'great anthropological interest'. I believe that the allusion to Homer's Tiresias is equally strong. Cer-

tainly there are many ways in which Eliot's questing figure is
implicitly related to Odysseus, or to Dante's Ulysses in old age sailing
to knowledge beyond the Pillars of Hercules. The meaning of
'throbbing between two lives' is somewhat ambiguous and many-
layered. The Ovidian myth suggests one aspect of the duality: he is
both man and woman, an epicene synthesis of all human experience;
a prophet who speaks out of a knowledge of all aspects of human
kind. Homer's Tiresias suggests another kind of duality, another
kind of comprehensiveness of experience; Tiresias as the prophet
who has travelled both worlds, this world and the next:

> (And I Tiresias have foresuffered all
> Enacted on this same divan or bed;
> I who have sat by Thebes below the wall
> And walked among the lowest of the dead.)

It would seem that the scene Tiresias *sees* is hardly worthy of so
distinguished a witness, the emotions expressed in this tawdry tale of
the bored and passive typist and her pimply guest too lacking in
wisdom and breadth of humanity. In the drafts the contempt and
arrogance is even more embarrassingly explicit: Pound comments
'Too easy' against:

> Knowing the manner of these crawling bugs
> I too awaited the expected guest . . .
>
> (*FT*, 45)

This is not the only place where Eliot compromises the tone of
prophecy with over-fastidious personal distaste, and not the only
time that Pound saves him from his worst excesses. 'I am no prophet'
said Prufrock, and it is, perhaps, only by mysterious elaboration that
Eliot himself seems to achieve the force of prophetic statement.
When the vision is seen clearly and the emotional tone assessed
calmly there is a terrible gulf between the persuasive skill of the poet,
his ability to carry the reader along with him, and the pernickety,
arrogant and narrow emotion.

What remains after the revisions is tighter and sharper, but no less
ugly, no more appropriate for the wise, all-suffering prophetic voice
of a Tiresias:

> He, the young man carbuncular, arrives,
> A small house agent's clerk, with one bold stare,

One of the low on whom assurance sits
As a silk hat on a Bradford millionaire.

This is good for a cheap laugh, an abrasive contempt that cuts more ways than one, but, in the end, debases the poet as much as his subject. If, as so many of Eliot's contemporaries felt, the poem expresses the disillusion and disorientation of a generation, it also expresses something of the silliness of the twenties, some of its snobbery and intolerance. If, as I have argued, it attempts to express another pattern of emotion, less characteristic of those troubled years, but belonging to the ancient ascetic tradition of thought and feeling, it is difficult to express one's sense of how much separates *The Waste Land* from the *Confessions* of St Augustine, the scriptures of the Buddha, the *Bhagavhad Gita*, or any of those touchstone texts to which Eliot returns so frequently, how much it differs from them in understanding and compassion. Its power, and pathos, is the power of mental, emotional and moral breakdown, the pathos of desperation, and that power breaks, and the pathos becomes of a different kind, in passages such as these.

But then the tone changes, and, fleetingly, a real beauty is caught, rich with the sense of unfulfilled possibilities, fulness of life and joyfulness of art at every corner of the city streets, waiting for recognition. It is a Romantic's sense of beauty, a teasing, Prufrockian joy: 'I know the voices dying with a dying fall/Beneath the music from a farther room', but nevertheless it is beauty:

Where fishmen lounge at noon: where the walls
Of Magnus Martyr hold
Inexplicable splendour of Ionian white and gold.

The Christian significances of this are clear: Magnus Martyr and 'fishmen' suggest irresistibly the passion of Christ and the early Christians. But it is Christianity seen with longing from outside, with the yearning of a child at a sweetshop window. Eliot more than once expresses the greatness of the gulf between potential of emotion and any actualization possible in life: the kind of beauty which he longs for here, and the way in which he longs for it, is so intricately bound up with his failure to accept what is immediately attainable that the desire becomes as suspect as the disgust. Characteristically Eliot is caught in an extreme form of the Romantic dilemma. An earlier, abandoned poem, 'Song for the Opherian', which contains a

[109]

phrase later used in 'The Fire Sermon' expresses very well this curious, frustrated state of consciousness:

> This thought this ghost this pendulum in the head
> Swinging from life to death
> Bleeding between two lives
> Waiting that touch that breath . . .

(*FT*, 99)

Indeed, the poem as a whole swings in its emotional tonalities between desire for something remembered or known imaginatively, a state of ecstasy which constantly recedes as one moves towards it, and a state of anguished disgust and contempt for present experience, a present experience soured by the tantalizing vision. Incidentally, 'Song for the Opherian' goes nearer to placing the remembered experience in time than any other: the deleted last lines read

> Waiting that touch
> After thirty years.

(*FT*, 99)

Eliot was thirty-three when this poem was published pseudonymously in *The Tyro*. Dante met Beatrice when he was nine (or said he did); Eliot seems here to admit to a more precocious beginning.

Unger, Drew and Grover Smith have remarked that the opening of the Thames-daughters passage briefly recalls Conrad's *Heart of Darkness* once again:

> The river sweats
> Oil and tar
> The barges drift
> With the turning tide
> Red sails
> Wide
> To leeward, swing on the heavy spar.

In Conrad's story the changing flow of tide is one of the powerfully ambiguous metaphors which runs beneath the story: Marlow has finished speaking of Kurtz and the final vision of horror which culminates desire, temptation and surrender:[9]

Marlow ceased, and sat apart, indistinct and silent, in the pose of a meditating Buddha. Nobody moved for a time. 'We have lost the first of the ebb,' said the Director, suddenly. I raised

[110]

my head. The offing was bared by a black bank of clouds, and the tranquil waterway leading to the uttermost ends of the earth flowed sombre under an overcast sky—seemed to lead into the heart of an immense darkness.

In *The Waste Land* the swing and change of tide has a rather different function. For Conrad's narrator it accompanies and expresses a new and sombre awareness of life, the realization of how fragile and superficial is the civilization which shapes our life and values. Eliot's river is equally sombre; but, despite its soiled and ugly surface, there is something in the shifting rhythms, so evocative of the water's restless flow, which points forward. Up to now *The Waste Land* has been remarkably static; such images of movement as we have had have been immediately qualified, or arrested by an abrupt hiatus. Now, even though the sexual encounters remain barren ones—the sad comedy of the Virgin Queen and her flirtation with Leicester, the occluded reference to Antony and Cleopatra on the Nile—the laconic rhythmical ease helps to shift our point of view; from this point the poem cannot possibly return to the *salon* of Madame Sosostris, the Lady's boudoir in 'A Game of Chess', the noisy pub, the typist's bed-sit. For Conrad's narrator the change of tide makes all directions become the same. In *The Waste Land* the change of tide makes direction become possible once more.

In one of those subdued and under-played allusions which are so characteristic of Eliot in *The Waste Land* Eliot associates his Thames-daughters with Dante's mournful La Pia, murdered by her husband after a loveless marriage:

> 'Trams and dusty trees.
> Highbury bore me. Richmond and Kew
> Undid me. By Richmond I raised my knees
> Supine on the floor of a narrow canoe.'

Once more there is a deliberately contrived ambiguity between death and sexual congress, the physical attitude of intercourse being described with weary, anaphrodisiac precision. This, together with the mockery of the language of male hypocrisy 'After the event/He wept. He promised "a new start"', and the disabused calm of 'I made no comment. What should I resent?' prepare for the psychic breakdown of 'On Margate Sands/I can connect/Nothing with nothing' (once more the faint intrusion of the autobiographical note

—Eliot had spent some time at Margate during his nervous breakdown).

The seduction is a kind of death; but while 'He promised "a new start"' imitates the hypocritical language of the seducer, it does, at the same time, ambiguously and tentatively, suggest a new beginning. After the disconnection, the breakdown, a brief, dry, hesitant attempt at wordless song, and then Augustine and the Buddha have their say:

>   la la
>   To Carthage then I came
>
>   Burning burning burning burning
>   O Lord Thou pluckest me out
>   O Lord Thou pluckest
>
>   burning . . .

'To Carthage then I came' is not, if you pay attention to the original context in St Augustine, a statement of arrival, spiritually speaking, but a confession of how far there is to go still:

> To Carthage then I came, where a cauldron of unholy loves sang all about my ears. I was not able to love yet, but I loved loving, and with secret love I hated myself for not loving. I sought for something to love, in love with loving, hating security, and hating a path that was not beset with snares.
>
> (*Conf.* X, 24)

The failure to 'connect' which the third Thames daughter laments is not simply failure to connect in thought or idea; it is failure to achieve love which renders all those graceless sexual episodes so empty and dry. But, of course, the allusion to St Augustine confuses by multiplying the ambiguities of the word 'love': necessarily Augustine stresses that word, so central is it to the Christian experience. Equally necessarily the Buddhist Fire Sermon makes no mention at all of love: the Buddha's Fire Sermon, with steady, exhaustive rhetoric, bids every man to rid himself of every attachment of sense, every attachment of mind, every attachment of any kind, and become as nothing. In their approaches towards asceticism Augustine and the Buddha are very different from each other, and it is only in a very superficial way, I believe, that one can say they point to the same thing; even in the most negative of Christian mystics the ecstatic experience of Christian Love is quite different in quality from the meditative silence of Buddhism. Eliot was equipped to understand the fire of Dante:

> Più non si va, se pria non morde
> anima sante, il foco. Entrate in esso,
> ed al cantar di là non siate sorde.
>
> (*Purgatorio*, XXVII, 11–13)

(O holy souls, none may go further unless the fire first bite. Enter into it, and do not let yourself be deaf to the singing there.)

but there are no harmonious angels in the Buddha's fire, no glorious, joyful saviour as in Malachi: 'for he is like a refiner's fire', and no God to exercise his continuous pastoral care, as in St Augustine:

> I resist seductions of the eyes, lest my feet, with which I walk on Thy path, shall be entangled, and I lift up my invisible eyes to Thee, that Thou shouldst deign to pluck my feet out of the net. Thou dost pluck them out continually, for they are trapped. Thou pluckest them out unceasingly.
>
> (*Conf.*, X, 24)

My argument is not against the verse itself, here, I believe: that stands by itself without any shoring. But by now Eliot's own notes have inextricably become part of the poem, and it is necessary at some point or other to protest at the facility of tone of 'The collocation of these two representatives of eastern and western asceticism, as the culmination of this part of the poem, is not an accident', suggesting as it does a didactic assuredness and completeness in the verse. The conclusion of 'The Fire Sermon' is, as it were, a dead end of feeling, with, as coda, a tentative, insecure and incompletely realized prayer that, by desperate means, something might be salvaged from the wreckage, and consolation from any source, east or west, is equally welcome.

'DEATH BY WATER'

Pound's pencil went through most of 'Death by Water'; eighty-three lines which give an account of a sea journey out from New England across the Atlantic, in a ship which is blown past the furthest northern islands to the Arctic glaciers. The narrative method is completely different from anything else in the poem; a plain but flexible blank verse, none of the abrupt elisions which we have come to think of as characteristic of Eliot, and yet, at the same time, none of the self-consciously clever pastiche which mars the original text of 'The Fire Sermon'. It is a seaman's yarn, relatively fresh and straightforward, which cuts through the static, neurotic complexities of the earlier sections with a promise of something much freer and more open.

It is difficult to say what our attitude to the cancelled passages would have been if Pound had persuaded Eliot to revise and to tighten rather than cut entirely. I think that perhaps we would have found the new manner in keeping with the emotional development of the poem, and welcomed the easy strength of the language.

As the poem stands in its final version Phlebas, the Phoenician sailor, arrives on the scene abruptly; an elision is implied, but the imaginative leap which seems to be demanded of the reader is perhaps too great, the ways in which the Phoenician sailor could relate to all that has gone before too many and various. Yet *The Waste Land* is what it is; the enigma is part of the withdrawn, secretive and uncommunicative manner of the whole poem, however that manner is arrived at, by design or because, through boredom, failure of energy, or Pound's pressure, Eliot was forced to a premature winding up of the complex process of the poem's creation.

The sailor's story was suggested by Dante's myth of Ulysses in *Inferno*, xxvi, 85–142, in which, in old age, Ulysses sails beyond the Pillars of Hercules, to test himself and his aged crew against 'l'esperienza/di retro al sol, del mondo senza gente' (the experience of the world without people beyond the sun). At last, in Dante's poem, Ulysses and his crew come within sight of the Mount of Purgatory, and a tempest springs up, whirling the boat around and sucking it down into the sea—the death by water prophesied for Odysseus by Homer's Tiresias. Three times it whirls around, and then sinks 'com' altrui piacque' (as it pleased another.)

For Dante the journey is a heroic one, but foolish and dangerous presumption. As Tennyson re-works the myth in the dramatic monologue 'Ulysses', the hero becomes an image of the Victorian lust for new experience, new knowledge:

[114]

I am a part of all that I have met;
Yet all experience is an arch wherethro'
Gleams that untravell'd world, whose margin fades
For ever and for ever as I move.

In comparing Dante's and Tennyson's versions Eliot praises Dante for 'the greatly superior degree of *simplification* of Dante's version. Tennyson, like most poets, like most even of those whom we call great poets, has to get his effect with a certain amount of *forcing*' (*SE*, 248). Under the direct and immediate influence of Dante, Eliot's version of the tale moves a good deal towards Dantesque 'simplicity'; it sounds for the most part, as Eliot says of Dante 'like . . . a well-told seaman's yarn'. But, in so far as it does move towards 'simplicity', it brings into relief how much of the rest of *The Waste Land* is 'forced'. Perhaps this is one of the reasons why Pound suggested its deletion, and why Eliot, at last, agreed to it. Furthermore, in its conscious approach towards 'simplicity' it doesn't go far enough. Eliot remarks of Tennyson's line about the sea which 'moans round with many voices' that, in comparison with Dante, it is too *poetical*. By contrast, he says, the simple 'as pleased Another' implies far greater depths (*SE*, 250).

It may be that when he wrote this essay on Dante, Eliot was remembering his own attempt at the same theme in 'Death by Water'. There, in a kind of belt-and-braces attempt to win complete security he borrows the best of both Tennyson and Dante:

> So the crew moaned; the sea with many voices
> Moaned all about us, under a rainy moon,
>
> (*FT*, 57)

and:

> And if *Another* knows, I know I know not,
> Who only know there is no more noise now.
>
> (*FT*, 61)

Curiously he neither 'simplifies' the Tennyson nor preserves the quiet economy and strength of the Dante; and the adaptation of Tennyson fits far better than that from Dante: the reference to *Another* becomes somewhat portentous and 'too *poetical*'.

This Ulysses myth encourages each poet to speak about the call of the unknown. Dante recognizes its power; part of the fascination of the *Divine Comedy* is the way in which it gives so detailed and concrete an account of a world of wonder beyond our daily experience; certainly he couldn't have written so interestingly about Ulysses' journey without a highly developed sense of wonder and instinctive longing for the strange and the new. It is, and he recognizes it, an essential human characteristic, but he is deeply enough a traditionalist, a conservative and classicist in temperament to believe that this expansive imagination must be held in check; that 'Another pleases' is a strong enough argument to satisfy our questionings. For Tennyson, the post-Romantic, the expansive imagination is just the thing; Ulysses is justified in throwing away his kingdom for it. For Eliot's 'Ulysses' there is only the horror of the journey, and no chance of knowledge at the end of it, or at least while he remains 'Ulysses'. In their contrasting ways, Dante and Tennyson see man as a blend of the natural and the heroic, who can and must aspire to something beyond the natural. For Eliot there has to be a break with the natural world before man can achieve that ultimate knowledge, that spiritual understanding, which (it is implied) is the only possible aim of the journey.

In some ways the journey resembles that of Conrad's Marlow in *Heart of Darkness* more than that of either Dante's or Tennyson's Ulysses. As Marlow travels further inwards into the heart of the continent; in this region of the mind which he discovers progressively as he moves further away from the world of cities and solid citizens, nearer and nearer to Kurtz and 'the horror', he and his companions seem little by little to lose their solidity and distinctness:[10]

> till you thought yourself bewitched and cut off for ever from everything you had known once—somewhere—far away—in another existence perhaps. There were moments when one's past came back to one, as it will sometimes when you have not a moment to spare to yourself; but it came in the shape of an unrestful and noisy dream, remembered with wonder. . . . When you have to attend to things of that sort, to the mere incidents of the surface, the reality—the reality, I tell you— fades. . . . We were cut off from the comprehension of our surroundings; we glided past like phantoms, wondering and secretly appalled . . .

There is no direct borrowing, but something like the same desperate nightmare vision controls the sea journey in the draft of 'Death by Water':

> We ate slept drank
> Hot coffee, and kept watch, and no one dared
> To look into anothers face, or speak
> In the horror of the illimitable scream
> Of a whole world about us. One night
> On watch, I thought I saw in the fore cross-trees
> Three women leaning forward with white hair
> Streaming behind, who sang above the wind
> A song that charmed my senses, while I was
> Frightened beyond fear, horrified past horror, calm,
> (Nothing was real) . . .
>
> (*FT*, 59)

and yet there is still a marked difference in tone. The tone of Eliot's verse is the tone of one still within the horror; Conrad contrives to make us feel the horror of dissociation and alienation fully, while at the same time achieving a reflective tranquillity, as of one who has really 'much seen and much endured', and grown to wisdom in the process.

However, there are various ways in which Eliot hints at a conclusion beyond the horror. The ambiguous image of the three women in 'the fore-cross trees', for instance, is in part a reminiscence of the sirens who sang to Odysseus, tempting him to destruction, while his men rowed on, their ears stopped, unhearing. But 'the fore-cross trees', while it has a specific nautical meaning, contains the submerged suggestion of the three crosses of the crucifixion in John's gospel, with the three Maries standing at the foot of the cross, and this prefigures the ambiguous hint that there might be a lightening of the terrible darkness:

> —Something which we knew must be a dawn—
> A different darkness, flowed above the clouds.
>
> (*FT*, 61)

In the original drafts all this prepares for the Phlebas passage which is now the whole of 'Death by Water', and directs the way in which we must read it to a much greater extent than anything in the final text.

The passage is, of course, an adaptation and translation of the last seven lines of 'Dans le Restaurant', Eliot's early French poem. That poem speaks in a vividly indirect way of the fading of an excited youthful vision of truth and reality, an ecstasy which is soiled and made tawdry as the memory grows old, and implies that all of us, like the sordid unwholesome waiter and the snobbish and irritable diner, share both the memory and its failure. In that context the figure of the drowned sailor acquires an other-worldly beauty; it is the might-have-been which continues to obsess the reflective memory: 'Those are pearls that were his eyes'; and equally a prolepsis of the marvellous 'sea-change/Into something rich and strange' which may crown the journey.

When the image is moved into the context of *The Waste Land*, its meaning is enriched. For one thing, various phrases are omitted, changed, or added. 'Un courant de sous-mer l'emporta très loin' becomes the more evocative 'A current under sea/Picked his bones in whispers', recalling, faintly, 'Of his bones are coral made'. Another phrase which is added in translation, 'entering the whirlpool' more firmly associates the fate of Phlebas the Phoenician with that of Dante's Ulysses. Both changes shift the meaning slightly, making the death echo or shadow, whether in a positive or ironically negative way we cannot immediately tell, a spiritual destiny, a wonderful rebirth. A further change:

> Gentile or Jew
> O you who turn the wheel to windward

introduces yet more echoes. The drowned sailor in 'Dans le Restaurant', as it were, closes the incident; all meaningful experience is placed in the past:

> Figurez-vous donc, c'était un sort pénible;
> Cependant, ce fut jadis un bel homme, de haute taille.

Whereas, in *The Waste Land*, there is a 'you' who continues the journey. Once more we cannot entirely be sure exactly how Eliot's pronouns work: 'you' does not seem to be addressed to the reader simply or entirely. And the phrase 'Gentile or Jew' very clearly recalls a note often struck in the Pauline epistles:

> For as many of you as have been baptized into Christ have put on Christ. There is neither Jew nor Greek, there is neither bond nor free, there is neither male nor female: for ye are all one in Christ Jesus.
>
> (Gal. 3: 27–28)

Thus, the episode of the drowned sailor points us gently towards the Christian theory of baptism and communion, to the transformation of old man into new, of separation into community. The ambiguities remain unresolved; but the cluster of images, hints, allusions, at least maps out the possible meanings and directions of failure and success.

Unresolved as the question is, it is one which has grown in intensity and complexity from a very early stage in Eliot's verse. At each venture into the problem Eliot uses some of the same images, though in every case when the question is explored, the images take different forms and, though they indicate similar territories, seem to point in different directions. The sea-cave image of the close of 'Prufrock', for instance, is one kind of wistful ambiguity:

> We have lingered in the chambers of the sea
> By sea-girls wreathed with seaweed red and brown
> Till human voices wake us, and we drown.

A manuscript poem, undated but probably written between 1913 and 1915, provides a bridge between 'Prufrock' and 'Dans le Restaurant'; the sea-imagery of 'Prufrock' returns, but in a new context. 'So through the evening' contains the first sketches of the queer, hallucinating journey of 'What the Thunder Said', as well as the first tentative use of the journey to Emmaus as an image for the anxious search for meaning of the dissociated mind in a hell of doubt and disorientation. The passage ends with the simile:

> As a deaf mute swimming deep below the surface
> Knowing neither up nor down, swims down and down
> In the calm deep water where no stir nor surf is
> Swims down and down
> And about his hair the seaweed purple and brown.
>
> So in our fixed confusion we persisted, out from town.
>
> (*FT*, 114)

But here the image of the man beneath water is one of the journey continued, in confusion and disorientation, but nevertheless continuing. 'Dans le Restaurant' gives us the journey completed, remembered, a failure which lies in the past. 'Death by Water' compounds the ambiguity; Phlebas the Phoenician is an image of something past and gone, but an image, a memory, which persists

[119]

in the mind of a traveller who continues the journey, both warning him of the way he may fail and hinting at a possible success.

A curious, half-realized play with words in the name 'Phlebas the Phoenician' does very little to help us *understand* the episode, merely increases our sense of puzzlement, and that is, perhaps, what is intended. 'Phlebas' is derived from the Greek *phleps*, meaning vein, of which *phlebas* is the accusative plural. And, as has often been pointed out, 'Phoenician', while evoking all the restless travelling of the great traders of the ancient world, suggests also the bird of re-birth, the Phoenix: the Greek for Phoenix and Phoenician are identical. So Phlebas the Phoenician is Mr Veins who is reborn. An odd locution, but not without a meaning if one remembers, for instance, Marvell's 'A Dialogue between the Soul and Body':

> A Soul hung up, as 'twere, in Chains
> Of Nerves, and Arteries, and Veins.
> Tortured, besides each other part,
> In a vain Head, and double Heart.

The poem is one to which Eliot would have responded with some-thing more than sympathy. Consider, too, the way in which Yeats was later to find in Byzantium the only possible retreat from 'the fury and the mire of human veins'.

'WHAT THE THUNDER SAID'

> After the turning of the inspired days
> After the praying and the silence and the crying
> And the inevitable ending of a thousand ways
> And frosty vigil kept in withered gardens
> After the life and death of lonely places
> After the judges and the advocates and wardens
> And the torchlight red on sweaty faces
> After the turning of inspired nights
> And the shaking spears and flickering lights—
> After the living and the dying—

(FT, 109)

So begins another of the fragments which Eliot bundled together with the original draft of *The Waste Land* and sent to Quinn: it seems to have been written at the same time as 'I am the Resurrection and the Life' and 'So through the evening', perhaps seven or eight years before it was adapted and stitched into the texture of *The Waste Land*:

> After the torchlight red on sweaty faces
> After the frosty silence in the gardens
> After the agony in stony places
> The shouting and the crying
> Prison and palace and reverberation
> Of thunder of spring over distant mountains

We may assume that all of these three fragments were responses to similar impulses; perhaps they were intended to be part of the same poem. Certainly each takes its starting point from the New Testament, and both 'So through the evening' and 'After the turning' treat the bereavement and the confusion of Christ's disciples after the crucifixion, perhaps as their subject, perhaps as metaphor for a more general human condition, or for a particular state of emotion, perhaps as a blend of all of these.

The longest fragment contrasts a state of transition, movement and chaotic uncertainty, a hallucinatory and frightening vision of a world of abnormality and illusion, with 'The one essential word that frees', the *logos* which gives meaning to the nightmare. (I have omitted some of the variant readings in the manuscript):

> So through the evening, through the violet air
> One tortured meditation dragged me on
> Concatenated words from which the sense seemed gone—
> —When comes, to the sleeping or the wake
> The This-do-ye-for-my-sake
> To the sullen sunbaked houses and the trees
> The one essential word that frees.
>
> (*FT*, 113)

'This-do-ye-for-my-sake' paraphrases the passage in I Corinthians where Paul speaks of the last supper of Christ and summarizes the origins of the Eucharist in it:

> For I have received of the Lord that which also I delivered unto you, That the Lord Jesus the same night in which he was betrayed took bread: And when he had given thanks, he brake it, and said, Take, eat: this is my body, which is broken

for you: this do in remembrance of me. After the same manner also he took the cup, when he had supped, saying, This cup is the new testament in my blood: this do ye, as oft as ye drink it, in remembrance of me. For as often as ye eat the bread, and drink this cup, ye do shew the Lord's death till he come.

(I Cor. 11: 23–6)

Paul's elaboration of this in the passages which follow links the theory of communion, through which the communicant re-enacts his communion with Christ, with the theory of baptism, which achieves the same end. The terms he uses here are familiar to us:

For as the body is one, and hath many members, and all the members of that one body, being many, are one body: so also is Christ. For by one Spirit are we all baptized into one body, whether we be Jews or Gentiles, whether we be bond or free; and have been all made to drink into one Spirit.

(I Cor. 12: 12–13)

It is, perhaps, from this point that Eliot moved towards the use of the Grail legend as controlling structural metaphor for *The Waste Land*. Whether or not there is much real continuity between pagan myths and the Christian legends of the Grail, it is certain that the Grail came to be associated with the cup used by Christ and His disciples at the last supper. The mediaeval mind was so steeped in allegory that it is inevitable that the search for the Grail should have been interpreted as a search for communion with Christ. And for Eliot, who was not a Christian when he wrote these fragments, but who found in baptism and Communion a living magical enactment of escape from isolation, incoherence and illusion, a way of discovering 'the one essential word that frees', the Grail legend would seem to be, if not good magic, at least excellent metaphor.

In this or some such way we have the origins of two of the three themes which Eliot tells us are employed in the first part of 'What the Thunder Said': 'The journey to Emmaus, the approach to the Chapel Perilous (see Miss Weston's book) and the present decay of eastern Europe'. The third theme is a more strenuous and energetic fulfilment of the tame conclusion to the fragment 'After the turning'. The bald emptiness of 'The world seemed futile – like a Sunday outing' is, as Bernard Bergonzi remarks, a kind of throw-back to the Laforguean manner of Eliot's first poetic exercises written at Harvard in 1909.[11] In re-shaping his material for *The Waste Land* Eliot contrives to give his sense of the sickness of the world more force by half-concealed reference to the aftermath of the Russian revolution; as in Yeats's 'The Second Coming' this is seen as portent more than accomplished fact: neither poets nor governments were able yet to think about Soviet communism calmly. For both Yeats and Eliot events in Russia were simply anarchy; for Eliot the anarchy was related to other anarchic moments of history, like the descent of the barbarians upon the city and empire of Rome; to anarchic moments in the soul; but above all to the advance of materialistic values which he saw as the new barbarism.

All these factors (and many more) culminate in 'What the Thunder Said', the section which Eliot, in a letter to Bertrand Russell, declared 'is not the best part, but the only part that justifies the whole' (*FT*, 129).

For all the obvious similarities, there is a world of difference between the fragment 'After the turning' and the opening of 'What the Thunder Said'. The fragment develops by rhetorical addition: expectation is roused by repetition of the same syntactical pattern— a simple enough rhetorical device—and the expectation is defeated. In 'What the Thunder Said' the rhetorical sequence is far more subtle; the verse moves on quickly from the opening pattern, pre-serving expectation, but without the stagnation—syntactical and emotional—of the fragment. And the expectation is fulfilled with lines sufficiently many-valued to justify the rhetorical pressure:

> He who was living is now dead
> We who were living are now dying
> With a little patience.

The verse here recalls Revelation: 'I am he that liveth, and was dead; and behold, I am alive for evermore' (Rev. 1: 18), especially since all that has gone before relies so heavily on our memories of the Passion of Christ. But the opening of 'What the Thunder Said' also accomplishes a distancing effect, so that the familiar images are, as it were, stretched to the point where they could include much that does not belong to the Christian tradition alone. First there is the sharply-focused close up 'After the torchlight red on sweaty faces', recalling the scene of Jesus's arrest—John 18: 3 gives us the torches—and suggests, perhaps, a composite or imagined painting of the faces huddled in the light. Then, with 'the frosty silence' and the 'agony in stony places', though they are equally specific in their reference to the passion, a gradual distancing begins to take place. Sharply defined harshness and cold gives way to distance and confusion: 'Prison and palace and reverberation'. And then the curious promise of 'thunder of spring over distant mountains', which reminds one much more of pagan sentiment than Christian gospel, effects the beginnings of an odd reconciliation: the specific content of Christian faith is dissolved in a larger myth. So, when we come to the question of life and death the passion of Christ blends in with other deaths and lives, the aspirations and promises of other religions and cultures. For instance, Eliot may have remembered Frazer on Osiris (a case of death by water) and the Pyramid texts which assure the dead Pharaohs that they, like Osiris, can expect to live for ever:[12]

> the dominant note that sounds through them all is an insistent, a passionate protest against the reality of death: indeed the word death never occurs in the Pyramid Texts except to be scornfully denied or to be applied to an enemy. Again and again the indomitable assurance is repeated that the dead man did not die but lives. 'King Teti has not died the death, he has become a glorious one in the horizon.' 'Ho! King Unis! Thou didst not depart dead, thou didst depart living.' 'Thou hast departed that thou mightest live, thou hast not departed that thou mightest die.'

The Bible is not lacking in similar words of comfort; but, perhaps because the language and sentiments of the Epistles are so profoundly influenced by the spread of Christianity amongst the gentiles, and began to deal with paradoxes of birth and death in a way rather more like the mystery religions of the Greek world, the language of comfort changed: 'Now if we be dead with Christ, we believe that we shall also live with him' (Rom. 6: 8). The doctrine of Paul is one of unity; a tribal sense of unity extended and adapted far enough to cover men from a thousand tribes or no tribe, and therefore developed beyond the notion of the unity of the tribe to the idea of the unity of man:

> For none of us liveth to himself, and no man dieth to himself. For whether we live, we live unto the Lord; and whether we die,

we die unto the Lord: whether we live therefore, or die, we are the Lord's. For to this end Christ both died, and rose, and revived, that he might be Lord both of the dead and the living.

(Rom. 14: 7–9)

Thus the poem has turned full circle to return to the same concerns which shaped 'The Burial of the Dead', but now seen in the context of a different kind of myth. The condition of being human is seen through the metaphor of the bereaved disciples of Christ; the present pain of living seen in the context of the promised second coming, and 'patience' becomes the key-note of the journey.

In your patience possess ye your souls. And when ye shall see Jerusalem compassed with armies, then know that the desolation thereof is nigh.

(Luke 21: 19–20)

He who was living is now dead
We who were living are now dying
With a little patience

Who are those hooded hordes swarming
Over endless plains, stumbling in cracked earth
Ringed by the flat horizon only
What is the city over the mountains
Cracks and reforms and bursts in the violet air
Falling towers
Jerusalem Athens Alexandria
Vienna London
Unreal

But the complex fusing process in 'What the Thunder Said' brings together still more from the common stock of images. Images of rock and water, of thirst and journeying through a desert would stand quite independently, would communicate immediately even to a person who did not share the hoarded stock of images held in trust by any European, supposing the person to know what rock and desert, water and thirst are. But for any man who is profoundly influenced by the cultural traditions of Judaism or Christianity there will be one association which can hardly be denied. The journeying of the Israelites across the desert:

[125]

and there was no water for the people to drink. Wherefore the people did chide Moses and said, Give us water that we may drink . . . And the Lord said unto Moses . . . thou shalt smite the rock, and there shall come water out of it, that the people may drink . . .

(Exod. 17: 2–6)

> Here is no water but only rock
> Rock and no water and the sandy road
> The road winding above among the mountains
> Which are mountains of rock without water . . .

At this point 'Come in under the shadow of this red rock' mutates in meaning retrospectively. 'Fear in a handful of dust' expands into the fear of the man lost in the desert, fear of death, not by water, but by lack of water. 'Death by Water' mutates too, being set beside the terror of dryness; and water, once an image of death, becomes an image of life and renewal (already hinted by 'thunder of spring over distant mountains').

At such a moment, when so many of the images which control and give substance to the earlier parts of the poem become fluid and shift into new meaning, the metaphor of the journey becomes peculiarly appropriate: meanings which have been, though complex, comparatively clear, become more and more ambiguous. We have at least the illusion that we are moving closer to the 'real' meaning. All *The Waste Land* is hints followed by guesses; Eliot continually exploits the human habit of longing for meaning; through rock with no water he leads us on with a sense of loss and unmeaning, but the unmeaning is of a kind which implies meaning, somewhere; less directly than in 'So through the evening', but the relative directness of that fragment gives it less force as an image of indirect and baffled search:

> The inspiration that delivers and expresses
> This wrinkled road which twists and winds and guesses.

(*FT*, 113)

For all its complex suggestiveness that there really is purpose in the journey, an end to it all somewhere in an unspoken Word, the passage is dominated by pain and difficulty. The movement, steady, persistent, though uncertain, gives direction, but terror, unease and deprivation are expressed in flat, weary cadences which settle in to a circling, trance-like utterance:

[126]

> If there were water
> And no rock
> If there were rock
> And also water
> And water
> A spring
> A pool among the rock
> If there were the sound of water only
> Not the cicada
> And dry grass singing . . .

The journey continues, if we are to believe Eliot's own note, with an allusion to an account of an Antarctic expedition, in which, when near exhaustion, it seemed to the explorers that there was one more member than could actually be counted:

> Who is the third who walks always beside you?
> When I count, there are only you and I together
> But when I look ahead up the white road
> There is always another one walking beside you

The experience is not an unfamiliar one, particularly to those who are near collapse from extreme weariness or anxiety, from emotional and spiritual, as well as physical distress. It is not always a consolatory experience, but sometimes a terrifying one; the old Greek notion of the Furies dogging the footsteps of the guilty, the 'panic' fear of something lying in wait, these too arise out of similar hallucinations or fears in moments of extreme stress. But experiences of this kind seem always to be associated, or at least are very easily associated, with the feeling of supernatural presences, whether benign or malign. Certainly Dostoevsky knew 'the third' who appears at such moments. In *The Brothers Karamazov* Ivan visits Smerdyakov, who is now very sick. It is Smerdyakov who struck the blow that killed Ivan's father, but there remains an ironic ambiguity about who was responsible for the murder. Smerdyakov speaks:[13]

> 'Aren't you tired of it? Here we are face to face; what's the use of going on keeping up a farce to each other? Are you still trying to throw it all on me, to my face? *You* murdered him; you are the real murderer, I was only your instrument, your faithful servant, and it was following your words I did it'.
> '*Did* it? Why, did you murder him?' Ivan turned cold.

[127]

Something seemed to give way in his brain, and he shuddered all over with a cold shiver. Then Smerdyakov himself looked at him wonderingly; probably the genuineness of Ivan's terror struck him.

'You don't mean to say you really did not know?' he faltered mistrustfully, looking with a forced smile into his eyes. Ivan still gazed at him, and seemed unable to speak.

Ach, Vanka's gone to Petersburg
I won't wait till he comes back,

suddenly echoed in his head.

'Do you know, I am afraid that you are a dream, a phantom sitting beside me', he muttered.

'There's no phantom here, but only us two and one other. No doubt he is here, that third, between us'.

'Who is he? Who is here? What third person?' Ivan cried in alarm, looking about him, his eyes hastily searching in every corner.

'That third is God Himself, Providence. He is the third beside us now. Only don't look for him, you won't find him.'

Academic discussion could never settle the question of just how much this, that or the other experience or memory or piece of reading contributed to the final result; it is in keeping with Eliot's own idea of the relationship between the individual and tradition that we can discern many echoes in his verse—and the echoes each person hears may be different—contributing to the total meaning. The 'third' in Dostoevsky is connected with guilt and judgment; that of Eliot with comfort and spiritual sustenance; but both of these ghostly presences, seen as it were, out of the corner of the eye, hint at a resolution which is as yet only *just* within the field of vision. And Eliot himself gives the clue to a memory which lies behind both Dostoevsky's 'third, between' and Eliot's 'third . . . beside you'. In the journey of the two unnamed disciples to Emmaus after the crucifixion Jesus appears: 'But their eyes were holden that they should not know him.' (Luke 24: 16) And in Paul's account of the wanderings of the tribes of Israel through the desert, the Jews were accompanied by a similar, ghostly presence: 'And did all drink the same spiritual drink: for they drank of that spiritual Rock that followed them: and that Rock was Christ' (I Cor. 10: 4). The passage is linked by the continued note of questioning:

'Who is the third . . .?' 'What is that sound . . .?' 'What is the city . . .?' and each question modulates the doubting cadence: in such a manner the only appropriate mode of language is question. The terrible outer chaos is only qualified by the thing half-seen, half-guessed, which disappears if you examine it too closely: 'the third beside you'; 'Murmur of maternal lamentation'; 'the city over the mountains' which shifts and changes in the distorting atmosphere, 'Cracks and reforms and bursts in the violet air'. Ambiguity is of the essence here. 'The city over the mountains' suggests many things— the new Jerusalem of Revelation 21: 2, Blake's 'Jerusalem', the Celestial City which is the end of the journey in *The Pilgrim's Progress*, the City of God which Augustine wrote of after Rome, that other great city, centre of the earthly world, had fallen to the barbarians. But in its context it is associated disturbingly with 'Unreal' cities, Jerusalem, Athens, Alexandria, Vienna, London, cities which, like Rome, take their turn as centres of power and wealth and intellect, and then, in turn, decay. And 'the third', he who glides 'wrapt in a brown mantle, hooded' is distinct from, but in some undefined way partly assimilated to 'those hooded hordes swarming/ Over endless plains', comforter and barbarian destroyers mimicking each other.

'Murmur of maternal lamentation' has its ambiguities too, suggesting, perhaps, the *Stabat Mater*, but containing more sinister possibilities as well, as does the woman in travail in Revelation: 'And she being with child cried, travailing in birth, and pained to be delivered' (Rev. 12: 2).

Some of these more sinister possibilities are allowed to develop in the passage, from line 376 to line 384, which incorporates the monstrous hallucinations of the fragment 'So through the evening':

> A woman drew her long black hair out tight
> And fiddled whisper music on those strings
> And bats with baby faces in the violet light
> Whistled, and beat their wings
> And crawled head downward down a blackened wall
> And upside down in air were towers
> Tolling reminiscent bells, that kept the hours
> And voices singing out of empty cisterns and exhausted wells.

A hallucinatory vision such as this has at the heart of it that blend of uniqueness and familiarity which all nightmares have.

But there is a prophetic voice from the past informing the whole passage. Jeremiah, upbraiding the people of Israel for their back-sliding into error, speaks of the journey towards the promised land, of how they had been brought safely through a waste land 'through the wilderness, through a land of deserts and of pits, through a land of drought, and of the shadow of death' (Jer. 2: 6), and yet now have deserted his cause:

> For my people have committed two evils; they have forsaken me the fountain of living waters, and hewed them out cisterns, broken cisterns, that can hold no water.
>
> (Jer. 2: 13)

Jeremiah goes on to speak of burning cities in the waste land: 'The young lions roared upon him, and yelled, and they made his land waste: his cities were burned without inhabitant' (Jer. 2: 15). And again he prophesies the destruction of cities by earthquake, in a passage which has some of the quality of hallucinatory unreality and formlessness which make Eliot's towers hang, mirage-like, 'upside down in air'. In the midst of this nightmare vision, there is the wail of 'maternal lamentation', crying the universal decadence and horror:

> For I have heard a voice as of a woman in travail, and the anguish as of her that bringeth forth her first child, the voice of the daughter of Zion, that bewaileth herself, that spreadeth her hands, saying, Woe is me now! for my soul is wearied because of the murderers.
>
> (Jer. 4: 31)

If we wish to understand the ambiguities of a passage like this we should look back through the rest of the poem, remembering how consistently ambiguous Eliot is in his attitude towards the notion of 'the image', how deeply he suspects the human habits of imagination, of image-making, while he himself, as a poet, is forced to use the image as a means of communicating:

> Son of man,
> You cannot say, or guess, for you know only
> A heap of broken images

'What the Thunder Said' gives an account of a journey under-taken in the aftermath of a death; a journey which seeks meaning.

The landscape is that of a world of broken images, of dry stones with no sound of water; images which distantly suggest some kind of comfort, like the shadowy 'third' and 'the city over the mountains', but can never be stabilized at the centre of vision, which change or disappear as you look at them; images of horror and corruption, freakish monsters and mirages; images of cities which are 'unreal'. The images steadily grow in their distortive quality; equally our sense that the journey is about to come to a conclusion grows.

The distortion reaches its peak with the hallucinatory fugue of lines 359–84, and then the tension and the illusion *appear* to dissolve and leave us with a comparatively bare and simple image:

> In this decayed hole among the mountains
> In the faint moonlight, the grass is singing
> Over the tumbled graves, about the chapel
> There is the empty chapel, only the wind's home
> It has no windows, and the door swings.

Bare and simple, comparatively, but still an image, and invested with some of the quality of *unreality* which belongs to the whole journey. It is only by contrast that the illusory quality appears to dissolve, only by a sleight of hand that we believe, briefly, that the journey is at an end and then recognize the disappointment.

The disappointment lies in the continued ironic ambiguities: nothing is settled yet. 'The grass is singing' may recall the prophecies of Isaiah:

> The voice said, Cry. And he said, What shall I cry? All flesh
> is grass, and all the goodliness thereof is as the flower of the
> field: The grass withereth, the flower fadeth: because the
> spirit of the LORD bloweth upon it: surely the people is grass.
> The grass withereth, the flower fadeth: but the word of our
> God shall stand for ever.
>
> (Isa. 40: 6–8)

The memory of Isaiah brings with it a promise of peace. The graves, too (if one accepts the rhetoric of resurrection) are scattered witness of the burial of the dead and thus of re-birth. The chapel is empty, 'only the wind's home'; but if you wish to interpret it so, the wind may be an image of life 'because the spirit of the LORD bloweth upon it'; almost all words for the spirit—anima, psyche, spirit itself—

contain the idea of breath or wind. 'Dry bones can harm no one', nor did they in Ezekiel when the Lord made him prophesy:

> So I prophesied as I was commanded: and as I prophesied, there was a noise, and behold a shaking, and the bones came together, bone to his bone. And when I beheld, lo, the sinews and the flesh came up upon them, and the skin covered them above: but there was no breath in them. Then said he unto me, Prophesy unto the wind, prophesy, son of man, and say to the wind, Thus saith the Lord GOD; Come from the four winds, O breath, and breathe upon these slain, that they may live.
>
> (Ezek. 37: 7–9)

So, in all sorts of ways the chapel is made to be a hint of new life rising out of death, the burial of the dead and the promised resurrection. But it is still an image, only half-focused, full of the most tortuous ambiguities of meaning; deliberately enigmatic, even to the cock:

> Only a cock stood on the rooftree
> Co co rico co co rico
> In a flash of lightning.

Peter's denial of Christ is what most readers will remember here, and rightly: thus the crowing of the cock twists the unease and doubt just a little further. But the image of the cock has many other associations. It is a bird of sacrifice: according to the *Phaedo*, Socrates' last words were about the sacrifice of a cock to Asklepios. It is a magical bird which drives away disease and demons. It is the bird of the dawn, announcing a new day. In the draft version, Eliot hinted at another connotation, making it 'a black cock', which, perhaps because of its black magic overtones, Pound disliked.

It is entirely up to the reader which of these associations is to count most, its sacrificial, heraldic, or other subtler aspects, and how they are blended in his response. What is more certain than anything else is that the crowing of the cock acts as a pivot to the whole poem; with its call the dryness and emptiness are resolved, the promise of 'thunder of spring over distant mountains' is fulfilled:

> In a flash of lightning. Then a damp gust
> Bringing rain.

The whole poem reaches its culmination in the voice of the thunder which follows the lightning. Eliot returns to one of the areas

[132]

of human history and learning which has fascinated him most since his early youth. In 'manipulating a continuous parallel' between the present and past worlds of imagination and belief (which yet remain alive within the contemporary mind) Eliot has sought to find shape and order, not just within the poem, but behind the anguish and the terror of living. The anguish remains, but now placed within a context so immense and ancient that the suffering is impersonalized, made part of the abiding pattern of suffering humanity; and personal tragedy becomes part of the divine comedy.

We may understand this better if, once more, we take account of the analogues in prophecy, and the repeated resort to the manner of prophecy, and the repeated play with the idiom and mannerisms of prophecy, which characterize the poem as a whole. The prophet stands, like Sweeney, 'at the hornèd gate', like Tiresias or the Sybil at the mouth of the underworld; and, if you accept the view of life in which prophecy (or indeed religious experience of any kind) is valid, then there is a sense in which you may think of any and every human as a kind of prophet, however imperfect and distorted his vision: every Sweeney his own oracle. But, as Samuel Johnson says in quite another context, 'gold may be so concealed in baser matter that only a chymist can recover it'. The problem faced by any man in trying to discover the truth of things is what skills, what habits of thought are most appropriate to the purpose. He has only his own experience to use, even if that contains in suspension the distillation of a million men's experiences—the experiences of other men are only usable in so far as they have in some sense become part of one's own experience.

We store up memorials of the past, never knowing to a certainty their precise status, whether they are experiences out of our own past; or experiences so transmuted by the process of memory that they no longer have much to do with our own past; or other men's experiences handed down to us; or other men's experiences so changed by naturalization, as part of the population of our minds, that they no longer have much to do with other men's pasts. So the incident in the hyacinth garden is a fusion of many things, and so complete has the fusion been that there is no point in trying to discover exactly what, or whose, the experience is, in terms of past time. All that we do know certainly is that it was Eliot's *as he wrote* the poem, and is ours *as we read* it: however it came to be as it is, it is what it is.

[133]

There remains the urgent instinctive drive towards prophetic truth, and the one positive way that Eliot can discover to satisfy it. That is to behave as if one is not simply oneself:

> What happens is a continual surrender of himself as he is at the moment to something which is more valuable. The progress of the artist is a continual self-sacrifice, a continual extinction of personality.
>
> (*SE*, 17)

and, whatever else this may mean, it means adopting a point of view in which one's own experience is only accepted as really valid when it is, or seems to be, in continuity with the experience of humanity as a whole, stored in its languages, its customs, its literature, its paintings, its buildings. The artist must behave as if all this is present *now*; not in a lumber-room of the mind, but present in such a way that it can *use* the mind of the artist to re-create itself.

But when we reach this stage we begin to find ourselves in country where the literature, the paintings, the languages and the customs, in their ideal order, imply something else precisely because of the ideality of their order. They imply something analogous to the tribal spirit which comprehends the whole of a tribe, living and dead, with all its complex organization, the patterns of its words and rites, its customs and its artefacts.

Thus, for Eliot, the nearest way to discovering a truth is to behave as if the whole of human experience, and beyond that a transcendent metaphysical truth, speaks with our voice; and our guide to this may be the most ancient and most persistent habits of belief: the traditional view, and the idiom which tradition most characteristically uses.

With the damp gust of rain there is a sudden shift from a dream landscape, a world of unreal objects and confused feeling, to an imaginative reconstruction of the very earliest stages of the development of that shared culture upon which the whole of European and Indian literature and philosophy and religion and civilization still depend. Even if, in some sense, equally unreal, the new landscape, with all its connotations, makes way for clear and powerful statement, statement invested with all the power and dignity which we associate with a most ancient past when myth and reality, gods and men, the two worlds, or 'two lives', of sense and spirit, seem to have been more intimately and essentially linked.

[134]

It was a world in which the speech of the gods and the immense reserves of power latent in wind and water, mountains and rivers, were so close to each other that they were seen as part of the same process. This sense of an other-worldly, inhuman power in the natural world, is something we can still feel, vestigially; the calm, dispassionate account of the energies latent in the material universe given by the scientist has never quite dispelled this primitive awe, and has never disqualified the poet from using it to suggest powers and energies, of a non-material kind, lying behind the whole of creation:

> Ganga was sunken, and the limp leaves
> Waited for rain, while the black clouds
> Gathered far distant, over Himavant.
> The jungle crouched, humped in silence.
> Then spoke the thunder
> DA

A big river is a powerful thing; given a name, and an unfamiliar one at that, it begins to acquire some of the quality of a primitive god. A jungle is something which fills us with awe, with the feeling of unknown presences and savage, teeming life (and this is especially true if we have never been in a jungle). When it is made to crouch, like a hunting animal, waiting for something, just as 'Ganga' waits, a curious tension of anticipation is created. The word, or syllable, which releases the tension, is given an unusual energy by the release. The process mimics the growing tensions of an approaching tropical or sub-tropical storm, and its release in the shattering thunder, with extraordinary accuracy.

Eliot refers us in his note to the *Brihadaranyaka Upanishad*, 5, 1. It may be significant that he refers us to the first Brahmana of the fifth Adhyaya, which is a philosophical investigation of the problem of appearance and reality, rather than to the second Brahmana, from which he draws the detail of the imagery.

The second Brahmana tells us of the Pragapati, the ultimate source of creativity and power, and his education of his descendants, Gods, men and Asuras (or demons). The gods ask their father for a word, and he gives them the syllable Da. The gods interpret this as *Damyata*, meaning control, or subdue the self. He gives the same answer, Da, to men, but they interpret it as *Datta*, which means give; the Asuras interpret the same answer as meaning *Dayadham*, sympathize or be merciful. It is then said that when the divine voice of thunder says DA, it means all these three things at once.

Eliot changes the order from control, give, sympathize to give, sympathize, control. There is some significance in this; Eastern asceticism has usually tended to emphasize subduing the self as the first step towards purification of motive; asceticism in the western tradition has always characteristically begun with a love affair: the giving of the soul to God.

'Giving' is what the ecstatic moment in the Hyacinth Garden was about; it is a variety of religious experience which tends to be, almost must be, spoken of through erotic imagery. This is how the commentators saw the Song of Solomon: 'a marriage song, which Solomon wrote in the form of a drama or song under the figure of the Bride, about to wed and burning with heavenly love towards her Bridegroom'. It is the essence of the *Vita Nuova* and the figure of Beatrice in the Divine Comedy. It is the basic metaphor of the Sufi poets, and of St John of the Cross, who takes his cue from the episode of the lover with hyacinths in the Vulgate Canticle, and the touch which the Bride remembers:[14]

> this touch of a spark which she mentions here is a most subtle touch which the Beloved inflicts upon a soul at times, even when she is least thinking of it, so that her heart is enkindled in the fire of love, just as if a spark of fire had flown out and enkindled it.

Even in his use of Eastern metaphors Eliot shows that the pattern of his emotional priorities is essentially Western, essentially Christian:

> *Datta*: what have we given?
> My friend, blood shaking my heart
> The awful daring of a moment's surrender
> Which an age of prudence can never retract
> By this, and this only, we have existed.

The 'giving' here is, in itself, ambiguous; it suggests at first reading a sexual indiscretion, and is meant to: the experience described, whatever it is, is certainly not entirely one of joy, but also of fear and danger, so entirely private that it is kept secret even in death. But there is no sense, except a very sentimental one quite out of keeping with the tone of the poem, in which one can say of sexual conquest or surrender 'By this, and this only we have existed'. The whole context of the poem (and of Eliot's other poems) suggest inescapably that this is yet another modulation of metaphors we have met elsewhere, the play with pronouns, 'I' and 'you' meeting in 'we', the sexual metaphor for the surrender of one aspect of the soul to the control of another. It is yet another account of the drama of the soul which poems like 'Prufrock', 'Gerontion' and the Quatrain poems deal with. The memory of the hyacinth garden, the encounter in the Lady's boudoir in 'A Game of Chess' are different phases of the same drama. The figure of Tiresias, in whom 'the two sexes meet' is a suggestive metaphor for the union of which all the episodes speak; a meeting which causes disharmony, pain, the anguish of dissociation, for such a person can never be satisfied with what he has in ordinary life. Like Dante, such a person must learn 'not to expect more from *life* than it can give or more from *human* beings than they can give; to look to *death* for what life cannot give' (*SE*, 275).

'*Dayadhvam.* I have heard the key/Turn in the door once and once only.' In a note at this point Eliot refers to Dante and F. H. Bradley. There is no need for me to comment on the juxtaposition, except to say that the peculiar, private world of isolation, in which 'every sphere is opaque to the others around it' which Bradley describes, changes as Eliot contemplates it, because it has become associated with so many other things, modified by a complex sensibility filled with fears and hopes which would have no place at all in Bradley's philosophical discourse. The prison, for Eliot, is the terrible sense of existential isolation; the key is the memory of a fleeting sense of release from that isolation, that which is referred to by the hyacinth garden, or by 'The awful daring of a moment's surrender.'

The image of Coriolanus remained with Eliot for several years. 'Triumphal March', the first part of 'Coriolan', has a chorus of plebeians watching the parade of military hardware and civic organizations to the temple, where the sacrifice takes place, 'the virgins bearing urns, urns containing/Dust/Dust/Dust of dust.' Amongst all this meaningless accumulation there is Coriolanus, a consciousness of a different kind from the plebeians. Notice how the language here recalls the idiom of the Song of Solomon:

There he is now, look:
There is no interrogation in his eyes
Or in the hands, quiet over the horse's neck,

[137]

And the eyes watchful, waiting, perceiving, indifferent.
O hidden under the dove's wing, hidden in the turtle's breast
Under the palmtree at noon, under the running water
At the still point of the turning world. O hidden.

Coriolanus, both here and in 'What the Thunder Said', comes to suggest a stillness and meditative detachment, the capacity to overcome the terror of isolation by the gift of contemplation.

'*Damyata*': we are returned to the image of the boat, which has recurred ever since the quotation from *Tristan und Isolde*. We must see it in the context of the voice of thunder saying DA (a word for the gods): *Damyata*—control or subdue the self. And yet there is a fundamental ambiguity about the image as Eliot uses it: the boat has left the shore, the journey continues, full of gaiety, but 'you' are left behind, just as in Tristan 'mein Irisch kind' lingers on the shore:

> The sea was calm, your heart would have responded
> Gaily, when invited, beating obedient
> To controlling hands.

Mixed with the gaiety, the sense of continued hope, there is the pathos and tender regret of lost opportunities. I do not believe the ambiguity can be solved, or that we should attempt to solve it: both emotions can be and are present in the one personality.

I have spoken of the 'muddle' of emotion that Eliot was in as he wrote *The Waste Land*; it may be said that, in one sense, the poem is *about* muddle, about tensions, unresolved ambiguities, which are, in the end, seen just as that, as a muddle of memory and desire, the portrait of a sensibility warped by 'Unreal emotions, and real appetite', reaching out for a half-glimpsed reality which always hovers on the borders of vision, tempting, teasing, leading the mind on and on through ever more sterile and confused states of feeling and thought, but never reaching conclusion. It may be said, too, that the structure of the poem, with its repeated withdrawal from communication, its deliberate obscurities and intermittent hysteria, its lapses from taste, its jerky discontinuities, represents, with some accuracy, such a state of mind.

It cannot be denied that *The Waste Land* is a difficult and unsettling poem. It is, as Eliot himself said, 'a piece of rhythmical grumbling'—though it is not 'just' that. It demands an extraordinary effort of attention from the reader, withdraws in a somewhat arrogant way from direct communication with him, and yet claims the reader as a fellow conspirator in failure. At times it struts with clever display; at other times it cowers before life with an abject maudlin fear; it betrays all the inconsistency and violence of mental instability.

And it is just because of these qualities that it re-shaped English verse, by its energy, impatience and wilfulness, its willingness to employ patterns of emotion, rhythm and idea which had so far been *tabu*. The very fact that it is, as it were, arrested, hastily put together before the poet himself knew how to complete the whole, is one of the things that makes it so important. It catches a disturbed and yet impressively creative mind in all its twists, turns, evasions, insecurities, self-doubts, in its moments of arrogance and hysteria, of nostalgia and self-pity as well as self-understanding; catches it putting together bits and pieces, stitching and patching. The twentieth century has made us all more aware of the difficulty both of beauty and of sanity, the predominance of the unformed, interim states of feeling and judgment over the stable and fulfilled, harmonious sensibility, if not in significance, at least in experience of fact.

Eliot himself recognizes this and expresses it in the final peroration, with 'These fragments I have shored against my ruins.'

Each fragment, in its own way, picks up one of the themes of the poem; as a whole the fragments suggest the chaotic fragmentation of emotion of the poetic experience. The nursery rhyme refrain 'London Bridge is falling down' summarizes the imagery of unreal cities, the anxiety about the collapse of civilized values, the sense of the absence of significance from real life, city life. Over against the collapse of the city, there is the tag from Dante, reminding us of the fire sermon, the Buddha's purifying fire as well as the purgatorial flame of Malachi, Dante and the Christian tradition. The half line from *Pervigilium Veneris*, 'Quando fiam uti chelidon', has a more complex effect. It resumes, briefly, the Ovidian theme of metamorphosis:[15]

> The maid of Tereus sings under the shade of the poplar trees
> so that you would think love songs came from her mouth, and
> not the complaint of a sister against a barbarous Lord. . . .
> She sings, we are silent: when will my spring come? when shall
> I be as the swallow, that I shall cease to be mute?

Like so many other poems in the allegorical mode to which it belongs, *Pervigilium Veneris* uses erotic imagery in a way which, though it loses none of its erotic flavour, implies spiritual love too; the refrain runs 'cras amet qui nunquam amavit quique amavit cras amet' (for those who have never loved there will be love tomorrow, those who have loved will love again), echoing Augustine's longing for love, and Eliot's continuing nostalgia for love remembered in a world of the loveless. 'O swallow swallow', remembered from Tennyson's *The Princess*, also touches on the theme of metamorphosis and transfiguration.

The characteristically enigmatic texture of Gérard de Nerval's verse seems to have depended a great deal on the use of alchemical symbolism and the symbolism of the Tarot. In his sonnet, *El Desdichado*, he has combined a quest theme with symbolism of this kind; the ruined tower is one of the Tarot cards, and thus 'La Prince d'Aquitaine à la tour abolie' touches *The Waste Land*'s pattern of metaphor and symbolism at many points.

The composite quotation from Kyd's *Spanish Tragedy* relates to the whole of *The Waste Land* in rather a different way. It has a function somewhat similar to the line in 'Gerontion': 'I have not made this show purposelessly', in a kind of retroflex comment on the action of the poem as drama, even melodrama.

In Kyd's play Hieronymo is Marshal of Spain. His son, Horatio, has been murdered by Balthazar and Lorenzo. Later they approach Hieronymo for help in entertaining the King of Portugal, and Hieronymo answers:[16]

> Why then, Ile fit you; say no more
> When I was yong, I gaue my minde
> And plide my selfe to fruitles Poetrie;
> Which though it profite the professor naught
> Yet it is passing pleasing to the world.

Hieronymo, like Hamlet, offers to produce a play as a means of exacting revenge. The Tragedy he produces is a disguised version of the story of Horatio, up to his death. Hieronymo contrives that each of the villains should play a part, but reserves the part of the murderer for himself.

Thus, 'Why then, Ile fit you' refers, allusively and indirectly, to *The Waste Land* as a kind of play within a play, an unreal mirage which yet distantly and disturbingly reflects the reality. 'Hieronymo's mad againe', the sub-title of the play in some editions, suggests, with the painfully acute self-consciousness which is so typical of the poem, the busy, self-centred energy, the note of hysteria and anguish, the confusion and insecurity of the poem.

After a repetition of the three injunctions of the thunder the poem ends with the formal conclusion to prayer in the Upanishads, like Amen as the Christians use it: 'Shantih, shantih, shantih'—the blessing or greeting of peace. It is a curious ending for a poem so little like the Upanishads in its moral and spiritual universe; but perhaps it points beyond the poem itself to an imagined or ideal resolution.

I suppose it would be near the truth to say that *The Waste Land*'s reputation has fallen more rapidly since the Second World War than the public reputation of any major poem in any similar period. It was at one time accepted uncritically, and it is good that it no longer should be so. It now seems, to more and more readers, increasingly irrelevant to contemporary experience. In the sense that it is irrelevant now, it always was. In the sense that it ever was genuinely relevant it will always continue to be so. It is simply that it is taking an unusually long time to accustom ourselves to the shock which this poem—like any great poem—produces. And of course this is partly the peculiarity of the poem's method; its extreme reserve, its extreme distrust, its anguished bullying of the reader.

CHAPTER FIVE

'WHERE THE DREAMS CROSS' FROM 'THE HOLLOW MEN' TO *MARINA*

Between 1922, when *The Waste Land* was published, and 1930, when *Ash Wednesday* and *Marina* appeared, Eliot was deeply preoccupied with certain problems; problems which were implied or expressed by *The Waste Land*, but find no resolution there. The fragmentary ending of *The Waste Land* concludes a collection of haunting insights from the literature of the past with words which betoken ritual and prayer; but the anguished cry of the poem lacks in every way the stability which ritual might have given it; lacks in every way the peace which is the object of prayer.

In these years Eliot moved steadily towards some kind of reconciliation of his role as a poet with the need for stability and peace; he became more and more convinced that literature in the absence of ritual order and magical or religious awareness was either impossible or absurd. In 1923 he wrote:[1]

> At what point, we may ask, does the attempt to design and create an object for the sake of beauty become conscious? At what point in civilisation does any conscious distinction between practical or magical utility and aesthetic beauty arise? . . . Surely the distinction must mark a change in the human mind which is of fundamental importance. And a further question we should be impelled to ask is this: Is it possible and justifiable for art, the creation of beautiful objects and of literature, to persist indefinitely without its primitive purposes: is it possible for the aesthetic object to be a *direct* object of attention?

It would seem obvious that reflections such as these are encouraged by Eliot's very deep interest in the work of anthropologists like

Frazer, Harrison, Murray and Cornford. Jane Harrison, particularly, was profoundly interested in the whole question of the relationship between art and ritual, and the basic impulses in man which give rise to both.

In 1921, Harrison returned briefly to the study of Greek religion after many years in which she was absorbed in other matters, and wrote her *Epilegomena to the Study of Greek Religion*. In this tiny but compact work she contrasts primitive theology and religious practice with the religion of today. Primitive religion, she observes, is lacking in what we should call the worship of a god. She goes on to try and understand what happened when primitive man began to make gods to worship. She calls upon the exciting new psychological thinkers of the day, particularly Jung, to support her conception of man as essentially an image maker, and it is possible that this idea contributed to the general pattern of *The Waste Land* which we have just discussed:[2]

> He cannot perform the simplest operation without forming some sort of correlative idea. It has been much disputed whether the myth arises out of the rite or the rite out of the myth, whether a man thinks something because he does it, or does it because he thinks it. As a matter of fact the two operations arose together and are practically inseparable.

In animals, Harrison argues, perception sets up an immediate two-fold reaction—at one and the same time the body acts, and the mind represents. But ritual actions, being human actions (and human actions at their most characteristic) are not simple in this way. She summarizes the central thesis of her earlier work, *Themis*, that rites are either 'an action redone (commemorative) or *pre*done (anticipatory or magical)'. This, she argues, is because in the perceptive processes of man, unlike those of the animal, there is a built-in delayed reaction; that in man 'perception is not immediately transformed into action'.

Here we come to the centre of her argument, and the point at which it is most directly relevant to our understanding of Eliot. It is, she says, in the interval between perception and action that almost all our mental life, and in particular all that gives rise to magic, theology, ritual and poetry, occurs:[3]

> Perception is pent up and, helped by emotion, becomes conscious representation. In this momentary halt between per-

ception and reaction all our images, ideas, in fact our whole mental life, is built up. If we were a mass of well combined instincts, that is if the cycle of perception and action were instantly fulfilled, we should have no representation and hence no art and no theology. In fact in a word religious presentation, mythology or theology, as we like to call it, springs like ritual from arrested, unsatisfied desire.

'THE HOLLOW MEN'

It would be fascinating to trace the links between Harrison's thesis and *The Waste Land*. But the relationship is, I believe, undeniable between Harrison's argument and 'The Hollow Men', a poem which grew out of the aftermath of *The Waste Land* and pursues some of its problems further:

> Between the conception
> And the creation
> Between the emotion
> And the response
> Falls the Shadow.
>
> *Life is very long*

The unmistakable echo of antiphonal church responses hints that 'The Hollow Men' is consciously verse designed as ritual. The ritual describes the pause between perception and action in many different ways; between the two falls 'the Shadow'; the interval of unsatisfied desire, inaction, unreality which delays the fulfilment. But '*Thine is the Kingdom*' cannot but carry with it some of the meaning it has in the Lord's Prayer to contend with the prayer of shadow to shadow. The end result is a highly ambiguous expression of the process which Harrison describes when she writes of the making of gods: 'We figure to ourselves what we want, we create an image and that is our god.'

Harrison develops, in her own highly individual way, Jung's contrast between 'directed thinking' and 'dream, or phantasy thinking'. Directed thinking has very little to do with magic, myth, religion or poetry, but phantasy:[4]

turns away from reality and sets free subjective wishes. . . . It is from this early infantile type of dream or phantasy thinking engendered by the fertility rite that primitive theology and mythology spring. 'The gods *are* libido,' says Jung boldly. . . . 'We imagine what we lack, the dying resurrected gods and heroes are but the projected hopes and fears of humanity.' . . . In like manner arises the myth. The myth is not an attempted explanation of either facts or rites. Its origin is not in 'directed thinking', it is not rationalization. The myth is a fragment of the soul life, the dream-thinking of the people, as the dream is the myth of the individual.

'Instead of the narrative method, we may now use the mythical method', wrote Eliot in his review of Joyce's *Ulysses*, and in the following year published three short poems under the general title of 'Doris's Dream Songs'. One of these, 'This is the dead land', was later used in the third part of 'The Hollow Men'. All three are intended as expressions of dream-consciousness, phantasy; but even more they are intended as criticisms of dream-consciousness as the characteristic state of human being, of the Doris in us all.

Like Joyce's Earwicker, Doris is everybody—the private dream hovers on the borderline of communal myth. But Joyce's sympathetic involvement in common humanity gives his characters a power to borrow from our private dreams as if we belonged to them: with Joyce we have the illusion that we are overhearing somebody dream; and the dream—half exploratory journey, half play of an engagingly creative nature—extends our awareness. Doris's Dream Songs, on the other hand, are generalizations about man's experience, his waking experience seen as dream which yearns towards a higher state of awareness. The generalizations are elaborated by a highly individual, even an eccentric mind: we are conscious, not of community with the dreamer, but of being told how somebody thinks about human thought and dream.

'The Hollow Men' arises out of the same generalizing process. Characteristically this involves allusions to a variety of sources, not only the usual literary sources, such as Conrad and Dante, the usual religious and anthropological sources like the Bible and *The Golden Bough*, but also popular myth. So the childish ritual of Guy Fawkes day with children gathering pennies for fireworks is one of the important structural metaphors, expressive of the ritual habit of human behaviour. And the last section parodies 'Here we go round the mulberry bush', a childish ritual game, converting the circularity of the ritual into a image for life in general. All this is part of an attempt to create a ritual and a myth which shall be a criticism and expression of the inadequacy of life.

It doesn't quite work. Ritual and myth, in the sense that both Harrison and Eliot think of these concepts, express communal experiences which are shared at a very profound level, reaching everybody in a community from the most highly sophisticated to the illiterate and the unthinking. 'The Hollow Men' could only appeal to a highly sophisticated audience which is ironically aware of popular ritual and popular myth, an audience, too, which takes pleasure in intellectual puzzles, and knows something about Dante, and a good deal else.

The meaning of the episode in the Hyacinth Garden and the figure of Tiresias in *The Waste Land* depended in part on the ambiguity of 'seeing': the sight of the soul and the sight of the natural body are contrasted. Paul is one of the points of reference in the tradition this embodies: 'For now we see through a glass darkly, but then face to face.' St Thomas Aquinas elaborates the distinction. Dante dramatizes the idea as he tells of his approach to the Heavenly Rose. He sees a river of light which seems to hold all the glory and wonder of eternity, but Beatrice tells him: 'The river and the topazes that enter and depart and the laughter of the grass are the shadowy prefaces of their true reality' (*Paradiso*, XXX, 76–8). Following Beatrice's advice he bathes his eyes in the river, and is able to see directly, 'face to face': 'as soon as my eyelids drank of it, the river's length seemed to turn into roundness. Then, as people under masks seem different from what they were before, if they take off the appearance which is not their own with which they disguised themselves, so the flowers and the sparks were changed before me so that I saw both courts of heaven manifested' (*Paradiso*, XXX, 88–96). He is therefore permitted to see the multifoliate Rose of the blessed in Heaven, a symbol of the unifying of many in one.

In 'The Hollow Men', then, there are two worlds, the 'here' and the 'there', 'death's dream kingdom' and 'death's other Kingdom'. 'Here' the hollow men live, perceiving only 'Shape without form, shade without colour' while 'Those who have crossed/With direct eyes, to death's other Kingdom' (significantly capitalized) can see face to face. 'Here' the hollow men are surrounded by images,

escape from reality by wearing 'deliberate disguises', just as Prufrock finds it convenient to 'prepare a face to meet the faces that
you meet', and as the young man in 'Portrait of a Lady' borrows
'every changing shape/To find expression'

> Rat's coat, crowskin, crossed staves
> In a field
> Behaving as the wind behaves
> No nearer

> Not that final meeting
> In the twilight kingdom.

People make images, scarecrows of themselves not only to scare
away others, but to scare away themselves, from a 'meeting'. They
project their own fears and hopes into images, which they worship
as the people of Israel did when they went whoring after strange gods;

> Here the stone images
> Are raised, here they receive
> The supplication of a dead man's hand
> Under the twinkle of a fading star.

'The eyes are not here/There are no eyes here', but 'there' is
peopled by those 'with direct eyes'. But the eyes are spoken of in a
strange way:

> There, the eyes are
> Sunlight on a broken column

The eyes 'here' are sightless among the dying stars;

> Sightless, unless
> The eyes reappear
> As the perpetual star
> Multifoliate rose
> Of death's twilight kingdom
> The hope only
> Of empty men.

'There', eyes do not just 'see' sunlight, or the image of the ultimate
beauty, they *are* it, they reappear *as* it. The act of seeing is one with
what is seen; and this is the 'final meeting' which is feared by the
blind.

The two lines 'The hope only/Of empty men' contain one of the
slipperiest ambiguities in Eliot's work. 'Religious presentation,

mythology or theology, as we like to call it, springs like ritual from arrested, unsatisfied desire', says Jane Harrison. The 'perpetual star', the 'multifoliate rose' are nothing but images; what they represent is a state of consciousness which those with 'direct eyes' *are*. So the images represent something unattained and unattainable: 'arrested, unsatisfied desire' for hollow men.

But there is just enough difference between 'hollow men' and 'empty men', between 'desire' and 'hope', to suggest a quite contrary interpretation. St John of the Cross, interpreting his own 'Dark night of the soul', describes that night as a purging, or emptying, both of the sense and of the spirit. Thus, hope of a real kind, not 'arrested, unsatisfied desire' might come from a deliberate emptiness.

Section V combines the echo of ecclesiastical ritual with that of the child's round game to express both the solemnity and the childishness of the dream state:

> For Thine is
> Life is
> For Thine is the

> *This is the way the world ends*
> *This is the way the world ends*
> *This is the way the world ends*
> *Not with a bang but a whimper*

The trailing, inconclusive diminuendo, with its broken syntax and rhythms, mimics the incompleteness of unsatisfied desire.

ASH WEDNESDAY

Ash Wednesday begins with an incantation which is equally broken; but the rhythms are the halting rhythms of a tentative beginning:

> Because I do not hope to turn again
> Because I do not hope
> Because I do not hope to turn

But this abandonment of hope is only hopeless in the sense that it rejects hope as a mode of living. Hesitantly, the voice which speaks explores the way towards a form of words, as if experimenting with a ritual which is not yet authorized by custom and usage, so that one must walk round the words to see their every implication: what do I mean by hope? What do I mean by turn?

Implicitly, this opening is an attempt to answer a question which cannot be completely answered; we can reconstruct the question either by looking at Eliot's biography or by looking more closely at the poem: inevitably the second kind of investigation will be far more complex than the first.

Ash Wednesday was begun in 1927, the year when Eliot entered the Church of England. The question asked by the poem is, on one level, simply why he made this decision, with all that the decision must entail for a deeply serious man: why the whole direction of life, from this point onwards, must be changed.

The history of the poem's genesis is complicated. The second section of it was published in the *Saturday Review of Literature* in December 1927, under the title 'Salutation'. The first and third parts followed in 1928 and 1929, and the three remaining parts were not published until the whole poem appeared in April 1930.

It would seem legitimate to suppose that the second part was written first, an eloquent and impassioned response, in the form of a complex private myth, to the new liberty, security, and sense of purpose given him by his conversion. The other sections arrived after reflection, providing a context for the very intimate and immediate sense of revelation in the second part; and yet the whole poem coheres so well that there is no feeling of discontinuity in tone or mood, no feeling that the other five parts are an afterthought or addition to the second. The poem grows out of the impulse which was satisfied in the second part, and is a record of the assimilation of its curious visionary quality into the whole pattern of life, the new direction which is taken after the decisive 'turning'.

Eliot has so far displayed a deep ambivalence towards ritual, looking at it, in one way, as a constricting force expressive of human inadequacy, but at the same time being fascinated by the way ritual orders language, thought and feeling. One of the effects of conversion is that Eliot must needs accept ritual as valid; and he does so without reservation, indeed with touching happiness.

Together with this goes a use of words, a new use of images. No longer the crabbed ellipses, the violent changes of tone, the somewhat hysterical facetiousness, the angular, restless rhythms which more than anything else had marked out Eliot to his contemporaries as the voice of his age. The rhythms of ecclesiastical ritual have entered into Eliot's voice to be adapted and transformed in an easy commerce of old and new. The conflict of the soul, in the poems up to and including 'The Hollow Men' has been dramatized with defensive irony as a protection against too much involvement; in *Ash Wednesday* he approaches that sweet Dantean ease which he praises so often in his critical work, and though, in a limited sense, the poem is an openly personal one—if one wished to play a word counting game one would find the first person singular repeated more than usually frequently—yet paradoxically the sensibility the poem expresses has far greater humility than any of the other poems so far. The tradition is assimilated in the poem (or, the poem assimilates itself *to* the tradition) in a much greater degree: it uses allusion no less than *The Waste Land*, for instance, but subsumes its memories into a moving singleness and strength.

Even though there is this greater sureness and harmony of tone, and in a real sense a shining clarity, there is need for elucidation, particularly of the second section. This will necessarily include some tracing of sources and allusions; what Eliot calls the 'embryology' of the poem. But more important than this we must establish what kind of experience the second section contains; by which I mean, not an experience outside the poem which the poem describes, but the experience which the poem itself is, and communicates.

We have already seen how Eliot stresses the way that poetry depends on 'the religious, ritual and magical view of nature.' In a review of a collection of American Indian ritual chants written as early as 1919, he had written of the need for poets to return to the primitive sources: 'For the artist is, in an impersonal sense, the most conscious of men; he is therefore the most and least civilized and civilizable; he is the most competent to understand both civilized and primitive.'[5] And, he implies, the poet is most likely consciously to pursue primitive aims and methods in a contemporary context. Jane Harrison and her colleagues helped to form his sense of the continuity between the primitives and the civilized in matters of religion and of poetry. In *Themis* she had written:[6]

A δρώμενον is as we have said not simply a thing done, not even a thing excitedly or socially done. What is it then? It is a thing *re*-done or *pre*-done, a thing enacted or represented. It is

[150]

sometimes *re*-done, commemorative, sometimes *pre*-done, anticipatory, and both elements seem to go to its religiousness. . . . The element of μίμησις, is, I think, essential. In all religion, as in all art, there is this element of make-believe. Not the attempt to deceive, but a desire to *re*-live, to *re*-present.

One could say of certain episodes in Eliot's poetry that they are, in this sense, commemorative: the episode of the Hyacinth Garden or that of the Rose Garden in *Four Quartets* embodies and protects a memory. There is no doubt that the second section of *Ash Wednesday* is prophetic in tone, magical in method, and tends towards ritual intonations; but it *commemorates* nothing: it is, in Harrison's terms, *pre*-done, a piece of anticipatory magic. Commenting on William Morris's 'The Blue Closet', in an essay written in 1942, Eliot observes:

It has an effect somewhat like that of a rune or charm, but runes and charms are very practical formulae designed to produce definite results, such as getting a cow out of a bog. But its obvious intention (and I think the author succeeds) is to produce the effect of a dream. It is not necessary in order to enjoy the poem, to know what the dream means; but human beings have an unshakeable belief that dreams mean something. . . . It is a commonplace to observe that the meaning of a poem may wholly escape paraphrase. It is not quite so commonplace to observe that the meaning of a poem may be something larger than its author's conscious purpose, and something remote from its origins.

(OPP, 30)

Something of the sort may, I believe, be said about section II of *Ash Wednesday*; Unger and others have traced much of its origins in allusions; we may re-construct a great deal more about the state of emotion in which the poem was written; but when 'Salutation' stood on its own, I doubt that Eliot himself really understood it: the rest of the poem is an effort to find its real meaning, as a manifestation of the strange enlightening crisis through which Eliot was passing in 1927, and as a 'high dream', a complex symbolical pre-figuring of a new direction.

The 'Lady' who is addressed is clearly related to Dante's Beatrice, and to the mediaeval cult of the Virgin Mary, and to the conventional Lady of Italian Renaissance imagery. Praz and Unger both point to the persistence in this tradition of the convention of earthly love: the sexual image is used to express, not so much the conflict of the soul, but the resolution of that conflict by an object of worship.

Thus, the first section of the poem was originally given the title 'Perch'io non spero' from a poem by Cavalcanti in which the poet bids his soul to worship his Lady, but to 'worship her/Still in her purity'; and, of course 'Perch'io non spero', (Because I do not hope) provides the first lines of the poem.

But there is a significant difference between the first and second sections: 'the blessed face' is a scarcely concealed reference to Dante's Beatrice: the poet renounces 'the blessed face':

> Because I know that time is always time
> And place is always and only place
> And what is actual is actual only for one time
> And only for one place

and this renunciation is of the essence of 'turning'.

Conversely, the second section is an address to the Lady, and contains a prayer to her. The paradox needs some explanation. We must first look a little longer at 'turning'.

Ash Wednesday, the first day of Lent, is a day of penitence, contrition and renunciation; a day set aside for the exercise of self-discipline, purification, and the dissolution of worldly attachments. It is a day for ascetics. Unger suggests, rightly, I believe, that *Ash Wednesday* represents Eliot's experience of the self-purifying processes described by St John of the Cross in his manual for the novice, *The Dark Night of the Soul*. Ash Wednesday has always had this kind of significance in the Christian calendar. Another of Eliot's favourite writers, Lancelot Andrewes, spoke eloquently on several occasions of the significance of the day. One of his favourite texts for the occasion was Joel 2: 12–13, 'Therefore also now, saith the Lord, turn ye even to me with all your heart, and with fasting, and with weeping, and with mourning: And rend your heart, and not your garments, and turn unto the Lord your God.' Another text he loved to develop was Jeremiah 8: 4–8.

> Moreover thou shalt say unto them, Thus saith the LORD; Shall they fall and not arise? shall he turn away, and not return? Why then is this people of Jerusalem slidden back by a perpetual backsliding? . . . Yea, the stork in the heaven

knoweth her appointed times; and the turtle and the crane and the swallow observe the time of their coming; but my people know not the judgment of the LORD.

So, on Ash Wednesday 1602, Bishop Andrewes preached a sermon in which he asked: 'What then, shall I continually "fall" and never "rise"? "turn away" and not once "turn again"? Shall my rebellions be perpetual?' And again, on Ash Wednesday 1619, he interprets the choice of the text from Joel by the makers of the Book of Common Prayer as betokening the need for 'a *solemn set returne, once in the yeare at least*':[7]

> And reason: for, once a yeare, all things *turne*. And, that once is *now* at this *time*; For, now at this time, is the *turning* of the yeare. In Heaven, the *Sunne* in his *Equinoctiall line*, the Zodiacque, and all the *Constellations* in it, do now turne about to their first point. The earth and all her plants, after a *dead Winter*, returne to the first and best season of the yeare. The creatures, the Fowles of the *Aire*, the *Swallow* and the *Turtle*, the *Crane* and the *Storke know their seasons*, and make their just returne at this time, every yeare. Every thing now turning, that we also would make it our *time* to *turne* to *God* in.

Doubtless Andrewes's superb rhetoric would attract Eliot, not least because Andrewes's sensitivity to the ancient symbolism of the cycling year; a symbolism which is more ancient than Christianity. But *Ash Wednesday* strives to express something beyond this flux and change 'Because I know that time is always time/And place is always and only place.' Thus, a 'turn' which is so decisive that it cannot be repeated can not be thought of in terms of time and place. 'The blessed face', the 'one veritable transitory power' may represent an experience which transcends time and place, but they are still only apparent in terms of time and place and memory. St John of the Cross warns the novice against being misled by images and visions: 'All these imaginings must be cast out from the soul, which will remain in darkness as far as this sense is concerned, that it may attain to Divine union; for they can bear no proportion to proximate means of union with God, any more than can bodily imaginings.'[8] An emptying of the imagination is the first stage:

> Consequently I rejoice, having to construct something
> Upon which to rejoice.

This leads naturally to the second section in this sense; that the song sung by the bones is sung out of emptiness; but paradoxically the method of 'Salutation' is richly fertile in images, images of grace and divine beauty of the kind rejected in the first section. It is as if Eliot, while wishing to preserve the record of the high dream and all its beauty, must warn us of taking it as anything more than it is.

I believe that Unger and other commentators have given us much of the correct embryology of the dream: the Lady is an image which arises from memories of Dante, Cavalcanti and the poetry of earthly love. The juniper tree refers to one of Grimms' tales, in which a stepmother murders a supernatural child and makes puddings of his flesh. Her daughter hides the boy's bones under a juniper tree and this death is followed by a resurrection—the boy reappears as a singing-bird, causes the death of the stepmother, and at last turns back into a boy. The bones recall Ezekiel 37, in which the Lord sets the prophet in a valley of dry bones, and says 'Son of man, can these bones live?' The Lord tells Ezekiel to prophesy unto the bones that God will bring life back to them:

> So I prophesied as I was commanded: and as I prophesied, there was a noise, and behold a shaking, and the bones came together, bone to his bone.
>
> (Ezek. 37: 7)

Ecclesiastes comes in too, as the source for 'the burden of the grasshopper' (Ecclesiastes 12: 4–5), and there are numerous other sources worth mentioning.

All these references are genuinely relevant and deeply interesting; but they do not *explain* it; the end result is something which 'explanation' can only satisfy if one's threshold of satisfaction is very low indeed. Rather than 'explain' we should attempt ourselves to experience the poetry as dream, while preserving our critical awareness: this mixture of collaboration and detachment is not impossible.

We might distinguish between the qualities of the dream in 'The Hollow Men' and the quality of this dream by using Jungian terms: the one is dominated by the shadow, the other dream by *anima*. A freer rein is given here to the magical or religious consciousness; a symbolic language is used to body forth the perception, but, while the detail gives meaning to the pattern, the detail is not the object of the pattern. The Lady and the bones, the leopards and the juniper tree are figures in somewhat the same sense as the numerals or figures

in a mathematical equation—vehicles which represent, not themselves, nor any definite thing, but intricate relationships. Somewhere
in the shape which is gestured by 'three white leopards' is 'Christ the
tiger' and Blake's Tyger, the Trinity, white as the colour of faith
and of chastity. Somewhere in the shape of their feeding on 'my legs
my heart my liver and that which had been contained / In the hollow
round of my skull' is the theory of the Eucharist, reversed; the idea
of communion in the singleness of Christ, the voiding of the spirit in
St John of the Cross and his theory of the negative way; one could
point in this way to relationships implied by each one of the images,
but none of these gestures will cover the meaning, which is in the
mythical experience, the high dream of the bones, the drama of the
myth as a whole.

Word play takes a part in the complex communication. Take, for
instance 'dissembled':

> And I who am here dissembled
> Proffer my deeds to oblivion, and my love
> To the posterity of the desert and the fruit of the gourd.

In one's first unwary readings one converts 'dissembled' into
'disassembled', or something of the sort, influenced by all the talk of
scattered bones. But 'dissemble' means to feign or give a false appearance: the word points to the unreality of 'I'; but at the same time
the shadowy 'disassembled' affects the meaning so that 'I' is at once
pretence and disconnection.

Another significant word play is: 'Let the whiteness of the bones
atone to forgetfulness.' The high rhetoric of the dream allows us to
pass over this at first, and at many subsequent readings, but the
question, What does it mean? is bound to press on us at some time.
To atone means to reconcile, literally to set at one, to compose into a
unity. The doctrine of the atonement is to do with the reconciliation
of God and man by Christ's sacrifice and their setting-at-one in
Christ. Here, the setting-at-one and reconciliation of the bones leads,
not to any dramatic re-birth, but to forgetfulness. The new beginning
prayed for is in a one-ness which is defined only negatively: it is
without memory and desire, without thought; in St John of the Cross's
sense entirely dry:

> Under a tree in the cool of the day, with the blessing of sand,
> Forgetting themselves and each other, united
> In the quiet of the desert.

There is an echo of a very familiar ritual form of words, the Lord's prayer in:

> As I am forgotten
> And would be forgotten, so I would forget
> Thus devoted, concentrated in purpose.

The faint yet recognizable mimicry of 'And forgive us our trespasses, As we forgive them that trespass against us', curiously dissolves the idea of forgiveness into forgetting. The syntax and rhythms of ritual give an unfamiliar weight to the words which makes us look at them with rather more curious attention than usual. For instance 'devoted' is seen to be far closer to its primary meaning of consecration in this context: 'forgetfulness' and 'atonement' makes the human (bones though he may be) a votive offering. The plain, natural meaning of 'concentrated' tends, in the peculiarly tense structure of this context, to move towards the meaning contained in its etymological structure: 'to bring to or towards a common centre of focus', thus anticipating the wheel and point imagery of Section V.

The liturgical incantation 'Lady of silences' continues the magical pattern:

> Lady of silences
> Calm and distressed
> Torn and most whole
> Rose of memory
> Rose of forgetfulness

Each paradoxical reconciliation acts as a kind of charm to produce a desired result—not to get a cow out of a bog, but to conjure a unity with magical symbols: Lady, leopards, juniper tree and bones, and now the Rose, and the Garden:

> The single Rose
> Is now the Garden
> Where all loves end

The musical structure of the section is that of a minuet and trio; the myth of the bones under the juniper tree returns; but there is a change:

> This is the land which ye
> Shall divide by lot. And neither division nor unity
> Matters.

Eliot has drawn a map of the soul's geography, in which the soul turns and wavers between the tropics, not able to decide which pole it should fly to for stillness and peace. The Rose of memory, the one pole, attracts with great power, but at the other side of experience there is an anticipated joy of entire forgetfulness. His prophecy is that once either pole is discovered, it will be both: Rose and Garden will be the same. Our experience remains one of division: but at the end of 'Salutation' he reaches the point, in his definition of humility, where even worried distinctions between separation and unity become trivial: this is the point at which the high dream of 'Salutation' loses its self-dependence, where it becomes necessary for Eliot to write the rest of *Ash Wednesday* to find the context for the high dream. The magical impulsion it imparts is not, finally, sufficient for the purpose, it is not a way to 'terminate torment': for those who entirely forget themselves, 'neither division nor unity matters'— 'Lord I am not worthy/But speak the word only'.

Consequently the high dream, a moment which seems out of time, is replaced by an image of movement, of time, space, and strenuous effort, the image of the stairs. Unger and others refer to St John of the Cross for the source of this image, citing the ten steps of the ladder in *The Dark Night of the Soul* II xix. There seems to be much better reason for citing a passage from *The Ascent of Mount Carmel*:[9]

> The stairs of a staircase have naught to do with the top of it and the abode to which it leads, yet are means to the reaching of both; and if the climber left not behind the stairs below him until there were no more to climb, but desired to remain upon any one of them, he would never reach the top of them nor would he mount to the pleasant and peaceful room which is the goal. And just so the soul that is to attain in this life to the union of that supreme repose and blessing, by means of all these stairs of meditations, forms and ideas, must pass through them and have done with them, since they have no resemblance and bear no proportion to the goal to which they lead, which is God.

And yet the visions which the climber sees in his slow, deliberate journey up the twisting staircase are not the 'meditations, forms and ideas' of which St John speaks. The image of the staircase is taken over from the Spanish mystic; the ascetic purpose is partly defined by the reference, but the symbolism which surrounds the image is quite

[157]

different. St John occupied himself with steady progress towards the goal; Eliot deals with the persistence of the passions, their continual hold upon the imagination:

> Struggling with the devil of the stairs who wears
> The deceitful face of hope and despair.

The high dream of 'Salutation' has, as it were, gone ahead, beyond the climber, and this is why, in some sense, it is suspect, beautiful though it is; in the meantime the climber remains aware of less aetherealized emotions; the dream plots the direction, but the labour and discipline are as yet far from accomplished:

> Blown hair is sweet, brown hair over the mouth blown,
> Lilac and brown hair;
> Distraction, music of the flute, stops and steps of the mind over the
> third stair
> Fading, fading; strength beyond hope and despair
> Climbing the third stair.

The lyrical rhetoric of 'Blown hair is sweet, brown hair over the mouth blown/Lilac and brown hair' is expressive enough of the nostalgia, with its rocking movement always circling back to the remembered image. Expressive enough, indeed, to make one uncertain about the strength of ascetic resolution. The hesitant, cautious movement of the long line 'Distraction, music of the flute, stops and steps of the mind over the third stair' makes the doubt stronger: 'strength beyond hope and despair' becomes of very uncertain tenure.

Section IV begins by speaking of a paradise, and those who inhabited that paradise; a garden which is in the past, which is remembered with wonder and joy and pain. In some sense or other we are bound to think of Adam and Eve; but 'Who' is kept indefinite in a very deliberate way. We cannot imagine Adam and Eve except by projecting some part of ourselves on to them; they are a grace and innocence and simplicity which we believe ourselves to have possessed some time, in some condition of existence. Perhaps that state never existed, either for man in general, or for ourselves in the childhood we really lived; but somewhere in all our private memories (memory is sometimes concealed desire) there is a state of innocent beauty and pleasure and peace, a state which our stubborn phantasies insist we have experienced at some time, long ago, and a state from which (at least in a perfect world of imagination), the experience of the human race began.

The state is very much the same as that which is described in the episode of the Hyacinth Garden; with one important difference. The ecstasy described there is a solitary joy: in *Ash Wednesday* it is a *society* of peace which is imagined or remembered, a society where harmony (moving, as in a pattern ritually remembered) is the spell or charm which creates the strength of the fountains, the coolness of the rock. Yet it is a past state; a dream of human innocence remembered or imagined among the clear simple colours; the white of faith, the green of hope, the violet of charity or love; the conventional colours of the theological virtues, and the blue of the Virgin Mary, the blue of heaven.

In the geography of the spirit which provides the structure of this part of the poem, this is the dream one starts from; but there is another dream too, 'in the time between sleep and waking.' The one dream, like a ritual or a myth, commemorates the garden of innocence; the other anticipates a fulfilment of that dream. The poem as a whole describes, not so much the dreams which lie at each pole of the spiritual universe, but the state of traverse between them.

> Here are the years that walk between, bearing
> Away the fiddles and the flutes, restoring
> One who moves in the time between sleep and waking, wearing
> White light folded, sheathed about her, folded.

It is the essence of faith, I suppose, to insist to oneself that, even if one's dreams are untrue, there yet remains a truth behind them; a truth which the phantasy shadows forth. A communal ritual, such as, for instance, the ritual of the Anglican dispensation, persuades by suspending one's disbelief in one's dreams. An unsupported human phantasy, shaped by a need for consolation or assurance, will fade very easily, appear or disappear as a mood changes; but if that dream is re-shaped by a continuing and repeated ritual participated in by others who seem to have the same dreams, something lasting and separate, something not simply one's own, seems to be made from the dream.

But the poet who creates a private ritual in support of the communal experience is faced by a different problem. He is, as it were, forced to *insist* on the need for

restoring
Through a bright cloud of tears, the years, restoring
With a new verse the ancient rhyme. Redeem
The time. Redeem
The unread vision in the higher dream.

Ash Wednesday as a whole has a curious kind of dependence upon
Dante: Dante too describes the spiritual impulsion of a life between
two dreams, the childish memory of Beatrice in *La Vita Nuova* and
the anticipation of heavenly grace, experienced with Beatrice as
guide and mediator, in 'Paradiso'. Beatrice is Dante's 'One who moves
in the time between sleeping' as well as she 'who walked between'.
But inevitably Dante's attitude to either dream is very different:
Hell is peopled by the sinners of Florence, Heaven a true society of
the blessed, and there is a real continuity for the dreamer between
the privileged community of the Rose and the complex, feuding,
disordered society of his own town. Eliot's universe is far, far more
personal and isolated; the idea of a blessed community of spirit,
though intensely desired, is a possibility remotely imagined, to be
conjured by magical rhetoric. The redemption of the pledge given
in time by the memory of innocent ecstasy is for Dante something
implied by the whole structure of the universe; for Eliot, never completely a catholic in this as in many other things, the pledge had to
be redeemed by a personal effort, and only by sealing off the meditative imagination against contamination by the world of time. For
Dante Florence was never an 'Unreal City'; and this made Heaven and
Hell all the more real. For Eliot it was a struggle to believe in anything, other than the tangled texture of memory and desire which was
his own personal hell.

The remembered image of innocence returns with:

The silent sister veiled in white and blue
Between the years, behind the garden god,
Whose flute is breathless, bent her head and signed
but spoke no word

—Eliot's attitude to the memory is made more complex by irony;
the sister and the garden god are, together, a complex of pagan
artifice and Christian piety, but *in themselves* meaningless. The flute
lacks the breath of life; the sister speaks no word; and yet both are
signs (together a more complex sign) which point towards a redemption of which they are symbolically the pledge.

[160]

In so far as the garden is a communal myth, a memory of the garden of Eden, 'And after this our exile' has a clear enough meaning, though a complex one, with all the paradoxes of the *felix culpa* making exile both a painful and a welcome thing. In so far as 'the word unheard, unspoken' refers to the Christian doctrine of the second person of the Trinity, the phrase has a clear, though complex meaning. Both images take on the colour of personal experiences; are ways of subsuming fears and hopes, feelings of isolation and inadequacy, in a conjuration of future peace.

The fifth section continues to speak of the transit between two worlds, or two dreams; the image of the exile of Adam becoming powerful in the structure of feeling. The contorted complexity of the first nine lines signals a kind of desperation with language. Sweeney complains 'I've gotta use words when I talk to you'; Harry in *The Family Reunion* has to bear with the knowledge that 'You will understand less after I have explained it':

> Words strain
> Crack and sometimes break, under the burden
>
> (*BN*, V)

The contrast between the word and the Word is at best a make-shift device, so ramshackle that it needs a typographic distinction to save it from unmeaning; but the very awkwardness of it serves to convey the desperation of exile. Twelve years after *Ash Wednesday* was published Eliot wrote that 'the poet is occupied with frontiers of consciousness beyond which words fail, though meanings still exist' (*OPP*, 30). So is everyone, or should be; and the frontiers are not always quite the ones which Eliot has in mind; yet it is appropriate that Eliot should call attention to the inadequacies of his own language at a point like this:

> If the lost word is lost, if the spent word is spent
> If the unheard, unspoken
> Word is unspoken, unheard;
> Still is the unspoken word, the Word unheard,
> The Word without a word, the Word within
> The world and for the world
> And the light shone in darkness and
> Against the Word the unstilled world still whirled
> About the centre of the silent Word.

[161]

The Word is, of course, the Word of the Gospel of St John: 'In the beginning was the Word'; and the *logos* of the Greeks from Herakleitos to the neo-Platonists. In a note to 'Second Thoughts about Humanism' Eliot remarks that Norman Foerster interprets the word too narrowly: 'Mr. Foerster's "reason" seems to me to differ from any Greek equivalent (λόγος) by being exclusively human, whereas to the Greek there was something inexplicable about λόγας so that it was a participation of man in the divine' (*SE*, 485), F. M. Cornford developed the notion of *logos* of Word in a way which appealed to Eliot: 'To the mysticism of all ages, the visible world is a myth, a tale half true and half false, embodying a *logos*, the truth which is one.'[10]

The 'word' and the 'Word' are ways of describing the two poles of the journey of exile; 'the lost word' the sign offered by the silent sister, the moment of inexpressible joy in the garden, and 'the Word' the fulfilment which they promise. The remembered dream shadows forth the Word; but for those in 'the years that walk between', neither are present substantially; they are 'unspoken, unheard', to the exile. Yet nevertheless they are 'Still' both in the sense that they continue to exist throughout the search; and in the sense that they are unmoving, outside the pattern of movement in time and space.

The wheel and point imagery derives from Aristotle ultimately; but the most immediate and affecting source is, as one would expect, in Dante; the concluding lines of *La Divina Commedia*:

> Ma già volgeva il mio disiro e il *velle*
> sì come rota ch'egualmente è mossa
> l'amor che move il sole e l'altre stelle.

(But already my desire and *will* were turned, like a wheel that spins evenly, by the Love which moves the sun and the other stars.) Thus, Dante's great discovery at the end of the 'Paradiso' is the reconciliation of Love and desire, of divine and human will. In terms of Eliot's rhetoric, a reconciliation of Word and word would be an equally liberating discovery.

The rest of section V, punctuated by the ambiguous line from Micah, evokes the restlessness of search with restless incantation, rhythms leaning forward, tumbling rhyme. Micah makes the Lord and his people at odds in 'the LORD's controversy' (Micah 6: 3); characteristically Eliot describes the human anarchy in terms of division: 'Those who are torn on the horn between season and season, time and time, between/Hour and hour, word and word, power and power' and in terms of persistence of will—those who 'are terrified and cannot surrender'.

'Although I do not hope to turn again'; the slight change at the opening of Section VI is significant; the repeated words are altered by all that has gone between, and the tiny loophole offered by 'although' for lyrical sweetness, for joy in the senses, makes the spiritual journey seem far more real, far less a matter of insistent rhetoric, than before:

> And the lost heart stiffens and rejoices
> In the lost lilac and the lost sea voices
> And the weak spirit quickens to rebel

The *frein vital*, the vital curb of which Babbitt speaks, has something substantial to restrain in Eliot's temper; the 'cry of quail and whirling plover', 'the salt savour of the sandy earth' have a sensuous sharpness which conflicts with the Virgilian tag: it seems that they exert too strong a nostalgic power to be the false dreams which issue from 'the ivory gates'. The tension generated by the conflict is placed at this point, just before the ending of the poem, with perfect judgment, to open the way to the resolving prayer, with its paradoxes 'Teach us to care and not to care/Teach us to sit still'. But the last line of all points us back into the experience which Eliot would have us believe is the only relief from this 'place of solitude where three dreams cross' (the dream of memory, the dream of anticipation, the dream of present experience); the only way of escaping the solitude of separation, and that is the ritual of the Church. The private ritual, the private myth, finally become merely tributary to the established ritual of the Church: 'And let my cry come unto thee' echoes many, many moments in the English rite, including the service for Ash Wednesday, but perhaps the clearest echo is from the *Preparation* for Communion, with its talk of 'turning' and 'quickening':

P. Wilt thou not turn again and quicken us, O Lord?
S. That thy people may rejoice in Thee.
P. O Lord show thy mercy upon us.
S. And grant us thy salvation.
P. Lord, hear my prayer.
S. And let our cry come unto Thee.

THE ARIEL POEMS

The first of the Ariel poems, 'The Journey of the Magi', was written in 1927, the year of Eliot's conversion and of the second section of *Ash Wednesday*. It exploits the theme of the journey which is also central to *The Waste Land*, but perhaps it is more immediately to the point to compare the transit it describes with the phrase from *Ash Wednesday*, 'this brief transit where the dreams cross.' Eliot takes as a mythical vehicle for his dramatization of the journey of the soul the journey of the Magi as described by Lancelot Andrewes: 'A cold coming they had of it at this time of the year, just the worst time of the year to take a journey in. The ways deep, the weather sharp, the days short, the sun farthest off, *in solstitio brumali*, the very dead of winter.'

Their journey is towards the Christ child; towards the evidence of Incarnation, or the entry of the divine spirit into the world and into the flesh. It is also a journey towards the New Testament, the new Covenant between man and God, which destroys the old dispensation. The mythical complex of which the journey is part can be taken as describing, not just a historical event (perhaps not *even* a historical event) but an event in the life of the soul; a death and rebirth in a spiritual sense. The poem was written in the year of Eliot's conversion: it is a kind of mythical record or re-enactment of that event.

The images seem to have evolved in a most interesting way. In *The Use of Poetry and the Use of Criticism* Eliot remarks:

of course only a part of an author's imagery comes from his reading. It comes from the whole of his sensitive life since early childhood. Why, for all of us, out of all that we have heard, seen, felt, in a lifetime, do certain images recur, charged with emotion, rather than others? The song of one bird, the leap of one fish . . . six ruffians seen through an open window playing cards at night at a small French railway junction where there was a water-mill: such memories may have a symbolic value, but of what we cannot tell, for they come to represent the depths of feeling into which we cannot peer.

(*UPUC*, 148)

Eliot's personal memories enter into the poem as they must; the water-mill, for instance, invested with an evocative power for him which is as little, or as much, 'understood' by ourselves as it is by Eliot. But the six ruffians change more radically: Grover Smith has pointed out the complex of echoing allusions to the soldiers casting lots for the garments of Christ (Matthew 27: 35) and to the blood money of Judas in 'Six hands at an open door dicing for pieces of silver'; the image which emerges from the process composes personal memory and the public memory of myth, convention and religious iconography into a peculiar compound. The prolepsis of the Crucifixion in 'three trees on the low sky' has somewhat the same effect: the extraordinary and boundlessly significant symbol sheathed in the most ordinary and unimpressive accidental image. Both the six hands and the three trees change aspect as one looks at them in different ways; with one eye open they *seem* to be unremarkable and insignificant memories; with the other, they *seem* to be conventional mythical icons; with both eyes opened they are a fusion of both, so that the marvellous and the ordinary are attuned in one vibrating chord.

The speaker returns to 'these Kingdoms' of the old dispensation, but as aliens: the ambiguous birth or death, of Christ, of an old world, of themselves, is a revelation which does not immediately end the journey. On the contrary, it initiates the journey, since it convinces him of the transitory nature of his existence, which awaits a final consummation: 'I should be glad of another death.' 'The dream crossed twilight between birth and dying' of *Ash Wednesday* VI lies between the dream of memory and the dream of anticipation, and is itself a dream: in the Magus's world of exile in his own kingdom Christ (a death and a birth for a world and a self) persists both as memory and anticipation. Alienation can only end with the fusion of the dreams in a new death.

'A Song for Simeon', written in 1928, is based upon the 'Nunc dimittis', or 'Song of Simeon' which follows the second lesson in the order of evening prayer. The prayer is taken from Chapter 2 of Luke, where it was revealed to Simeon 'that he should not see death, before he had seen the Lord's Christ' (Luke 2: 26). Simeon comes to see the Christ child and says 'Lord, now lettest thou thy servant depart in peace, according to thy word: For mine eyes have seen thy salvation, Which thou has prepared before the face of all people' (Luke 2: 29–31). Joseph and Mary marvel at this, and Simeon prophesies to Mary, 'this child is set for the fall and rising again of many in Israel;

[165]

and for a sign which shall be spoken against; (Yea, a sword shall pierce through thy own soul also,) that the thoughts of many hearts may be revealed' (Luke 2: 34–5).

This poem is not, however, a simple revision and augmentation of Simeon's prophecy: it is in only a limited sense another Song *of* Simeon, though the voice which speaks is in some sense Simeon. 'Simeon' speaks of his own age; of his own realization that he must accept a spiritual destiny which is less dramatic and joyful than that of the saint: 'Not for me the ultimate vision'. The prophetic mood of Simeon in the Bible story enables him to prophesy the ministry and suffering of Christ and the grief of Mary—this foreknowledge makes him the first to attain salvation by that ministry, the first Christian. Being the first Christian he is able to foretell the troubles and sufferings of the Christian community because he is at one with that community. But he is a very special case. He is the only Christian whose participation in the Community does not involve participation, while in life, in the suffering and death of Christ and the glory of His resurrection. He may prophesy the Crucifixion, but only in anticipation. Whilst every other Christian enacts the martyrdom within his own life—as the prime condition of his life as a Christian—Simeon only *sees* (in the sense that Tiresias, or any other prophet *sees*) the passion and the ecstasy. Thus, his position is a paradox piled on a paradox: he misses the ecstasy but wins the peace of salvation; he misses the pain and the glory of the Christian's life, but suffers the weariness:

> I am tired with my own life and the lives of those after me,
> I am dying in my own death and the deaths of those after me.

He is, in the same senses as Tiresias and Gerontion, 'old man', and in his life exists within the old covenant, but by a very extraordinary grace, by prophecy of the new life, *knows* the new world 'Before the time of cards and scourges and lamentation . . . Before the stations of the mountain of desolation/Before the certain hour of maternal sorrow', that is to say before the act of redemption in the passion. He therefore is and is not an image of the Christian; the ways in which he is say something about the Christian condition; his prophecy of those ways in which he is not, but others will be Christian, says everything else that it is necessary to say.

The complex perception which gives rise to the figure of Simeon ensures a moving and accomplished poem, an intentness and a dignity of utterance which is quite remarkable. The quiet gravity of the first movement, with its irregular slant rhymes imposing a ghostly echo of a formal structure (perhaps, too, an echo of the windless calm in which the aged Saturn waits described by Keats in the opening of the first 'Hyperion') seems to repeat the description of the waiting-period at the end of an old life in 'Gerontion', but transforms it with a tranquillity which is not within reach of that tense and puzzled poem. The Roman world, the world of the old dispensation, continues to move in its accustomed ways, the hyacinths blooming in the return to the repeated natural rebirth, but slowly, coldly, with entranced hesitance—'The winter sun creeps by the snow hills'—reflecting the old experience and the new knowledge of the speaker. Simeon, too, is in transit between two worlds; the world itself is in transit between two states: not only does 'memory in corners' survive, awaiting the change, but 'dust in sunlight', the debris of change flecking the weak light of the winter sun, waits for the wind.

The quiet strength of the poem enables the allusions to be used in such a way that the mind is held back, forced to pause and consider; take for instance, '(And a sword shall pierce thy heart/Thine also)'. This is an allusion in Luke also: Simeon, addressing Mary, foretells her grief and Christ's—Christ will be pierced through the side by the soldier's sword; she also will suffer as if by the sword '(Yea, a sword shall pierce through thy own soul also.)' But in the new context the words extend in their meaning to cover the sufferings of all Christians, who praise and suffer, who bear the derision as well as sharing the glory of the passion.

'Animula' appeared in 1929. Again, it is a poem about the condition of transit; of immediacy and innocence of experience which we, as adults, seem to remember in our childhoods. There are three stages in the poem. The first is introduced by an adaptation of Dante, 'Issues from the hand of God, the simple soul', and traces the distorting process by which the immediacy of childhood experience is disrupted into distinction and relation. The second stage, introduced by a parody of the first line 'Issues from the hand of time the simple soul', laments the inadequacies of the human condition, the fearfulness and lack of purpose and direction which mark the human dream. The third stage is a prayer in which stock figures of the displacement of human energy are made to stand for the whole of humanity in its failure to achieve reality.

The quotation from Dante is spoken by Marco Lombardo, one of

[167]

the spirits who is being purged of wrathfulness on the third terrace of Purgatory. He laments the degeneracy of the times, and asks Dante to pray for him. Dante asks what the cause of earthly vice is, whether it is decreed by heaven or proceeds from the inherent vice of man. Marco sighs and reproaches him for blindness, for thinking in terms of necessity rather than in terms of free will. He then says:

> Issues from the hand of him who cherishes her before she exists, in the manner of a little child that plays, now weeping, now laughing, the simple soul, who knows nothing, save that moved by a joyful maker, she turns willingly to whatever delights her. First she tastes the savour of a trifling good; there she is deceived, and runs after it, if no guide or rein turns her love aside. So it was necessary to put law as a curb, necessary to have a ruler, who could at least discern the tower of the true city. Laws there are, but who puts his hand to them? None.
>
> (*Purgatorio*, XVI, 85–98)

Dante follows the psychological pattern of Aquinas, and adopts a late mediaeval concept of the nature of kingship and law. Eliot's psychology is somewhat more modern, entails a closer and more attentive observation, and is not concerned with political or legal commentary. But, like Dante, he is concerned to explore the relationship between free will and environmental circumstance.

Experimental observations of a kind which were already beginning when Eliot wrote 'Animula' tend to support his account of the growth of perception in a child, but the spirit of Eliot's account is more Augustinian than clinical, and the development he describes is very much in keeping with his own speculations in *Knowledge and Experience*. The child begins by being conscious only of the disorganized sense perception; as it begins to move and to respond to the world around it, response is immediate and unreflective—'Advancing boldly, sudden to take alarm,/Retreating to the corner of arm or knee'—the verse renders with delicacy the lack of the 'space between the impulse and the reaction' of which Jane Harrison speaks. 'Between the emotion/And the response/Falls the Shadow' for the Hollow Men, but it takes time for the child to reach that stage. In the interim sense and action, thought and feeling, reality and the imagination interpenetrate each other—sense is confounded with sense ('the fragrant brilliance of the Christmas tree'); emotion is immediate and unselfconscious; the story and the common reality merge into each other ('What the fairies do and what the servants say'). But as the child enters into the responsibilities of the adult state distinctions are forced upon him—' "is and seems"/And may and may not, desire and control,' distinctions which warp the immediate impulse by subjecting it to reflection. The mental life of the child warps in the process, makes living into pain, and causes the retreat into dream —and we have already discussed the idea of the dream in Eliot's poetry enough to make further discussion of it unnecessary. These processes 'Curl up the small soul in the window seat/Behind the *Encyclopaedia Britannica*'—cause it to withdraw into second-hand experience, analytical and reflective rather than direct and truthfully immediate.

'Issues from the hand of time the simple soul'—time distorts what God creates, but does not make the soul any the less simple. The harmony of impulse and action which allows the infant to grasp at kisses and toys, accepting without question the offered good, which allows him to seek comfort and reassurance so innocently and un-selfconsciously, which allows him to accept pleasure as his right and without question, is destroyed. For once in his poetry Eliot approaches some part of the way towards a Blakean or Lawrentian sympathy towards the natural impulse as against the distortion of 'civilised' convention.

Perhaps the poem does not have the energetic suggestiveness of Eliot at his best, and perhaps the impulse towards religious and philosophical investigation dominates a little too much, somewhat enervating the verse. But nevertheless it shows a most sensitive awareness of childish perception and the problems of growth and life: within its limits it works well enough.

Each of the Ariel poems so far has been centred around a drama-tis persona—the Magus, Simeon, Marco, old men, dying or dead, whose actions or words have been taken as a mythical vehicle for the expression of some incident or stage in the development of the soul, or in the case of 'Animula', the whole life of a disordered soul from creation to death (or birth) and after. Each of them is a new and different discovery of the ambiguity of death and birth. The little soul of 'Animula' lives first 'in the silence after the viaticum.' The 'viati-cum' is the Eucharist administered to one who is dying; the Latin word means provisions for a journey. And the final line, with its sub-stitution of birth for death, again stresses the ambiguity, the idea that death is the beginning of a journey out of a dream state into a reality.

[169]

The dramatis persona whose history is the mythical vehicle in 'Marina' is another old man, Pericles. In Shakespeare's *Pericles* both Thaisa and Marina have suffered a kind of death and rebirth, Pericles a kind of death by separation. His reunion with Marina his daughter, and later Thaisa his wife, effects a resolution of human pain and suffering into new life. The Pericles myth is combined with the Senecan myth of Hercules by an epigraph from *Hercules Furens* in which Hercules awakes from a mad fit which the jealous Juno has thrown him into, and wonders where he is. In the course of his insanity he has shot his own children with poisoned arrows. The composite Pericles/Hercules who is the persona, then, is awaking from a dream. As Hercules he is half aware of the most terrible, unforgiveable sinfulness in the madness of his dream world. As Pericles he is aware of the resolution of suffering and loneliness, a return to sweetness and peace through an extraordinary grace.

The whole poem echoes and develops the questioning mood of the Senecan epigraph, from the breathless, unpunctuated incantation of 'What seas what shores what grey rocks and what islands' (mimicking the repeated lap of water on the hull) to the end; and it is this wondering uncertainty, this tentative, entranced movement, which gives the poem much of its evocative power.

Consider the ambiguities of this:

What is this face, less clear and clearer
The pulse in the arm, less strong and stronger—
Given or lent? more distant than the stars and nearer than the eye

Whispers and small laughter between leaves and hurrying feet
Under sleep, where all the waters meet.

Our attention is caught first by the hesitant step of the words (continuing the wave-lapping movement of the opening lines), so that we, too, seem to be suspended between near and far, between new understanding and greater mystery. There are, as one would expect, a whole host of metaphysical, theological and literary memories suspended here: Marina is, one might say, another Beatrice figure, a 'blessed face' like that of *Ash Wednesday*, an image which bears in some sense or other the grace of God. And the ambiguities of this gracious image, one might say, are precisely the ambiguities which Christian doctrine would discover in the divine presence, immanent yet transcendent, 'more distant than the stars and nearer than the eye'. But if these things matter at all to us as we read the poem, they are subdued, merged into something more fundamentally interesting than any doctrine or metaphysical idea; a lightly suggested tone or mood, a phase of thought or feeling which, perhaps, lies behind most religious nostalgia. It's an image which Eliot frequently returns to, this elusive whispering and laughter of children in a garden; not because it means, or is intended to mean, anything firm or definite, in the sense that any doctrine or philosophical idea is intended to have meaning. By its elusiveness the image prompts the reader to recall images of his own, memories, or something less catchable than image or memory—moods, shapes of feeling—which nevertheless may be as distinct as can be as episodes in the reader's experience. The poem exploits our own memories of a dream world, and our sense of the unresolved, the wonderful, which so often envelopes our memories of dreams, and so often dominates the period between sleep and waking.

But there is another accent in the poem too, a far more distinct accent: 'Those who sharpen the tooth of the dog, meaning/Death . . .', and what follows, with its repeated heavy emphasis on 'Death', tolling out at intervals on its own separate line. In a poem so full of delicate uncertainty this kind of emphasis destroys the finely attuned poise so rudely that its dramatic and emotional rightness of purpose must be absolutely secure.

But dramatically it is wrong. It is far too deliberate and heavy a rhetoric for the imagined situation; too plainly it is an elaborate embroidery of the words 'sensuality', 'pride', 'sloth' and 'lust' because by themselves those words would sit too baldly. And it is emotionally wrong: the assertive negative morality doesn't fit with the air of tentative discovery. And, most important of all, the failure of tone here may seed some doubts about the validity of the rest of the poem. Delicate uncertainty of tone may collapse into cultivated vagueness of expression if we are not prepared to co-operate, and this poem, depending as it does upon our own memories imaginatively re-creating dream and waking, depends peculiarly upon the co-operation of the reader.

CHAPTER SIX

'STRIFE WITH SHADOWS'
THE PLAYS

'A Dialogue on Dramatic Poetry' (1928) is deliberately open-ended and inconclusive; unlike Dryden's essay it does not contrive the victory of one debater over the other participants, but its tendency is obvious enough. Eliot gives his clearest support to E's contributions:

> I say, with the support of the scholars whom B mentions (and others), that drama springs from religious liturgy, and that it cannot afford to depart far from religious liturgy. . . . when drama has ranged as far as it has in our own day, is not the only solution to return to religious liturgy? And the only dramatic satisfaction that I find now is in a High Mass well performed. Have you not there everything necessary? And indeed, if you consider the ritual of the Church during the cycle of the year, you have the complete drama represented. The Mass is a small drama, having all the unities; but in the Church year you have represented the full drama of creation.
>
> *(SE,* 47–8)

E expresses the point in its simplest and most challenging form; but B, more cautious and more critical in temper, is ready to supply the qualifications which are needed (and which E accepts.) The drama of the Mass is not a spectator sport: the celebrants and the congregation are *participants*:

> and that makes all the difference. In participating, we are supremely conscious of certain realities, and unconscious of others. But we are human beings, and crave representations in which we are conscious, and critical, of these other realities. We cannot be aware solely of divine realities. We must be aware also of human realities. And we crave some liturgy less divine,

[172]

something in respect of which we shall be more spectators and less participants. Hence we want the human drama, related to the divine drama, but not the same, as well as the Mass.

(*SE*, 49)

This is the core of Eliot's dramatic theory; related in the proper way to certain other assumptions and prepossessions it is also the core of his theory of Literature. From the beginning his poetry had tended towards dramatic expression. *The Waste Land*, for instance, shows considerable formal skill in the management of very diverse speech rhythms; the shifts in tone and idiomatic pattern in the second half of 'A Game of Chess' from line 111 to the end, for instance. In *The Waste Land* or 'Portrait of a Lady' he is feeling his way towards the possibility of a poetic drama which of all art forms (as he declared in 1920) 'is perhaps the most permanent, is capable of greater variation and of expressing more varied types of society than any other.'[1]

SWEENEY AGONISTES

This unfinished work, begun in 1924, shows that Eliot was very conscious of the need to develop a mode of drama which should be an intelligent response to the age itself; to address, not just the most perceptive and intelligent among his audience, but to discover a form which should make his dramatic statements intelligible on many levels. As Eliot wrote in 1920, 'A dramatic poet needs to have some *kind* of dramatic form given to him as the condition of his time . . . by a "kind of dramatic form" one means almost the temper of his age (not the temper of a few intellectuals); a preparedness, a habit, on the part of the public, to respond in a predictable way, however crudely, to certain stimuli.'[2]

At this time the conventions of the music-hall seemed to offer the best means of achieving a form which would be immediately apprehensible to all. He suggests the idea in several essays written in the early twenties and in 1923 he pays tribute to a great artist of the music-hall in his essay 'Marie Lloyd', speaking of her strength and dignity, and lamenting the decay of the music-hall under the onslaught of the cinema. Film lacked what, for Eliot, was the one essential virtue of the music-hall; the way in which it offered a degree of natural, unforced, audience *participation* which middle-class theatre, and indeed all middle-class art, lacked: 'The working man who went to the music-hall and saw Marie Lloyd and joined in the chorus was himself performing part of the act; he was engaged in that collaboration of the audience with the artist which is necessary in all art and most obviously in dramatic art' (*SE* 458).

Music-hall, then, offered a way of achieving two of the most important functions of dramatic art: that it should entertain, and that it should draw the audience into collaboration with the artist. But Eliot was impelled, like many other artists of his time, to seek a more respectable model. He didn't turn to the far East, as Yeats and Pound turned towards the Noh play, or as Eisenstein did to the Kabuki theatre; he chose to return to something far more central to the ritual, magical and religious traditions of the West: to Aristophanes. But Aristophanes as interpreted by 'the scholars whom B mentions', Jane Harrison, Gilbert Murray and F. M. Cornford; particularly as interpreted by F. M. Cornford in *The Origin of Attic Comedy* (1914).

Eliot attempted to imitate the racy, alert dialogue of Aristophanes, not by copying the original rhythm patterns, but by substituting the rhythms of rag-time. This grafting and welding of modes was designed to produce a many-layered form of dramatic communication in which there would be something for everybody:

In a play of Shakespeare you get several levels of significance. For the simplest auditors there is the plot, for the more thoughtful the character and conflict of character, for the more literary the words and phrasing, for the more musically sensitive the rhythm, and for auditors of greater sensitiveness and understanding a meaning which reveals itself gradually . . . I once designed, and drafted a couple of scenes, of a verse play. My intention was to have one character whose sensibility and intelligence should be on the plane of the most sensitive and intelligent members of the audience; his speeches should be addressed to them as much as to the other personages in the play —or rather, should be addressed to the latter, who were to be material, literal-minded and visionless, with the consciousness of being overheard by the former. There was to be an understanding between this protagonist and a small number of the

audience, while the rest of the audience would share the responses of the other characters in the play.

(UPUC, 153-4)

The passage displays Eliot's aristocratic bias, the measure of condescension which he could not avoid in attempting to develop a
popular ritual form. *Sweeney Agonistes,* even if it had been finished,
would almost certainly never have succeeded as a popular play
because of this. The modern equivalents of Aristophanes and Shakespeare, the great film-directors from Griffith, Eisenstein and Chaplin
onward, would never dare to show such contempt for their audiences;
they would be found out too quickly, or rather their art would die
before they were found out: audience participation is in the end less
important than respect for, and understanding of, the audience.

We are to understand, then, that there is a profound meaning in
Sweeney Agonistes for the sensitive and intelligent among us to discern. A hint as to the essential meaning is given in the title (an
adaptation, of course, of the title of *Samson Agonistes*). Agonistes
means 'in conflict'. The play is about Sweeney, the double man of the
quatrain poems, pink, broad-bottomed, as gross and fleshly as the
hippopotamus, but by the absurd paradox of human existence a
hero comparable with Agamemnon or Theseus, sharing something of
the divine: Sweeney, in conflict. The nature of the conflict is suggested by the two epigraphs which, like the title, were added when
the fragments were published in 1932: 'Orestes: You don't see them,
you don't—but I see them: they are hunting me down, I must move
on. Choephoroi' and 'Hence the soul cannot be possessed of the
divine union, until it has divested itself of the love of created beings.
St. John of the Cross.'

Orestes is hounded by the Furies who are invisible except to the
one they follow, punishing him for violating the law of the universe.
Sweeney as Orestes is driven by a kind of knowledge which sets him
apart from other men, and enables him to *see* more than others. 'You
suffer from a sense of sin, Miss Coplestone? / This is most unusual,'
says Reilly in *The Cocktail Party*—and Sweeney is unusual in the
same way. The Aeschylean epigraph hints at the nature of the conflict; the epigraph from St John of the Cross hints at the nature of a
possible resolution, and the means by which resolution must be
achieved. The juxtaposition of the two as joint epigraphs for what is
called 'an Aristophanic melodrama', suggests a continuity between

the religious element of Greek drama, Christian mystical thought and the play itself.

The ideal content, and its relation to the tradition, would have been expressed in terms of the formal structure; the whole play, when completed, would have aimed at being a ritual expression of certain religious patterns of idea and feeling. In 1933 Hallie Flanagan wanted to produce the play, and wrote to Eliot for help. Eliot answered, sending various stage directions, hints about production, and an epilogue; most important of all he advised her that she must read F. M. Cornford's *The Origin of Attic Comedy* before attempting to stage the play. Cornford analyses the structure of Aristophanic comedy in a way which, very clearly, Eliot used as the basis for the structure of *Sweeney Agonistes*.

(1) A *Prologue*, which is expository. (2) The *Parodos* or entry of the Chorus. (3) What is now generally called the *Agon*, a contest between two combatants. The first part ends here, and between the first part and the second part there is (4) the *Parabasis*: 'a long passage which cuts the play in two about half way through its course and completely suspends the action.' The Parabasis is a static choral interlude which seems to modern readers to disrupt the dramatic illusion unnecessarily. Sometimes, however, the matter is complicated by there being two Parabases and two Agons, often interspersed with other scenes. After the Parabasis there is always (5) A scene of *Sacrifice* and (6) A *Feast*. There follows (7) a Festal Procession, or *Komos*, and a union which Cornford calls a *Marriage*. The pattern varies somewhat from play to play, says Cornford; for instance the Sacrifice, or Feast, or both, are sometimes interrupted by a series of unwelcome intruders or impostors who are chased away by the protagonist. But the basic structure of Agon, Sacrifice, Feast, Marriage, Komos remains, and this 'canonical plot-formula preserves the stereotyped action of a ritual or folkdrama, older than literary Comedy, and of a pattern well known to us from other sources.'[3] The pattern is that of vegetation ritual. The protagonist represents the spirit of the year, as does the cognate priest-king in Frazer, and Harrison's *eniautos diamon*. The agon is a dramatized conflict between the representative of the vegetation god and his antagonist upon which the renewal of fertility and therefore the life of man depends. The conflict is often represented as conflict between day and night, or life and death, or black and white, or summer and winter, good and bad, or the old king and the new. The protagonist must

win the conflict, of course, and his victory in the Agon is celebrated by a ritual sacrifice and feast, and then by a procession culminating in his marriage with the representative of the earth-goddess.

In the fragments of *Sweeney Agonistes*, we have a 'Fragment of a Prologue' and the 'Fragment of an Agon'. The Prologue fragment is divided by nine knocks at the door or on the floor signalling the entry of the Chorus; the first stage of the Parodos. Thus, in Cornford's scheme the Prologue proper is the scene between Dusty and Doris. Its function is an oblique introduction of the major characters and themes. The *dramatis personae* are introduced by the drawing of the cards, just as, in *The Waste Land*, Madame Sosostris's ritual mumbo-jumbo with the tarot pack introduces obliquely the *dramatis personae* and formal structures of the poem. It will be noticed that doubt is expressed about the identities of the personae represented by three of the cards. The King of Clubs, says Dusty, is Pereira, but Doris says it might be Sweeney. The Queen of Hearts, says Doris, is Mrs Porter, but Dusty says it might be Doris. The Knave of Spades, says Doris, is Snow, but Dusty says it might be Swarts. Neither Pereira nor Mrs Porter enter into the action in the fragments we have, but Swarts and Snow do; they act as a pair like the conventional Tambo and Bones who accompany the nigger minstrels on the bones. They are a pair, but in a highly conventionalized contrast; their names mean Black and White. It is legitimate to assume that Sweeney and Pereira are a contrasted pair and so are Doris and Mrs Porter.

The drawing of the cards also prefigures incidents in the play. The four of diamonds looks forwards, perhaps, to the feast scene: 'A small sum of money, or a present/Of wearing apparel, or a party.' The three prefigures news of an absent friend, Pereira. The six seems to look forward to the Agon, or conflict: 'A quarrel, an estrangement. Separation of friends.' The two of spades foretells a death; the coffin, which Doris is sure is her own. But the coffin is curiously associated with a wedding, the culmination of the 'canonical plot-formula':

> No it's mine. I'm sure it's mine.
> I dreamt of weddings all last night
> Yes it's mine. I know it's mine.

The remaining card, the Knave of Hearts, looks forward to the Parodos which immediately follows, for it introduces Sam, the leader of the Chorus.

The Parodos is not complete. The individual members of the Chorus are introduced; there is some idle chatter which suggests well enough the 'material, literal-minded and visionless' nature of its members, but they do not go into the song and dance routine we should expect from an Aristophanic music-hall melodrama. As yet, Swarts and Snow are absent too; we could expect them to enter before the Agon begins and entertain us, as Tambo and Bones should, with their cross-talk patter act as well as accompanying the Chorus on the bones.

The Agon is not complete either. Presumably the Parodos has ended with another series of knocks and Sweeney has entered; the flirtation with Doris cannot begin as abruptly as it does here. We cannot be sure, either, that the Agon ends with the fragment as it stands, or indeed that the conflict which must characterize the Agon has even begun. Cornford's analyses of the plot structures of Aristophanes make it quite clear that the Agon proper is often delayed, and prepared for by various other scenes. In *The Frogs*, for instance, six scenes, an ode, an antode and a chorikon intervene between the Parodos and the Agon; and in that play even the Parabasis occurs between Parodos and Agon. Any guesses we may make about how Eliot intended to develop the structures provided by Cornford must depend upon whether we can accept that Doris is the true antagonist. If she is not, then Pereira is waiting in the green-room to fulfil the function. We cannot hope to settle the question with the information which is available, but we can outline some alternatives.

Sweeney has appeared in the quatrain poems as a double man, on the one hand sensual and gross, on the other hand with something of the divine in him, like the heroes Agamemnon and Theseus with whom he is compared (and Samson, with whom he is implicitly compared in the title of the play.) In *The Waste Land* he plays Actaeon, a version of the dying god to Mrs Porter's Diana, the earth goddess. The punning element of 'Sweeney Erect' has already suggested his phallic rôle and linked him to the Dionysian heroes of comedy who used to appear with an enormous mock phallus strapped on to their costumes.

Doris has appeared in the last stanza of 'Sweeney Erect', one of the inmates of Mrs Turner's 'house'. Again, in *Sweeney Agonistes*, she is a courtesan, or kept woman, her flat paid for by the mysterious Pereira. She has appeared in 'Doris's Dream Songs' also, as one caught in the interval between the idea and the reality, living in 'the Shadow' of hope and despair.

We have seen how the sexual metaphor is used in Eliot's poems from 'Portrait of a Lady' onwards; how Eliot continually builds myths of parting in which the male persona rejects the female persona in order to seek his destiny.

If the fragment which we have here is the substance of the Agon, then the conflict is between Sweeney as hero of the spirit and Doris as attachment to a world of dream, phantasy and illusion, and the union or marriage which Cornford insists is necessary to the canonical plot-formula will be, as Doris foretells in the Prologue, a wedding which involves her own death; a death which enables the hero to go on to seek for higher things. In the sly spoofing epilogue which Eliot wrote for Hallie Flanagan there is one phrase which suggests this conclusion—'the wedding-breakfast of life and death'. There are further hints of this in Sweeney's teasing of Doris:

DORIS: That's not life, that's no life
                Why I'd just as soon be dead.
SWEENEY: That's what life is. Just is
DORIS: What is?
                What's that life is?
SWEENEY: Life is death.

Sweeney's invitation to the cannibal isle is not exactly a proposal of marriage; but then seduction and elopement have done duty for marriage in *The Waste Land* already; and the elopement prefigures both the scene of sacrifice and the scene of feast, linking the two with a reference, however jocular, to religion:

DORIS: I'll be the missionary
      I'll convert you
SWEENEY: I'll convert *you*!
      Into a stew.
      A nice little, white little, missionary stew.

Finally, Sweeney's boredom with 'Birth and copulation and death', his sense of the ambiguity of life and death, is expressed by the story of the man who did the girl in: 'He didn't know if he was alive/ and the girl was dead/He didn't know if the girl was alive/and he was dead . . . For when you're alone like he was alone/You're either or neither/I tell you again it don't apply/Death or life or life or death.' What Sweeney *sees* ('You don't see them, you don't—but I see them') is the state of death-in-life; and the solution of death in life prefigured throughout the play is a death-wedding: a life-in-death, which resembles the ritual marriage prescribed by Cornford as the culmination to the Aristophanic comedy.

Perhaps it would be better to arrest the enquiry into the probable structure of the play at this point. It can help us to discover themes and possibilities within the fragments we have; it can also help us to relate *Sweeney Agonistes* to Eliot's later experiments with drama, and recurrent themes in his verse. But the fact remains that *Sweeney Agonistes* is a fragmentary experiment, and that the significance of the experiment lies more than anything else in the way it breaks away from the conventions of the contemporary stage. Conventional dramatic structures are abandoned. Even more strikingly, the conventional approach to dialogue is abandoned. Rhythmical patterning plays a far greater part in the structuring of dialogue than narrative convenience. The seriousness of the comedy (obscured by the fact that the argument is not completed) lies, not in overt discussion of contemporary problems by the characters, but in an oblique, stylized allusiveness. These departures from convention over-taxed Eliot's dramatic skill as *The Waste Land* had almost over-taxed his skill as a poet, and Arnold Bennett, for whom he wrote the play, was not equipped to play the Pound for Eliot. Before he could make any progress in drama Eliot was forced to retreat from experiment a little, and learn a great deal more about the actual practice and potential of the theatre.

MURDER IN THE CATHEDRAL

The Rock is a failure, an uneasy association of modes in which a crude expressionism alternates with rather flaccid experiments in the choric mode. Eliot's ear for the rhythms and intonations of British working class speech which had served him well in *The Waste Land* II fails him: the language of the workmen in *The Rock* is self-conscious parody, and though Eliot's intention is far more sympathetic to his subjects than it is in 'A Game of Chess', the final result is a far more contemptuous debasement of the dialect than in *The Waste Land*, where the cockney speech at least has a kind of vigorous flatness and sloppiness.

As E. Martin Browne has made clear, the difficulties in producing a pageant of this kind were immense.[4] The mixture of modes did not escape attention at the time of production. *The Times* review, quoted by Browne, begins 'The theatre, that long-lost child of the English Church, made a notable reunion with its parent last night. Mr Eliot's pageant play looked first to liturgy for its dramatic form, though wisely imitating also the ready and popular stage modes, such as music-hall, ballet and mime . . .'[5] The combination of modes in *Murder in the Cathedral* is far more integral to the purpose and the sentiment, and though it must always remain a rather special case in the drama, the play is an astonishing success. In 'Poetry and Drama' Eliot speaks of the audience which crowds into religious festivals, expecting to be 'patiently bored and to satisfy themselves with the feeling that they have done something meritorious' (*OPP*, 79). *Murder in the Cathedral* is a special case partly because Eliot does not accept the easy way out offered by such a complaisant audience, and faces the problems of religious drama with courage and intelligence; but also because Eliot is sympathetically aware of the needs and problems of his audience, and this forces a greater directness and paradoxically, despite the special limitations of the spectators, a greater universality. While it is true, as Eliot said in his essay on 'Marie Lloyd', that the artist needs 'the collaboration of the audience with the artist' (*SE*, 458), it is equally true that the audience needs an artist who is temperamentally capable of collaborating with *them*, and in these special circumstances Eliot discovers the skill. He declared in 1934: 'With the disappearance of the idea of intense moral struggle, the human beings presented to us both in poetry and prose fiction today . . . tend to become less real. It is in fact during moments of moral and spiritual struggle . . . that men and women come nearest being real' (*After Strange Gods*, 64). In any usual sense of the word both *Sweeney Agonistes* and *Murder in the Cathedral* are far from 'realistic', but (whether or not *Sweeney* would have achieved it) it is this special kind of realism which both were aiming at. However, the struggle or conflict is not expressed simply in terms of a character study. The drama is focused upon Thomas and in one sense the conflict is within him; in another sense it is in all the characters as they participate in the action; in another sense it is intended to be in the audience in so far as they are drawn into the play to participate in the drama themselves. Thus we must be aware as we experience the drama that, just as all the men and women of *The Waste Land* meet in Tiresias, so all the characters in *Murder in the Cathedral* reflect or represent potential or actual states of Thomas's being—tempters, priests, knights and chorus—and that he in turn is the focus of the drama of the whole community. And Thomas's agon and pathos, his conflict and suffering, are made into a communal experience to be entered into by the modern audience, just as is the apprehension and then the joy of the chorus and the sophistries, the crudenesses and destructiveness of the tempters and the knights:

> But for every evil, every sacrilege,
> Crime, wrong, oppression and the axe's edge,
> Indifference, exploitation, you and you,
> And you, must all be punished. So must you.
>
> (*CP*, 31)

The last sentence is spoken directly to the audience. But though Eliot assumes and declares the responsibility of every one of us in a community of guilt: 'the sin of the world is upon our heads . . . the blood of the martyrs and the agony of the saints/Is upon our heads,' the responsibility has its credit side too—we share in Thomas's guilt but may also share ritually in the triumph of his martyrdom; his death may bring new life to the community of which we are part.

Murder in the Cathedral is the play which most clearly declares its ritual origin: it was designed for performance in a place of worship and Eliot himself has declared that its versification owes something to *Everyman*, a play which has equally clearly departed not very far from the original liturgical impulse. But its formal structure, like that of *Sweeney Agonistes*, seems to be modelled upon an anthropological interpretation of Greek drama. Cornford's *The Origin of Attic Comedy* is an application to Aristophanic comedy of the general line of investigation opened up by Gilbert Murray in his 'Excursus on the Ritual Forms Preserved in Greek Tragedy' which was published in 1912 as part of Jane Harrison's *Themis*.[6] Murray conceives of the origin of Greek tragedy as aetiological ritual—the celebration of the supposed historical cause of a current ritual practice. *Murder in the Cathedral* is not precisely an aetiological ritual in this sense, but it does commemorate the historical origin of the shrine of St Thomas, an object of pilgrimage and of veneration for Christians for many centuries. Murray, like Cornford, argues that whatever particular event is celebrated in Greek drama, and whichever hero is protagonist, the *Sacer Ludus* is essentially and originally in celebration of the death and resurrection of the dying god, most typically in his manifestation as Dionysus. As in his poems Eliot conflates the pagan and the Christian myths, reconstructing and enriching the Christian myth with pagan parallels. Thomas's pathos is, as, in a sense, are the sufferings of all the Christian martyrs, an imitation of Christ. Thomas's agon, his exchanges with the four tempters, is partly modelled on the temptation of Christ by Satan in the wilderness. But there is no need to repeat here the ways in which Eliot and the anthropologists who influenced him found parallels between the Crucifixion and the passion of the dying fertility god, between Christ's temptation and the motif of the testing of the hero in ancient myth.

Here, then, is Murray's analysis of the prototypical elements of Greek tragedy, with comments on their adaptation in *Murder in the Cathedral*. Eliot's play begins with a *Prologue* or exposition scene which is present in all Greek tragedies except for *Supplices* and *Persae*. Then, following Murray's pattern, there is '1. An *Agon* or Contest, the Year against its enemy, Light against Darkness, Summer against Winter.' In *Murder in the Cathedral* the antagonist is split into four tempters, but as is made clear in many ways, the four are merely different manifestations of one antagonist. After this Eliot has an Interlude, Thomas preaching on Christmas morning. Then follows, as in Murray's analysis: '2. A *Pathos* of the Year-Daimon, generally a ritual or sacrificial death, in which Adonis or Attis is slain by the tabu animal, the Pharmakos stoned, Osiris, Dionysus, Pentheus, Orpheus, Hippolytus torn to pieces'—or, in *Murder in the Cathedral*, Thomas is stabbed to death by the four Knights. In Greek tragedy the Pathos rarely occurs on the stage, so Murray's next stage is '3. A *Messenger*' announcing the death. Since Eliot acts out the Pathos in the play itself the scene is replaced by the address of the four Knights, justifying their actions as in a public meeting. Then in Murray's scheme comes: '4. A *Threnos* or Lamentation. Specially characteristic, however, is the clash of contrary emotions, the death of the old being the triumph of the new.'[7] This describes precisely the last scene of *Murder in the Cathedral*.

Murray goes on to add sections 5 and 6, the *Anagnorisis* and the *Theophany*, but argues that, in the prototypical tragedy, these elements were reserved for the Satyr play which follows the trilogy, and that when the custom of the Satyr play was discontinued, not all tragedians elected to assimilate these two elements into the tragedy.

In *Murder in the Cathedral* Anagnorisis and Theophany are absent, though one might think of Thomas's eventual canonization as being a historical consummation of these elements.

The adoption of Murray's analysis of tragedy has some curious and important results. Since the neo-Classical period of criticism the theory of tragedy has commonly been based upon Aristotle's *Poetics*. The range of possible interpretations of Aristotle has been very wide indeed and many, perhaps most, writers of tragedies have used Aristotle second-hand, depending upon critical middlemen or imitating and adapting their contemporaries or predecessors. But certain prescriptions for tragedy have retained their classic status, and many of them are ignored by Eliot in *Murder in the Cathedral* and to a lesser extent in *The Family Reunion*. In Aristotle's scheme 'The change of fortune should be not from bad to good, but, reversely, from good to bad. It should come about as the result not of vice but of some great error or frailty' (*Poetics*, XIII). Both Thomas and Harry triumph over error and frailty and move from bad to good. 'A perfect tragedy . . . should, moreover, imitate actions which excite pity and fear' (*ibid.*, XIII, 2), 'through pity and fear effecting the purgation of these emotions' (*ibid.*, VI, 2). In *Murder in the Cathedral*, pity and fear are the staple emotions of the Chorus, and are evoked from the audience too, perhaps, but the victory of the hero is so nearly complete that it removes him beyond the reach of pity and fear, making those emotions irrelevant; our pity and fear are transferred from the hero to the Chorus and the Knights. In *The Family Reunion* too, we may feel pity and fear for Harry at the beginning, but the hero goes beyond them, neutralizing both emotions; it is Amy who suffers the fall and excites pity and fear in the audience, but she cannot be considered the hero of the play.

In Aristotle's classification, then, neither *Murder in the Cathedral* nor *The Family Reunion* can be considered a true tragedy. There are very few tragedies which can; Shakespeare's tragedies do not observe the unities of place and time and are very liberal in their interpretation of unity of action, for instance, whereas Eliot is fairly meticulous about all three unities. But the 'rules' which Eliot breaks are 'rules' which have not often been broken by dramatists working consciously within a tragic tradition (at least since Aristotle, for Greek tragedies themselves very often do not fit the Aristotelian prescriptions). It may be asked how Eliot, the champion of tradition, could ignore such well established conventions. The answer is that he felt that he was observing and respecting the tradition in a much more fundamental way than the neo-Aristotelian, searching for the essence of tragedy in its ritual function and its communal purpose. It follows from this view of tragedy that purgation of pity and fear should be secondary motives; that the principal effect of the tragedy should be participation of the audience in the protagonist's victory over his self; the welding of the audience into a community which has no use any more for fear and pity. 'The Mass is a small drama, having all the unities', but it fails to meet Aristotle's other specifications in much the same way as *Murder in the Cathedral* does.

The *dramatis personae* of the Mass are the celebrant, the communicant and the congregation as chorus, but the end of the drama is the absorption of each persona into one who is present in all the personae, Christ. And the history of each hero, whether the all-embracing heroic figure of Christ or those who imitate his history, the communicants and the celebrants, is not decline and fall, but a symbolic death and triumphant rebirth. To call the Mass a drama is in a way a piece of coat-trailing, but it does suggest various ways in which the experience of drama and specifically tragedy may parallel the experience of the Mass, and the way in which both experiences might have grown from certain persistent human habits and needs. And the tendency of Murray's argument is to confirm the parallels and to suggest the existence of pre-Christian parallels for Christian rituals in the daimon dance and seasonal myths.

It follows naturally enough from the structural basis suggested by Murray that there should be implicit reference throughout *Murder in the Cathedral* to the symbolism of vegetation ritual. The first chorus, for instance, establishes a seasonal symbolism very clearly:

Since golden October declined into sombre November
And the apples were gathered and stored, and the land
  became brown sharp points of death in a waste of water and mud,
The New Year waits, breathes, waits, whispers in darkness.

(CP, 11)

It is the waste land of winter; but, as in *The Waste Land*, the barrenness of winter has at least the comfortableness of something known and the Chorus fear the unexpected which will begin the destructive cycle again: 'Now I fear disturbance of the quiet seasons.' The extraordinary incident which the Chorus awaits with fear that it will disturb the comfort of barrenness is, in point of time, the new year.

[185]

In the pagan metaphor this is precisely the time of the agony of the dying god; the winter solstice when the new year struggles with the old. In the Christian metaphor it is the time of Christ's birth, when an old world ends and a new begins. The foreboding of the Chorus anticipates the struggle of Thomas the hero with his king, a death, and a re-birth of the spirit: conflict is sensed as disaster, as something passively to be borne:

> Some presage of an act
> Which our eyes are compelled to witness, has forced our feet
> Towards the cathedral. We are forced to bear witness.
>
> (*CP*, 11)

In the state of consciousness which the Chorus manifests at this point this action, *any* action, must be performed by somebody else. They imagine themselves to be simply spectators of the drama—and in this they represent the audience who watch them. The season of sacrifice has to be renewed by repeated martyrdom, but somebody else's:

> Come, happy December, who shall observe you, who shall preserve you?
> Shall the Son of Man be born again in a litter of scorn?
> For us, the poor, there is no action,
> But only to wait and witness.
>
> (*CP*, 12)

However, Eliot is not prepared to allow either Chorus or audience to be entirely spectators; the drama is shaped towards ritual purposes, and ritual inevitably involves participation: it is the way in which the tribe or the community re-affirms and re-creates the consciousness of its identity—and the struggle, the suffering and the triumph of the hero are its own agon, pathos and theophany. The Chorus in its forebodings recognizes this, leading the audience gently into the recognition:

> O Thomas, return, Archbishop; return, return to France.
> Return. Quickly. Quietly. Leave us to perish in quiet.
> You come with applause, you come with rejoicing, but you
>   come bringing death into Canterbury:
> A doom on the house, a doom on yourself, a doom on the world.
>
> (*CP*, 15)

Their fears are a kind of response to the speech of the third priest; his speech in its turn is a reconciliation of the blind fears of the first priest and the blind hopes of the second. The third priest employs the wheel symbolism which has become familiar to us in *Ash Wednesday*: 'The wheel has been still, these seven years, and no good./For ill or good, let the wheel turn./For who knows the end of good and evil?' As against the Chorus's desire to avoid the drama, the third priest welcomes it, knowing how much good and evil interpenetrate each other, how necessary the process which is feared and desired; how the reconciliation is impossible without the conflict. In another sense the priest is recognizing the *magical* functions of Thomas. The wheel has been still for seven years, the period of Thomas's absence; his return imparts movement to the wheel of change, as the agony and the passion of the dying god in the ancient myths causes the cycle of the seasons to begin anew.

Thomas enters, announcing the paradox of action and suffering which underlies the drama of agon and pathos, and the paradox of the rôle of the Chorus (and the audience) in the drama, the half perceived necessity of *participation* in his own action and suffering in order that action and suffering may be transcended:

> They know and do not know, what it is to act or suffer.
> They know and do not know, that action is suffering
> And suffering is action. Neither does the agent suffer
> Nor the patient act. But both are fixed
> In an eternal action, an eternal patience
> To which all must consent that it may be willed
> And which all must suffer that they may will it,
> That the pattern may subsist, for the pattern is the action
> And the suffering, that the wheel may turn and still
> Be forever still.
>
> (*CP*, 17)

In one sense, Thomas is an agent; his return sets the wheel in motion again. In one sense he is a patient; he suffers himself to be killed. But in another sense he is neither, since neither his action nor his suffering proceed from his own personal will; they proceed from the pattern of God's design. A similar distinction is made in Richard Hooker's *The Laws of Ecclesiastical Polity*,[8] between 'natural agent' and 'voluntary agent'. Man possesses free will, but his ability to act voluntarily is given him so that he can obey the natural law, that eternal order which Thomas calls 'the pattern' which is at once 'an eternal action' and 'an eternal patience.' The moral struggle, then, which takes place in the agon, is between Thomas and his personal will, and Thomas's triumph is the destruction of his will so that he becomes neither agent nor patient, but instrument. The Chorus know and do not know; precisely because of this they are involved in that struggle; and Eliot draws in the audience through the Chorus.

So, when the fourth Tempter throws back Thomas's words in his face: 'You know and do not know, what it is to act or suffer' (*CP*, 27), he presents the Christian with the ultimate challenge of complete submission: 'Now is my way clear, now is the meaning plain' means 'I shall no longer act or suffer, to the sword's end.' E. Martin Browne gives the most cogent interpretation of the fourth Tempter's omission of one of the phrases which Thomas uses, 'for the pattern is the action/And the suffering';[9] the Tempter converts the wheel from something centred around a positive and all-embracing purpose into a dead automatic mechanism, making both action and suffering meaningless forms. For Thomas—and for the Christian—both action and suffering are absolutely central to existence, and bound in with the whole process of meaning and purpose. But not action and suffering of the individual self. The point is developed in the Interlude, where Thomas says that martyrdom 'is never the design of man; for the true martyr is he who has become the instrument of God, who has lost his will in the will of God, and who no longer desires anything for himself, not even the glory of being a martyr.' Of course this is a statement of both Christian sentiment and doctrine. But in the way it is stated it bears a very close relationship to the underlying philosophy of the *Bhagavad Gita*. 'He who seeks non-action in action. . . ./He whose every undertaking is without desire or purpose, and whose work is burnt up with the fire of knowledge, is called learned by the wise./When he has abandoned attachment to the fruit of actions, ever contented and without support, even though he is occupied in action, he performs none.'[10]

This, then, is the subtlety and power of the fourth Tempter who lies behind all the other three: that whereas the first three represent past stages of Thomas's being, states which Thomas has learned to recognize, the fourth Tempter (the unexpected one) reflects Thomas's state at the present moment. Thomas forecasts the nature of the agon before it begins:

[188]

For a little time the hungry hawk
Will only soar and hover, circling lower,
Waiting excuse, pretence, opportunity.
End will be simple, sudden, God-given.
Meanwhile the substance of our first act
Will be shadows, and the strife with shadows.

(CP, 18)

But the fourth Tempter defeats expectation; he is no shadow chal-
lenger, but Thomas's stubborn, continuing personal will and pride
embodied in its most dangerous form. Sensual ease promised by the
first Tempter; temporal power under the king, promised by the
second; power over the minds and hearts of the people, promised
by the third; these appeals to the will are easily turned aside; but
even the Tempters who promise them hint at the ultimate temptation:
'I leave you to the pleasures of your higher vices' says the first
Tempter, and the second, 'Your sin soars sunward, covering king's
falcons.' The first three temptations parallel Satan's temptation of
Christ in the desert to satisfy his physical hunger (Luke 4: 3–4) and
to enjoy the kingdoms of the world (Luke 4: 5–6). The fourth exploits
the lust for the spiritual power of the miracle, as Satan tempted
Christ to cast Himself down from the pinnacle of the temple. The
fourth temptation is to a *voluntary* martyrdom, a willed martyrdom,
rather than an inevitable martyrdom as part of the grand design.

According to this pattern of ideas, then, the pathos is not strictly
the suffering of Thomas; it is, however, the necessary suffering of
the Chorus and the community to bring about a purgation of the
world. The intimate relationship between the Chorus and Thomas is
beautifully expressed by E. Martin Browne when he tells of the new
discoveries which he made when playing Thomas in an 'emergency
version' of *Murder in the Cathedral* in the early years of the Second
World War:[11]

His long silent struggle with despair as the Tempters surround him is carried on in isolation until the women succeed
in breaking through to him. It is their intuition that 'the Lords
of Hell are here' which reveals to him the nature of his danger.
It is their plea:

O Thomas Archbishop, save us, save us, save yourself
that we may be saved;

[189]

Destroy yourself and we are destroyed.

which calls forth from him the power to banish the Tempters.

But their intuition is ambiguous: in the two lines which Browne quotes from page 30 of *Collected Plays*, both 'save' and 'destroy' can and do bear entirely contrary meanings in a complex ambiguity— 'They speak better than they know.' Instinctive, unreasoning fear of the hellish forces which cling round Thomas impel them to ask for a return to the drab but secure routine which existed before Thomas's return, and to ask that he should save himself by running away. They fear their own destruction through his. But Thomas recognizes the obverse of the ambiguity, the sense in which the lines mean that only by his martyrdom, only by his destruction as a self may the women of Canterbury be destroyed and saved through destruction. The Chorus speaks of the defilement of the world by conflict at the beginning of Part II: 'war among men defiles the world, but death in the Lord renews it,/And the world must be cleaned in the winter, or we shall have only/A sour spring, a parched summer, an empty harvest.' Again Eliot hints at Greek myth in his Christian parable: Thomas is playing the role of *pharmakos*, the ritual scapegoat who is driven away by the people of the tribe in a symbolic purgation of evil. It is also a role which Christ plays in the drama of the mass: 'Agnus dei, qui tollis peccata mundi, miserere nobis.' The symbolic sacrifice of the *pharmakos* ensures the success of the world's harvest; Thomas as *pharmakos* renews the sacrifice of Christ. But, if Thomas the individual is in one sense a functionary in a social ritual, the social ritual is also image for the drama of the individual. Thomas, like Sweeney or the male *persona* in *The Waste Land*, is the aspect of any soul which is capable of the ultimate spiritual adventure; he is surrounded by other aspects of any soul. The Tempters are part of him; the Chorus and the Priests are part of him, as he is of them. And the Knights are doubles of the Tempters: Eliot, on E. Martin Browne's suggestion, arranged that in the original production Knights and Tempters should be played by the same actors and, as Knights, wear a reminder of their previous appearances as Tempters. As Tempters they can harm him, for they represent the destructiveness of his own will; as Knights they cannot harm him for with the renunciation of his will he is as incapable of suffering (in his own person) as of action. But they can, and they do, continue to exercise their role as tempters. Thomas has completed his agon and won the conflict; the agon persists in the natural man, and the conflict is transferred to the audience. That is why, in the scene following the pathos, Eliot has the Knights turn round and address the audience directly, forcing the audience into total participation, challenging them to face temptation, to undergo an agon of their own. In his new rôle of fourth Knight the fourth tempter is again the most subtle, with his question, '*Who killed the Archbishop?*' It is said that in the original performances there were murmurs of agreement at the fourth Knight's sophistries, implicitly convicting Thomas of the gross spiritual pride of courting martyrdom, of suicide for the sake of glory. There is no wonder that this should be so; in this ironic age it is difficult to imagine any other motive than pride for such a martyrdom. The Knights represent a far more *modern* sensibility than Thomas, but Thomas acts, or Eliot makes him act, in a way which would appear insanely perverse to almost any modern audience:

> You think me reckless, desperate and mad.
> You argue by results, as this world does,
> To settle if an act be good or bad.
> You defer to the fact.

> (*CP*, 45)

The audience is called upon, whether it knows it or not, to make a choice between two mutually incompatible standards of judgment. On the one hand, a way of judgment in which one examines and assesses cause and effect, the evidence of the senses and the probabilities suggested by experience. On the other hand a way in which judgment is reserved for God:

> It is not in time that my death shall be known;
> It is out of time that my decision is taken
> If you call that decision
> To which my whole being gives entire consent.
> I give my life
> To the Law of God above the Law of Man.

> (*CP*, 46)

This is partly understood by the Chorus, who still lament the disturbance which they have feared since the beginning 'How how can I ever return, to the soft quiet seasons?' (*CP*, 47), but recognize that 'this is out of life, this is out of time,/An instant eternity of evil and wrong.'

[191]

Thomas's temptation is in one way a kind of Purgatory. But throughout the play the pull of Hell is felt. The interior Hell is an important theme in Eliot's verse implicit in 'Prufrock', *The Waste Land* and 'The Hollow Men', and explicit in plays like *The Family Reunion* and *The Cocktail Party*. The history of Hell has never been fully written: if one were to attempt to trace the changes in its geography and significance from ancient times to the present day one would be forced to write half the history of the human mind, and of the religious sensibility. At first it was another place, a distinct location, a place to be feared and abhorred, but normally beyond the living experience of humanity. A hero or a dreamer could enter Hell and return; he could triumph over the terror and return to the living world a being more than human, capable of action and of speech which could restore and refresh the world; but he would leave behind him a place which remained powerful, independent, with its own king, its own laws, its own separate reality. Some time during the Renaissance Hell began to migrate. It is always implicit in the anagogical reach of meaning of *La Divina Commedia* that Hell, like Purgatory, the earthly Paradise, and Heaven, has its place in the heart of the living human being. During and after the Renaissance man became more and more interested in himself; God became mysteriously divided, being both within man and utterly beyond him, and Hell began to lose its boundaries. Christian mysticism sought a state of being on earth as like as possible to heavenly beatitude; as a natural corollary Hell tore up its frontier treaties and became a state of mind, capable of existing wherever there was a man or angel capable of experiencing evil. The discovery of the inner Hell became most terrible for those who were torn between the religious and the humanist way of seeing. Marlowe made Mephistophiles tell Faustus:

> Hell hath no limits, nor is circumscribed
> In one self-place; for where we are is Hell
> And where Hell is, there we must ever be.
> <div align="right">(<i>Doctor Faustus</i>, Scene 5)</div>

Browne, in *Religio Medici* had written: 'The heart of man is the place the devils dwell in: I feel sometimes a hell within myself.'[12] And Milton seemed to be well acquainted with Hell when he wrote of:

> A mind not to be chang'd by place or time.

[192]

> The mind is its own place, and in itself
> Can make a heaven of hell, a hell of heaven.
>
> *(Paradise Lost,* I, 253–5)

and:

> Which way shall I fly
> Infinite wrath and infinite despair?
> Which way I fly is hell; myself am hell;
> And in the lowest deep a lower deep,
> Still threat'ning to devour me, opens wide,
> To which the hell I suffer seems a heaven.
>
> *(Paradise Lost,* IV, 73–8)

In *The Cocktail Party*, the traditional *motif* reasserts itself in a very clear verbal reminiscence; Edward Chamberlayne says to Lavinia:

> What is hell? Hell is oneself,
> Hell is alone, the other figures in it
> Merely projections. There is nothing to escape from
> And nothing to escape to. One is always alone.
>
> *(CP,* 169)

Martin Browne tells us that at the dress-rehearsal of *The Cocktail Party* before the Edinburgh Festival production 'Eliot leaned over and whispered: "Contre Sartre". The line, and the whole story of Edward and Lavinia, are his reply to "Hell is other people" in *Huis Clos*.'[13] Or, one might say, the response of the poet of tradition to an existentialist heterodoxy. Sartre's brand of existentialism subverts humanism by a bitter inversion; Eliot's newly humane Christianity subverts humanism equally, but by enfolding it within a religious tradition, which gains its mature strength from the tongues of the dead through seven centuries of speech, from Dante to our own troubled world.

In *Murder in the Cathedral*, the notion of the interior Hell is expressed with an unusual power and energy by the Chorus, Eliot achieving in his own way what he had praised Dante for doing, in a very different way, in the *Inferno*: 'It reminds us that Hell is not a place but a *state*; that man is damned or blessed in the creatures of his imagination as well as in men who have actually lived; and that Hell, though a state, is a state which can only be thought of, and perhaps only experienced, by the projection of sensory images' *(SE,* 250).

The long Chorus which begins 'I have smelt them, the death-bringers' *(CP,* 41–3) evokes this horror and sense of corruption more

powerfully, perhaps, than the prophecies of Hell in *The Waste Land*
—certainly far more effectively than the threadbare and miscellaneous
images which Harry uses to describe the personal Hell in *The Family
Reunion*: 'One thinks to escape/By violence, but one is still alone/In
an over-crowded desert, jostled by ghosts' (*CP*, 66). Harry excuses
the inefficiency of his language for describing the horror by saying
'I talk in general terms/Because the particular has no language.' But
the Dante essay is right: Hell can only be thought of in particular
terms; certainly a particularity of reference is the only way in which
the horrifying conviction of the Chorus of the immanence of Hell
and the obscenity which lies beneath all sensual experience can be
expressed.

In one way Eliot goes further in expressing the total range of
human experience than any other poet ever has done (only in one
way—there are other ways in which the range of experience expressed
is severely, even cripplingly, limited.) While Thomas expresses the
highest reaches of the human conflict, the Chorus here expresses a
range of human experience in which the intellect is no longer important—a state of feeling in which the sensitive faculties are so
hyperacute and so all-embracing that their experience becomes the
experience of all creation. The passage stretches our sensory imaginations as far, even further than our spiritual imaginations are stretched
by Thomas's martyrdom:

I have lain on the floor of the sea and breathed with the
    breathing of the sea anemone, swallowed with the
    ingurgitation of the sponge. I have lain in the soil
    and criticised the worm. In the air
Flirted with the passage of the kite, I have plunged with the
    kite and cowered with the wren. I have felt
The horn of the beetle, the scale of the viper, the mobile hard
    insensitive skin of the elephant, the evasive flank of the fish.
I have smelt
Corruption in the dish, incense in the latrine, the sewer in
    the incense, the smell of sweet soap in the woodpath, a
    hellish sweet scent in the woodpath, while the ground
    heaved. I have seen
Rings of light coiling downwards, descending
To the horror of the ape.

(*CP*, 42)

Even though the passage stretches to include images of exaltation, the predominating effect is of corruption and obscenity which is every bit as disturbing as the savage horror of Swift at his most destructive. The cascading freedom of the rhetoric resembles St John Perse, whom Eliot had recently translated, but the vision in all its horror is peculiarly Eliot's own. It is the natural complement of the vision of reconciliation which is expressed through Thomas's martyrdom— no vision of Heaven can exist without an equally acute vision of Hell, no exaltation of spirit without a consciousness of death which stretches beyond a personal fear into a consciousness of the horror of all creation. It is a terrible sickness that is expressed here; but then perhaps religious exaltation demands and implies a terrible sickness, an extension of the consciousness beyond the bearable limits of experience. It is 'mind-bending' in the current phrase; though bending the mind need not end in permanent distortion, but in a shaping of experience into a new order better able to cope with the less dramatic but more central and stabilizing emotions which we conventionally call health.

The whole passage is the most obvious attempt Eliot ever made to fulfil the requirement which Rémy de Gourmont made of great poetry and which Eliot summarizes in his essay on the Metaphysical poets: 'One must look into the cerebral cortex, the nervous system, and the digestive tracts' (*SE*, 290).

> What is woven on the loom of fate
> What is woven in the councils of princes
> Is woven also in our veins, our brains
> Is woven like a pattern of living worms
> In the guts of the women of Canterbury
>
> (*CP*, 42)

The pattern of *personae* in *Murder in the Cathedral* is somewhat like the conventional pattern of the organization of the state developed by the ponderous Menenius and the first citizen in *Coriolanus*, I, i (following Paul in I Corinthians 12) in which the head, the eye, the heart, the arm of the state depend upon the seemingly inactive belly storing and sending life 'through the rivers of your blood,/Even to the court, the heart, to the seat o' th' brain.' It is the part of the sensuous imagination which the women of Canterbury play; and their rôle is as necessary to Thomas as Thomas is to them. The rôle is played, as we have seen, by the women of *The Waste Land*, and the

triumph of the questing male *persona* would be their rape, desertion
and death. The same curious and arresting metaphor occurs in another, equally extraordinary and disturbing form in *Murder in the
Cathedral*. Here the women express their own foreboding of death
in terms of rape, the experience of total humiliation and desecration
of the body, but in terms which relate physical lust and spiritual
longings. It's curious how Thomas himself is ambiguously implicated
in the pattern of rape—for this hellish agony of the spirit is the
necessary counterpart of his triumphant pathos:

> Nothing is possible but the shamed swoon
> Of those consenting to the last humiliation.
> I have consented, Lord Archbishop, have consented.
> Am torn away, subdued, violated,
> United to the spiritual flesh of nature,
> Mastered by the animal powers of spirit,
> Dominated by the lust of self-demolition,
> By the final utter uttermost death of spirit,
> By the final ecstasy of waste and shame.

> > (*CP*, 42–3)

The hint of Shakespeare's 129th sonnet, 'The expense of spirit in a
waste of shame/Is lust in action' in the last line helps to place the
particular quality of the emotion in its context. Shakespeare's sonnet
on the treachery of desire agrees well with the sentiment of 'The
Hollow Men' and *Ash Wednesday* on the state of dream perception
between memory and anticipation, 'The place of solitude where
three dreams cross.' The sonnet ends:

> Before, a joy propos'd; behind, a dream.
> All this the world well knows; yet none knows well
> To shun the heaven that leads men to this hell.

But Thomas comforts the women of Canterbury with the assurance
that this knowledge of Hell is a necessary moment, still using sexual
imagery, the imagery of the orgasm, but equally the imagery of St
Theresa's ecstasy, to express a resolution of Hell in knowledge of
Heaven:

> This is your share of the eternal burden,
> The perpetual glory. This is one moment,
> But know that another

Shall pierce you with a sudden painful joy
When the figure of God's purpose is made complete.

(CP, 43)

As is to be expected, the play ends with a Threnos (in which are dissolved ghostly elements of the suppressed Anagnorisis or recognition scene and Theophany or appearance of the God). As one would expect from Murray there is a clash of contrary emotions, sorrow and affirmative joy blending. Affirmation predominates: for instance the Chorus return once more to their characteristic pattern of animal imagery, not now in the horrified flinching imagination of obscene contact, but in a triumphant Gloria: even those who deny God affirm Him simply by living: 'all things affirm Thee in living; the bird in the air, both the hawk and the finch; the beast on the earth, both the wolf and the lamb; the worm in the soil and the worm in the belly./Therefore man.' But affirmation is a difficult note as yet for Eliot to strike. In *Murder in the Cathedral* Hell is still known better than Heaven, and the pain of Purgatory more clearly felt than its joy.

THE FAMILY REUNION

In *The Rock* and *Murder in the Cathedral* Eliot had written for rather special audiences. Two years after the production of *Murder in the Cathedral* Eliot was having doubts about the wisdom of writing for audiences of such special character: 'People think of religious plays as they think of pageants—as performances which give a great deal more pleasure to people taking part in them . . . than to the audience.'[14] In his next play Eliot attempts another marrying of modes: music-hall and pageant and the mystery play are left behind; the common element of all the structures, Greek drama, remains, and Eliot embarks upon an attempt to combine the structures of Greek tragedy with the only commercially viable form of theatre at that time, middle-class comedy. The setting is a family house rather than a cathedral; a member of an aristocratic family is the hero, rather than a saint and martyr. And the language of *The Family Reunion* is, in parts at least, a slightly self-conscious attempt to cast the idiom of the middle-class comedy into the mould of verse. The result is a very odd, in some ways an absurd hybrid, which has neither the superficial ease of the drawing-room comedy nor the dignity, concentration and rhythmical power of *Murder in the Cathedral*. But, for all its awkwardness of conception and laboriousness of execution, it has a power which can be measured by the painfulness of reading it or seeing it staged; a power which rises from the thick, knotted complexities of fear, doubt and longing which lie beneath it, though they are never transformed into the kind of expressive unity which we demand of great art.

The structure of Greek tragedy as described by Murray can be discerned beneath the surface, and as has been pointed out by many commentators there are parallels with Aeschylus' *Oresteia*. In a way the parallels are mainly a structural convenience, and the images and motifs are so completely transformed that we can almost ignore their origin. For instance, as in Aeschylus, the Furies are converted into the Kindly Ones. But the meaning of the *Erinyes* in Aeschylus is so completely bound up with the pattern of Greek religious thought and symbolism and with the structure of the Greek mind and Greek society that they achieve a collective reality which is immediately valid to any member of the Greek society. In Eliot's play they are projections of an individual's sin and guilt, and the only possible reaction of a modern audience to them is a conviction of their unreality. In Aeschylus, as in Eliot, the problem of sin and expiation is one which affects a whole family. But in Aeschylus the family is conceived of as an actual historical continuity: in Eliot each member of the 'family' is a representation or manifestation of a stage of human consciousness, the 'family' a representation of the human condition as a whole. Thus, though this play declares its Greek origins more overtly than any of Eliot's other plays, it is less profoundly shaped by the Greek analogy than either *Sweeney Agonistes* or *Murder in the Cathedral*.

It is, however, in several ways, an attempt to re-cast the materials of the two earlier plays. Sweeney, the 'one character whose sensibility and intelligence should be on the plane of the most sensitive and intelligent of the audience', is transformed into Harry, and surrounded by characters who are 'material, literal-minded and visionless' to perform the choric function. But Harry is in Hell, and Hell blinds him to anything but fear, contempt, loathing and disgust; unlike Sweeney he needs help, the support, comfort and understanding of Agatha and Mary, and the steady faithfulness of Downing. Like

Sweeney, Harry is haunted by guilt; the guilt is to do with 'doing a girl in', and his entry is marked by the quotation from Aeschylus which was used as epigraph for *Sweeney*: '*You* don't see them, but I see them.' His exit, to follow the bright angels, parallels the other epigraph to *Sweeney*: 'Hence the soul cannot be possessed of the divine union, until it has divested itself of the love of earthly things.' Harry divests himself of Wishwood: the punning name indicates the delusive state of human desire and hope, wish and would. In the process he destroys the one character who keeps 'the family' together, Amy: the name, from the Norman French 'amée', 'loved', is another word-play—she represents the loved attachments which bind Harry, the consciousness of the family, to the world.

In other ways *The Family Reunion* re-casts some of the materials of *Murder in the Cathedral*. Harry returns to the scene of his past after an absence of eight years, as Thomas returns after seven, to find (what he knew already) that it is not the same place because he is not the same person. And he returns to suffer the persecution of ominous figures who pursue him from his past life, not, as in *Murder in the Cathedral*, to tempt and to kill, but to warn, to terrorize and to convert. Like Thomas he is faced with a challenge to make the final renunciation of the self; though here the stress is not so much upon the renunciation of the *will* as upon the renunciation of earthly ties, affection for the ghosts of family and ghosts of place.

As in *Murder in the Cathedral* seasonal imagery plays an important part in the opening scene. One of the subtitles which Eliot considered for the play was 'Vernal Equinox', which would suggest the critical point of time at which both the year and the hero break out from the darkness into the light. There are several more or less direct allusions to *The Waste Land*, particularly in Ivy's talk about going south for the winter. Again, as in *Murder in the Cathedral* the time is a waiting season: Amy waits for spring and fears the end of time and of sunlight:

O Sun, that was once so warm, O Light that was taken for granted
When I was young and strong, and sun and light unsought for
And the night unfeared and the day expected
And clocks could be trusted, tomorrow assured
And time would not stop in the dark!

(*CP*, 57)

The opening scenes revolve around the dominating force of Amy—

[199]

the family as a whole revolves around Amy, whose sheer force of *will* keeps both family and house alive. 'The tragedy is the tragedy of Amy, of a person living on Will alone', as Eliot wrote to E. Martin Browne while the play was still being revised.[15]

> I do not want the clock to stop in the dark.
> If you want to know why I never leave Wishwood
> That is the reason. I keep Wishwood alive
> To keep the family alive, to keep them together,
> To keep me alive, and I live to keep them.
>
> (*CP*, 59)

Critics have been puzzled by Eliot's statement in *Poetry and Drama* that Amy is the only completely human being in the play with the exception of Downing. Their puzzlement arises, perhaps, from the ambiguities of the word 'human'. Eliot attached a very special meaning to the word, ever since the time when he was strongly influenced by Babbitt's humanism. Harry begins as a hunted animal, but his vision takes him, eventually, beyond the simply human; Agatha and Mary, in their different ways, grow beyond humanity. Charles, Gerald, Ivy and Violet are masks rather than people (but then, so are many people) who have accepted a comfortable disguise, a comfortable routine of feeling and action which leaves them below the fully human level. They are not all treated with complete contempt. In a letter to Martin Browne, Eliot, with mild irony, expresses his 'affection for Charles (as the figure most like myself)'; indeed his easy indolent Tory clubman manner is an attractive mask. Amy exists between these two groups; she cannot accept all that is around her with the complacence of Charles, Gerald and the rest; she can conceive of the possibility of time ending, of Wishwood disintegrating, as they cannot. But her greater understanding only confirms her in hope and fear; her longings give rise to the power and determination of her will. She is not able to achieve the state of consciousness which Harry, Agatha and Mary are able to achieve; a detachment from time, a renunciation of desire, of hope and fear, a willingness to abandon Wishwood and all that it stands for; so her sole purpose is to keep the clocks turning, to keep Wishwood alive, to keep the family together: and this *is* being human, or one aspect of it. Downing is the other aspect: a faithful humility in service of the spirit—but we will discuss this later.

So Amy possesses, not the generosity and warmth that most of us associate with the word 'humanity', but a tenacious, possessive hold upon life, upon living in terms of time, memory, will, hope and fear. She is, in a way, heroic, but heroism is imposed upon her by her limitations. And, for all her fierce will and her powerful, limiting grasp upon all her family, especially the poor captive Mary, she has pathos too.

The play ends with the fulfilment of Amy's fears. Her last words, offstage, are 'Agatha! Mary! come! The clock has stopped in the dark!'—a too-predictable set of last words which is characteristic of the nervous insistence of the author upon his symbolic structures. And in the final ritual of prophetic runes which are the last words of the play, directly after the death of Amy, the symbol is repeated once again. Agatha and Mary move *clockwise* around a birthday cake (Amy's birthday cake, to suggest that her death is really a birth), blowing the candles out one by one until their clockwise movement can no longer be seen in the dark.

The final rune repeats the imagery of the knot unknotted and the cross uncrossed which has appeared before, in the previous runic ritual of Part II, Scene 2, where Agatha associates herself with the Eumenides by stepping into the window embrasure. The unknotting of the knot is quite literally the *dénouement* of the play:

> Completing the charm
> So the knot be unknotted
> The cross be uncrossed
> The crooked be made straight
> And the curse be ended
>
> (*CP*, 122)

and involves two things which are intimately related—the death of Amy and the departure of Harry. Harry's departure achieves the ending of time, the disintegration of Wishwood, and thus the death of Amy. Within the family, a complex image of the whole state of man's consciousness, Amy is the will to live, the attachment to hope and desire, to Wishwood; but Harry is the consciousness of the family, the faculty which is capable of spiritual fulfilment. Thus Agatha can predict that Harry's flight through purgatory can resolve the enchantment of the whole family. It is curious the way in which Agatha, in this passage from Part II, Scene 2, identifies 'we', herself, Harry and the other members of the family too, as the writer of the story. This does not suggest merely that Eliot used the family as an image for himself (though this is, inevitably, part of the case); it makes every man the author of the drama, makes every man contain 'the family' within himself:

> What we have written here is not a story of detection,
> Of crime and punishment, but of sin and expiation.
> It is possible that you have not known what sin
> You shall expiate, or whose, or why. It is certain
> That the knowledge of it must precede the expiation.
> It is possible that sin may strain and struggle
> In its dark instinctive birth, to come to consciousness
> And so find expurgation. It is possible
> You are the consciousness of your unhappy family,
> Its bird sent flying through the purgatorial flame.
>
> (*CP*, 105)

Amy dies, Harry goes; thus in one way the play could be entitled 'The Family Disintegration'. We have to decide in what sense, apart from the superficial one that all the members of the family are called to assemble at Wishwood 'at Amy's command, to play an unread part in some monstrous farce', is the play really about 'Reunion'?

The 'unity' from which the family disintegrates is in any case a superficial appearance; the family was racked by terrible tensions even before Harry was born, and it is only Amy's terrible, tenacious will which holds together a crumbling Wishwood so that it shall be exactly as it was when Harry left.

The history of Harry, 'the consciousness' of this unhappy family, is bound up with his relationships with four women. Amy, the actual mother, is, as we have seen, a being living in terms of time, memory and will. She is 'aimée', the loved, the ties of affection which bind the consciousness to 'wish' and 'would'. Balanced against the actual mother is Agatha, an ideal or spiritual mother, whose name comes from the Greek ἀγαθός, 'good'. Her intervention helps Harry to release himself from the ties of Amy and from the state of Wishwood.

Amy wishes Harry to marry Mary. When Harry returns he remembers the freedom that he shared with Mary, the 'hollow tree in a wood by the river' of the childish innocent world. But the simplicity and innocence is only in memory: the Wishwood he associates with her is 'a place/Where life was substantial and simplified—/But the simplification took place in the memory.' In his rebellion against Amy's power Harry turns his back upon the memory, and on Mary too, and enters into the restless chaos of the world with his marriage to the fourth woman, Lady Monchensey. But his return cannot be to the innocent memory, however much Amy wills it. The innocent memory remains a dream; Harry is between two dreams, one of them a dream of the past which he shared with Mary; the other of a future which Agatha can assist him to fulfil. So 'when the loop in time comes' (and, as Agatha says in the Prologue before Harry's entry, Harry returns 'to creep back through the little door') the image of innocent beatitude, the garden shared with Mary in their memories, is no longer sufficient. In the meantime Harry has lost innocence, he has experienced sin and must expiate it; he cannot creep back into the hollow tree, but must follow the narrow and difficult path pointed to by the Eumenides. A letter to E. Martin Browne commenting on an early version of the play helps to clarify Eliot's intentions. Marriage has given Harry:

> a horror of women as of unclean creatures. The scene with Mary is meant to bring out, as I am aware it fails to, the conflict inside him between this repulsion for Mary as a woman, and the attraction which the *normal* part of him that is still left, feels towards her personally *for the first time*. This is the first time since his marriage ('there was no ecstasy') that he has been attracted towards any woman. This attraction glimmers for a moment in his mind, half-consciously as a possible 'way of escape'; and the Furies (for the Furies are *divine* instruments, not simple hell-hounds) come in the nick of time to warn him away from this evasion—though at that moment he misunderstands their function. Now, this attraction towards Mary has stirred him up, but, owing to his mental state, is incapable of developing: therefore he finds refuge in an ambiguous relation —the attraction, half of a son and half of a lover, to Agatha, who reciprocates in somewhat the same way.[16]

Agatha has known the garden as well; it is this memory of blessedness which unites Harry, Mary and Agatha and commits them to a life which is in some way outside Wishwood, even if it is spent in constant 'wanderings in the neutral territory/Between two worlds', never entirely leaving behind the one or completely achieving the other. So she is able to speak, as it were, in an antiphonal exchange with Harry in Part II, scene 2, sharing the memory, not only of beatitude, but also of exile:

I only looked through the little door
When the sun was shining on the rose-garden:
And heard in the distance tiny voices
And then a black raven flew over.
And then I was only my own feet walking
Away, down a concrete corridor
In a dead air.

(*CP*, 107)

The reminiscence of 'Burnt Norton' is clear; indeed it is better to postpone detailed discussion of these images until we deal with 'Burnt Norton'. It is sufficient to say that the remembered vision of innocence is a prelude to, and cause of, exile, as exile is a prelude to, and cause of, fulfilment of the vision. Harry can say to Mary 'You bring me news/Of a door that opens at the end of a corridor,/Sunlight and singing'; but this only arouses the Eumenides—even as Mary consoles Harry: 'You can depend on me./Harry! Harry! It's all *right*, I tell you', the Furies choose to make their appearance (*CP*, 83). At this point the memory of innocence and the knowledge of sin are separate; but both are necessary constituents which must unite into one before Harry, the consciousness of the family, can fly free. And this can only be accomplished with the help of Agatha. Mary can revive the memory of innocent joy in Harry, but she cannot change the minatory aspect of the Eumenides; this has to wait until Harry and Agatha come together and share, not just innocent memory, but consciousness of a purgatorial exile, and consciousness that we can never return but must go on: 'We do not pass through the same door/Or return to the door through which we did not pass', says Agatha (*CP*, 107), and this shared knowledge is enough to transfer the burden of all the family from her shoulders to his, and to change the Eumenides from Furies into Kindly Ones.

Harry's assumption of the burden: 'The burden's yours now, yours/The burden of all the family'—is the point of Reunion spoken of in the title. Like Thomas, Harry has undergone his temptations; rejected the way offered to him by Amy, rejected the way offered to him by Mary, accepted the way of Agatha and the Eumenides. He accepts the burden, as Agatha says, 'chosen/To resolve the enchantment under which we suffer.'

Only Harry can undertake the journey, Agatha and Mary can see the Eumenides, can perceive a state of existence beyond Wishwood.

[204]

They can join Harry in trance-like exchanges of words; they can help him to achieve his destiny. They can also practice the necessary rituals. But they cannot, like Harry, travel through Purgatory. One other character shares some of their skills. Downing can *see* the Eumenides: 'You soon get used to them', he says—'There's no harm in *them*,/I'll take my oath.' Downing is a curious conceit: with a certain awkward condescension Eliot suggests through him that there are those who might see the truth without suffering the angular insecurities, the tortured and hyper-acute sensibilities of the Wishwood household. It is a way of modifying the high-pitched, over-insistent note of *The Family Reunion*, and suggesting that there are many ways of understanding. The attempt doesn't quite succeed, but it is there, and leads towards a more successful attempt to express the same purpose in *The Cocktail Party*.

THE COCKTAIL PARTY

The plot of *The Cocktail Party*, like that of *The Family Reunion*, is developed from that of a specific Greek play, Euripides' *Alkestis*. Murray classifies *Alkestis* not as a tragedy but as a Satyr play which, 'coming at the end of the tetralogy, represented the joyous arrival of the Reliving Dionysus and his rout of attendant diamones at the end of the Sacer Ludus.'[17]

However, Eliot has combined the satyr play with a sub-plot, centred around Celia, which reflects the pattern of tragedy as Murray analyses it, though her agon is somewhat irregular in that it is played out within herself in the Consulting Room with Reilly as referee and adviser rather than antagonist. Her pathos, as is typical of Greek tragedy, is off-stage, and needs a messenger, Alex, to announce it, and in the threnos there is, fittingly, 'the clash of contrary emotions, the death of the old being the triumph of the new.' The anagnorisis and theophany are somewhat eccentric in that they involve the revelation that Reilly, Julia and Alex have been a kind of godly fifth column all along. But theophanies in Harley Street consulting rooms would tend to be somewhat unconventional, however you contrive them.

In the Alkestis myth, Admetus, king of Pherae, is rescued from death by Apollo, on condition that he finds a substitute to die in his place and satisfy the Fates. He asks his mother, his father and all his relations to submit to this sacrifice for him, but only his wife Alkestis will do so. As the play opens, Alkestis is on the point of death, but Hercules intervenes, struggles with Death, and brings Alkestis back to the land of the living. Eliot says that the play began to take shape when he began to wonder what would happen after Alkestis came back from the dead. Admetus is transformed into Edward Chamberlayne; Alkestis becomes Edward's wife Lavinia; Hercules becomes Sir Henry Harcourt-Reilly, and the Chorus is modified, almost out of all recognition, into Sir Henry and his satyric companions, Julia Shuttleworth and Alexander MacColgie Gibbs, 'the Guardians'.

In some senses Edward Chamberlayne derives from a misreading —a perfectly deliberate, not a mistaken misreading—of the character of Euripides' Admetus. Any modern reader is bound to be struck by the apparent self-centredness and lack of humour of the King of Pherae. Not only is he content to let his wife die to preserve his own life, but he berates his father at length for failing to offer to die instead of her. Euripides and his audience would have understood Admetus' dilemma as a real conflict of responsibility between the sacred duty of a king to live and rule, and duty to family. But Eliot chooses to ignore this in fashioning Edward out of Admetus. Lavinia, on the other hand, bears remarkably little relationship to the noble, martyred Alkestis. She is a female parallel to Edward, and Celia takes over the character of the selfless martyr who is willing to meet death. The character who bears most resemblance to his parallel in Euripides is Sir Henry, who keeps all the boisterous eccentricity of Hercules as satyr-god, but his functions in the play are entirely different from those of Hercules. Like Hercules he is semi-divine, or at least semi-inhuman, and like Hercules he fights with death; but the *agon* is not his, as it is for Hercules in *Alkestis*; Sir Henry is not actor but instrument, who aborts a spiritual death in order to give his patients the chance to undergo 'the process by which the human is/Transhumanized' (*CP*, 193).

As in the case of Harry, the trouble begins for Edward with the death of a woman; or at least in Edward's case her desertion. In *The Waste Land*, *Sweeney Agonistes* and *The Family Reunion*, rape, desertion or death of a woman is connected in one way or another with the sense of sin, the denial of the body, or the beginning of a spiritual journey: the complex is discernible too in one form or another in 'Portrait of a Lady', 'La Figlia che Piange' and some of the quatrain poems. Lavinia's desertion leaves Edward with a choice to make; as the Unidentified Guest (Reilly) tells him

> If there's no other woman
> And no other man, then the reason may be deeper
> And you've ground for hope that she won't come back at all.
>
> (*CP*, 132)

—and it is clear already that the choice which Edward has before him hasn't quite the same options as that before Harry; Edward is far too mediocre, hasn't the stamina or the imagination for tragedy or martyrdom. And yet it is a choice, and is made a choice by his allowing new disturbing elements into the pattern of life.

> let me tell you, that to approach the stranger
> Is to invite the unexpected, release a new force,
> Or let the genie out of the bottle.
>
> (*CP*, 133)

In Act II, just after Celia's agon with Reilly, Julia returns to speaking about the problems of Edward and Lavinia:

> All we could do was to give them the chance.
> And now, when they are stripped naked to their souls
> And can choose, whether to put on proper costumes
> Or huddle quickly into new disguises,
> They have, for the first time, somewhere to start from.
>
> (*CP*, 193)

Edward's choice is whether to build defensive mechanisms of self-deception all over again or to cope honestly with his own inadequacies, adapt to the world as it actually is rather than to hide from it. The Unidentified Guest warns Edward of some of the unpleasant experiences which he will encounter on the way:

> There's a loss of personality;
> Or rather, you've lost touch with the person
> You thought you were. You no longer feel quite human.
> You're suddenly reduced to the status of an object—
> A living object, but no longer a person.
>
> (*CP*, 134)

This describes something very close to a pattern of mental sickness well known to psychology but in Eliot's scheme of things it is not quite the same thing that the psychologists would make of it—a sickness, certainly, but less of a sickness than the comfortable state which it replaces. It is close to the state of barren emptiness which both Harry and Agatha remember as exile from the garden in *The Family Reunion*; a first stage and a necessary stage in a process of transvaluation. For Edward the process of transvaluation cannot be heroic (as it is for Celia or Harry) but it is for him a tough and demanding experience and one which demands real courage, a recognition of the fact that others exist besides himself. Edward must win his way out of Hell as well, but not to a point where he relinquishes humanity; to a point where he becomes human. In an interview for *Horizon* in 1945 Eliot was asked 'How would you, out of the bitter experience of the present time, wish mankind to develop?' and answered: 'I should speak of a greater spiritual consciousness, which is not asking that everybody should rise to the same conscious level, but that everybody should have some awareness of the depths of spiritual development and some appreciation and respect for those exceptional people who can proceed further in spiritual knowledge than most of us can.'[18] To define the problems of the sub-heroic he finds it necessary to set them side by side with the typical case history of the saint and martyr; the satyric anti-hero by the side of the tragic heroine, Celia: 'There are different types. Some are rarer than others' says Reilly, speaking to Celia. In the beginning their emotional histories are somewhat similar—like Edward, Celia begins with a feeling of isolation; 'An awareness of solitude', and the failure to succeed in loving and being loved. Reilly tells Edward that he is incapable of love, and

> To men of a certain type
> The suspicion that they are incapable of loving
> Is as disturbing to their self-esteem
> As, in cruder men, the fear of impotence.

> (*CP*, 181)

To Lavinia he says that her greatest shock was when 'You had come to see that no one had ever loved you./Then you began to fear that no-one *could* love you.' But Celia doesn't need to be told of the problems of love; she discovers them for herself:

> Can we only love
> Something created by our own imagination?

[208]

Are we all in fact unloving and unlovable?
Then one *is* alone, and if one is alone
Then lover and belovèd are equally unreal
And the dreamer is no more real than his dreams.

(*CP*, 188)

Throughout the play Eliot remains sceptical about the possibility of what is ordinarily called love; but in another way the play is devoted to the idea of love and the possibility of love. Like Eliot's other heroic characters Celia experiences, and, more important, becomes aware of, the dream-like state of consciousness in which desire for something unknown motivates the heart; in which a remembered ecstasy remains a poignant and elusive part of experience never fulfilled in the ordinary world. These poignant memories combine, in a pattern which by now is quite familiar, with the feeling that the world is unreal: 'I have no delusions—/Except the world I live in seems all a delusion!' Further, they are combined with 'a sense of sin.' Thus in her mind the memory of ecstasy is felt as the reality which confirms the unreality around her:

Nothing again can either hurt or heal.
I have thought at moments that the ecstasy is real
Although those who experience it may have no reality.
For what happened is remembered like a dream
In which one is exalted by intensity of loving
In the spirit, a vibration of delight
Without desire, for desire is fulfilled
In the delight of loving. A state one does not know
When awake. But what, or whom I loved,
Or what in me was loving, I do not know. (*CP*, 189)

Eliot returns here once again to memories of St John of the Cross, especially his account of the divine touch or spark which enkindles the soul. More directly, the passage recalls a sentence from St Augustine which was quoted in the first chapter: *Nondum amabam, et amare amabam, quaerebam quid amarem, amans amare*: indeed, Celia's state of mind closely resembles Augustine's in that period of exhaustion and anguish before he gave himself entirely to Christianity—his weariness of life, his longing for an undefined love, his acute sense of the aimlessness and unreality of his old existence. Both allusions combine to suggest Celia's first hesitant steps on to the path of asceticism.

Edward's history is implicitly compared with Celia's, but the fact that he cannot achieve any extraordinary spiritual destiny does not mean that his career within the play is one of failure: quite the contrary. Eliot's concern here was more than anything else to define the kind of success which is possible to mediocrity—a task which is more difficult, perhaps, than the definition of sainthood. Edward achieves at least a measure of self-understanding and self-criticism, a sense of the dangers and limitations of the will:

> The self that wills—he is a feeble creature;
> He has to come to terms in the end
> With the obstinate, the tougher self; who does not speak,
> Who never talks, who cannot argue;
> And who in some men may be the *guardian*—
> But in men like me, the dull, the implacable,
> The indomitable spirit of mediocrity.
>
> (*CP*, 153)

It is this access of self-criticism which makes it possible for Edward to say at the end of the play 'Now I think I understand . . .' Lavinia, too: in the last scene Lavinia complains that she doesn't want to go on with the party. Reilly tells her 'It is your appointed burden.' She accepts this—she has to; but in the very last line of the play she is able to say: 'Oh, I'm glad. It's begun.'

The guardians are instrumental in the process. In the first version this is made explicit; Julia tells Reilly 'You, for your part, must not take yourself too seriously./You are only an instrument.' The use of the word 'instrument' is, of course, very similar to the use of the word in *Murder in the Cathedral*. Guardians are not, as it were, graduated students themselves. Julia reminds Reilly that they are ignorant of the actual journey which Celia undertakes:

> O yes, she will go far. And we know where she is going.
> But what do we know of the terrors of the journey?
> You and I don't know the process by which the human is
> Transhumanized: what do we know
> Of the kind of suffering they must undergo
> On the way of illumination?
>
> (*CP*, 193)

They do not know the process, not because they remain human, but because they have never been human: if 'transhumanization' means

[210]

a weak 'self that wills' coming to terms with a 'tougher self', the Guardians cannot experience it—they are the tougher self embodied. Martin Browne tells us how Edward's line about the tougher self as *guardian* came to be written. Originally the line read 'And who in some men may be the *daemon*, the genius.' Browne objected that the phrase would be confusing and somewhat opaque to the theatre audience, and suggested the line as it now stands. The same change, from 'daemons' to 'Guardians', was made in Celia's toast at the end of Act 1, scene 2 (*CP*, 154).[19]

In literature the longing for spiritual comfort and spiritual union takes many forms, but characteristically poets dramatize the longing by a figure who is at once human and yet representative of something beyond the human. Beatrice plays the part in Dante, Agatha has a broadly similar function in *The Family Reunion*. In a cancelled passage of *The Cocktail Party* Julia says, 'We are earth-bound spirits, Henry, frontiersmen;/We can help those who are elected, and we are allowed to know/The moment when we can show them the first stages.'[20] In another way, though, the guardians are like another figure in Eliot's work, who seems, as we have seen, to be another satyric, and at the same time satiric, version of the God-bearing figure: Mr Eugenides of *The Waste Land*.

The Cocktail Party, like the *Alkestis*, is a satyr play, and it is appropriate that its representatives of man's participation in the divine should have their farcical side too; and the link with the Smyrna merchant of *The Waste Land* is made by the re-appearance of the serio-comic symbolism of the one eye of the spirit. Reilly sings the song about the one-eyed Riley; and the curiously insistent business about Julia's spectacles which have one lens missing stresses the point.

The job of constructing a spiritual Mafia, an Alcoholics Anonymous for those who are trying to kick the habit of life, or at least to moderate the addiction, is an extraordinarily difficult one—it offers far more problems, for instance, than the creation of Agatha in *The Family Reunion*. Eliot is far more successful in *The Cocktail Party*: more successful because he brings to the play a new humanity, sympathy and tolerance of attitude, and therefore a lightness and gaiety in his approach to spiritual problems. And yet one must express one's reservations; the success, if it is a success, is only narrowly achieved. The relaxation of tone, the abandonment of the high-pitched, nervous note of stress which characterized *The Family*

[211]

Reunion creates problems of another kind. Celia's martyrdom has to be off-stage, not only for technical reasons, but because too violent an incident would disrupt the easy association of comedy and seriousness, the illusion of the extraordinary present within the very ordinary. But martyrdom is meaningless without suffering, so Eliot is forced to contrive the melodrama of crucifixion near an ant-hill. Even this is not enough; he must make Reilly assure Edward and the audience that she really did suffer:

> I'd say that she suffered all that we should suffer
> In fear and pain and loathing—all these together—
> And reluctance of the body to become a *thing*.
> I'd say she suffered more, because more conscious
> Than the rest of us.
>
> *(CP*, 209–10)

This illustrates the basic weakness of *The Cocktail Party*—the didactic content isn't fully realized in the action, and the author is forced to resort to assertion rather than dramatic representation to convey his point. It's not possible to react to the news of Celia's death with either horror or joy; because it doesn't really happen in the world which is created for us on the stage. Celia's death is carefully stylized myth; we know this and react to it with carefully stylized responses; an almost smug satisfaction seems to be demanded instead of a complex of horror and joy such as the horror and joy which the Chorus so finely expresses in *Murder in the Cathedral*.

Another effect of this general relaxation of tension and humanization of interest is that there is less of an attempt to pattern the language densely than in the earlier plays. In much of the dialogue of *The Cocktail Party* the division into verse lines is not very much more than a typographical convention, enabling the author to establish a slightly different mode of control over the intonation and stress patterns of the player's voice than he would have if he were writing in prose. But there are moments, as Jones points out, where, with no unseemly awkwardness of transition, the basic verse pattern is used as a vehicle for a more intense and impassioned utterance, as in Celia's speeches in the consulting room. The flexibility of the medium is such that passages like these have greater impact than anything in *The Family Reunion*, where the verse constantly strains after effect, and so only a narrow range of emotional tonalities is possible.

In *The Cocktail Party* Eliot has given up the attempt to force the

participation of the audience in the drama which he sets as his aim in
'A Dialogue on Dramatic Poetry'; the audience is merely a collection
of spectators, and despite Eliot's careful attempts to preserve an air
of realism as a vehicle for the profounder themes, the play seems
stagey and remote now, only a few decades after its first production.
It doesn't wear half so well, for instance, as Oscar Wilde or George
Bernard Shaw, who knew how to create conventions of artifice which
carried just so much conviction as was needed, no less and no more.
They demanded assent much less than Eliot does; Eliot would have
us *believe* much more, but to demand such assent some convention is
needed which is much more effective, not simply in form but in
emotion, a convention which carries its own authority. The 'some
kind of dramatic form' which Eliot has gravitated towards as the only
available vehicle for the drama is the threadbare convention of middle-
class comedy, and Eliot's genius was not precisely of the kind which
was needed to transform the convention, to make it strong or durable,
or to replace it with something entirely new.

THE CONFIDENTIAL CLERK

The Confidential Clerk is also based upon a Greek play, the *Ion* of
Euripides. There are many parallels between the two plays. As Jones
points out 'Ion is diffracted into Colby Simpkins and B. Kaghan.
Their fathers are a musician and a poet respectively, music and poetry
both being skills of Apollo.' One might add that there is a further
product of the diffraction process, Lucasta Angel, whose father is a
disappointed potter, as Colby Simpkins's and B. Kaghan's fathers
are an unsuccessful organist and an unsuccessful poet. Sir Claude
plays the part of Xuthus, Lady Elizabeth of Creusa, Mrs Guzzard of
Pallas Athene, and also of the high priestess who brings Ion/Colby
up. Eggerson takes over some of the functions of the high priestess
too, offering Colby the chance to return and live the rest of his life as
musician in the temple at Joshua Park. But, old retainer though he is,
he loses all the functions of the old retainer in the *Ion*; the plot to
kill Ion is dropped from the action, and the plot, the characters, the
action, the tone and the manner are changed so much that to follow
the analogies too far is a waste of energy. It is as if Eliot has left an

elaborate trap for the unimaginative to fall into; in its plotting the play is really more like *The Comedy of Errors*; in its farce it sometimes resembles a blunted Oscar Wilde, and in its final resolution into reconciliation and harmony it faintly mimics the late comedies of Shakespeare.

The essential theme of the play is summed up by Colby in the last Act when he announces his intention to leave the Mulhammer household and become a musician. He says to Sir Claude:

> You've become a man without illusions
> About himself, and without ambitions.
> Now that I've abandoned *my* illusions and ambitions
> All that's left is love. But not on false pretences:
> That's why I must leave you.
>
> (*CP*, 289)

Like *The Family Reunion* and *The Cocktail Party* it is about the process by which people may be weaned from illusions about themselves and the world they live in, and how love can only begin to exist when the illusions are gone. Eggerson remains a stable point of reference throughout the play; in one way or another everybody else is in a state of illusion. Even Mrs Guzzard, who creates illusions, or at least allows them to persist, is herself living a vicarious illusion in her ambitions for Colby. Sir Claude is in no doubt about Lady Elizabeth's capacity to deceive herself when he tells Colby:

> Why, it wouldn't surprise me if she came to believe
> That you really are her son, instead of being mine.
> She has always lived in a world of make-believe,
> And the best one can do is to guide her delusions
> In the right direction.
>
> (*CP*, 234)

But he has no realization of his own capacity for self-deception. When Colby wonders, 'If we all have to live in a world of make-believe,/Is that good for us?' Sir Claude answers, 'If you haven't the strength to impose your own terms/Upon life, you must accept what it offers you.' The alternatives he recognizes are the wrong ones: either to engineer the illusions you want or to accept those that you cannot avoid. Colby's final decision to go to Joshua Park is a far more true exercise of choice in that it is an abandonment of the illusion.

Colby, in fact, never quite accepts the illusions which he is offered as a way of living in the Mulhammer household. He remains aware that he is not entirely the person that he is expected to be; that the process of adaptation has something false and incomplete in it.

Sir Claude recognizes the ways in which Colby is beginning to repeat his own experience, splitting into a double personality, the public rôle of financier or confidential clerk and the secret, private world of the failed artist. And he encourages Colby in the deception, reminiscing about the way in which his private collection transports him into another world in which he experiences:

> an agonising ecstasy
> Which makes life bearable. It's all I have.
> I suppose it takes the place of religion:
> . . .
> I dare say truly religious people—
> I've never known any—can find some unity.
> Then there are also the men of genius.
> There are others, it seems to me, who have at best to live
> In two worlds—each a kind of make-believe.
> That's you and me.
>
> (*CP*, 238)

It is precisely the ecstasy, the standing aside from oneself for a brief moment of joy, that is suspect because it breeds make-believe; precisely this living in two worlds which is the barrier which stands in the way of unity.

When Sir Claude says that he has never known any truly religious people he means merely that he is unable to recognize truly religious people for what they are. If Colby's history is comparable in some ways to that of Harry in *The Family Reunion*, but muted in tone and more recognizably part of an actual world, Eggerson bears a similar relationship to Harry's servant Downing. Colby talks with Lucasta about the secret garden in a way which is similar to Harry's conversations with Mary, and like Harry he learns that he has to reject the withdrawal into the innocent vision. However, there is a difference, and an important one, between the experience of Harry with Mary and the relationship towards which Colby and Lucasta approach in their scene together. Colby is far more conscious of the deceptions which are implicit in his private world: he needs no Agatha to push him through into singleness of purpose, because he already recognizes, at least partially, the delusion, and the way in which Eggerson has transcended it:

> What I mean is, my garden's no less unreal to me
> Than the world outside it. If you have two lives
> Which have nothing whatever to do with each other—
> Well, they're both unreal. But for Eggerson
> His garden is part of one single world.
>
> (*CP*, 246)

Colby, in short, is able to recognize what Sir Claude is incapable of recognizing, that Eggerson, in his quiet adaptation to the world, in his singleness of vision and humility, is one of the 'truly religious people.' Colby hoards his music, Sir Claude his private pottery room, they clutch their secret worlds as a child clutches a security blanket; Eggerson is practical enough to grow marrows and beetroot in his garden: for him the garden is part of life, not an escape from it.

Sir Claude's longing for Colby as a son is a longing to share his private dream with somebody else, to recognize his own illusions in another. As we have seen, Colby is unable to accept the part forced upon him completely. The process by which he works his way out of the part he is expected to play into a part he chooses for himself is advanced by his conversation with Lucasta. Like Sir Claude, Colby longs for someone to share his private dream; Lucasta seems to offer herself as somebody who can share it with him. But she doesn't really; she offers him what he offers her, the chance to communicate with another person; and understanding other people is understanding oneself:

> LUCASTA: I think I'm changing.
>   I've changed quite a lot in the last two hours.
> COLBY: And I think I'm changing too. But perhaps what we call
>   change . . .
> LUCASTA: Is understanding better what one really is.
>   And the reason why that comes about, perhaps . . .
> COLBY: Is, beginning to understand another person.
>
> (*CP*, 247)

The way the pair share each other's sentences, recognizing their own thought in another's words, dramatizes the communication, the meeting, not in a private garden but in a moment of love. Playing to Lucasta, for Colby 'was neither solitude nor . . . people' (*CP*, 242);

[216]

but even this measure of fulfilment in mutual understanding is not the right path for Colby. This is why B. Kaghan is able to say 'I'm your guardian angel,/Colby, to protect you from Lucasta'—sympathy and communion between the foundlings is no substitute for the much wider and deeper communion which Colby seeks at last in the service of God through music.

However, the experience of understanding another leads to his determination to disentangle the fantastically complex knot of illusion which surrounds everybody in the play, and Mrs Guzzard, the *dea ex machina*, is called in to set everything straight. Only one person remains dissatisfied with the resolution in the end; but there is a hint that even Sir Claude will reach some understanding at last in his final appeal to Eggerson, the one character who is quite undisturbed by self-deceit and illusion: 'Eggerson! Do you really believe her?' at which Eggerson nods, and the curtain falls.

The play is a curious one; there are moments at which the farce is engaging; there are moments when the reflective passages strike one as having a maturity which is greater than in any of the earlier plays though just as often they seem ponderous and laboured. But the farce and the passages of reflection never entirely mesh with each other; it is perhaps too obvious that Eliot is using farce as a vehicle for moral teaching, sweetening the pill with a condescension which is both irritating and awkward. Eliot still seems to be incapable of treating his audience with uniform respect, and so juggles humour and ponderous wisdom with a self-consciousness which undercuts both. Perhaps it is only another way of putting this to say that the wisdom is never expressed in action, only in talk, and that the farcical bits are merely a relief from seriousness, not a natural extension of it.

THE ELDER STATESMAN

The plot of Eliot's last play derives remotely from Sophocles' *Oedipus at Colonus*, but there is no need to stress the relationship. As several commentators have pointed out, the ghosts from Lord Claverton's past who return to haunt him bear a faint relationship to the Eumenides of the Oresteian trilogy and *The Family Reunion*—again the parallel can be over-stressed. Martin Browne comments very appropriately on the ways in which *The Elder Statesman* differs so markedly from the history of Oedipus:[21]

> *Oedipus* is a whole man, who belongs to an age which holds certain firm convictions about the nature of man; his experience of life, painful as it has been, has brought him steadily nearer to peace of spirit. He is a figure of majesty because he is completely himself. The process of the play is the final establishment of this completeness. Eliot is writing in an age of shifting sand, in which man yesterday and man today are two different beings.

We may add that the Oedipus plays were written for a community so closely-knit, so homogeneous, with so much shared in the way of assumptions about man and the universe, religious beliefs and mythical memories, that Oedipus the man was not simply a man. The plays, and their hero, are a way of focusing the total experience of the Athenian community, representing and re-presenting a communal understanding of the interpenetration of the human world and the divine world, the fate of every man in the context of eternity. Oedipus is a hero, and his humanity lies in his heroic function. When Eliot attempts the hero, the heroic function disbars humanity —in two senses: in the sense that the hero is deliberately shown to be beginning a process in which he transcends human-ness; but again in the sense that our world is shy of heroism, finds it difficult to believe in the extraordinary destiny, at least in literature. In life, perhaps, there are just as many heroes, but the accent of modern art is ironic in tone, ambiguous in method; the modern audience is bafflingly diverse and incoherent in emotion, thought and knowledge. When a man is presented on the stage he is not (and we know he is not) *all* of us, as in a sense Oedipus was all Athens; so he cannot be the means by which a whole community experiences the resolution of their hopes and fears, the satisfaction of their spiritual longings.

Eliot's plays gradually develop from the heroic to the ironic mode, and, so deeply has the ironic mode taken root in our sensibilities that we can say that, for all practical purposes, this means they gradually become more human. *The Elder Statesman* is Eliot's most human play, the one in which he is least concerned with improbable adventures of the spirit which fail to convince because they depend upon ideal longings of a kind which can no longer be effectively realized in a dramatic action. It is in one sense Eliot's most personal play, in another sense his most impersonal, if his remarks in the essay 'Ben Jonson' are to be taken as a description of true impersonality:

> The creation of a work of art, we will say the creation of a character in a drama, consists in the process of transfusion of the personality, or, in a deeper sense, the life, of the author into the character. This is a very different matter from the orthodox creation in one's own image.

(*SE*, 157)

In all the other plays there is an element of wilful insistence in dealing with matters which Eliot all too clearly didn't understand well enough to convey them in dramatically effective ways. The exception is, perhaps, *Murder in the Cathedral*: the dramatization of a saint and martyr's career can more easily succeed in cases where the dramatic form approaches so close to ritual that the assent of the audience is won almost before the play begins. To dramatize an extraordinary religious sensibility without such a specially prepared audience was a task beyond Eliot's dramatic skills. He did not possess the immediate instinctive understanding which enables the great dramatist to seek and find the way in which assent for the extraordinary can be *won* from his audience. And it took him all his life to move towards the understanding that the ordinary is extraordinary enough; that the painful difficulties of understanding self and understanding others are as fit subjects for the most serious kind of drama as martyrdom or total renunciation of the world.

As we have seen, the humanizing of Eliot's drama began with a gesture in *The Family Reunion*: Downing, the faithful servant, the ordinary man, is able to see the benevolence of the Eumenides long before Harry. In *The Cocktail Party* Celia's history is not central to the play, which is much more concerned with the adaptation of the mediocre Edward and Lavinia to the problems of life. *The Confidential Clerk* goes a stage further, and is concerned with problems of self-deceit and illusion, with understanding and love, much more than spiritual heroism. *The Elder Statesman* is the conclusion of the process; there is no suggestion of any of the characters proceeding to an extraordinary spiritual destiny; the end of the play is quiet and peaceful atonement for a life of error. It is a drama of confession and absolution *in extremis*, of love through human understanding rather than love through self-destruction; at the last Eliot gives human love its proper place in the scheme of things without any undue fuss or strain.

The play is weak dramatically, but expresses a newly won personal strength and tranquillity, and I for one find it very moving for this reason. Eliot married his second wife in 1957; the marriage brought him extraordinary happiness which is reflected in innumerable ways in this play, but as Martin Browne remarks 'Eliot himself was as yet an amateur in happiness.' The poem of dedication to his wife is possibly the least guarded, most open poem that he ever wrote, the one in which he takes the least trouble to wear the armour of irony, farce, or learned allusion. Picasso once said of himself that as a child he was able to draw like a Titian or a Rubens, and that he had spent the rest of his life learning to draw like a child; here Eliot, at seventy, has at last learnt how to write like a seventeen-year-old. It doesn't matter in the least that the poem isn't a very good one; it is simple, ingenuous and unforced, and though simplicity, ingenuousness and unforcedness are not the greatest virtues for a poet, they are necessary for the complete human being. It is in a curious way comforting that they should make a tardy appearance like this, right at the end of Eliot's career.

Many critics have pointed out how the play seems to dramatize the 'gifts reserved for age' which the 'familiar compound ghost' predicts in 'Little Gidding' II:

> And last, the rending pain of re-enactment
> Of all that you have done, and been; the shame
> Of motives late revealed, and the awareness
> Of things ill done and done to others' harm
> Which once you took for exercise of virtue.
>
> (*LG*, II)

It is equally interesting to notice the way in which reminiscences of Eliot's earlier work keep on returning, but placed in a different context by the new vantage point. Mrs Carghill, for instance, reminds the reluctant Lord Claverton of an incident on the river which is strongly reminiscent of the 'nymphs' and 'loitering heirs of City directors' of *The Waste Land*, 179–80, and of the lament of the three Thames-daughters in lines 292 to 306 of the same poem. There's a pointed reference to the title of 'The Hollow Men' too, in '"That man is hollow." That's what she said./Or did she say "yellow"? I'm not quite sure' (*CP*, 321). And later there is a curious reminiscence of 'Dans Le Restaurant' and 'La Figlia che Piange' in:

> But you touched my soul—
> Pawed it, perhaps, and the touch still lingers
> And I've touched yours.
> It's frightening to think that we're still together.

The reminiscences of earlier poems do not carry any particular or deliberate symbolic weight; they are not insistent like the symbols of *The Family Reunion* or *The Confidential Clerk*. Eliot is writing words for an old man and his ghosts, words in which the ghosts bring back a painful pattern of memory. In the process ghosts from Eliot's own past visit him: 'And I wonder how they should have been together' becomes 'It's frightening to think that we're still together', and by a more radical change, 'Je la chatouillais' and 'Il est venu nous peloter un gros chien' are conflated into, 'you touched my soul—/Pawed it perhaps'.

These various reminiscences of lines from poems of the past recall, for a sensitive reader, not so much the detail of the earlier poems, but a mood, an accent. They recall the elaborate ironies, the dazzling and startling shifts of tone, the clever evasiveness, the slight hysteria of Eliot's verse in the years between, say, 1912 and 1924. Claverton confesses, 'What I want to escape from/Is myself, is the past' (*CP*, 337), but realizes through Michael's failings the cowardice of the attempt. The pyrotechnics of Eliot's earlier verse often clearly were designed to dazzle the eye so that the fear and sickness of the soul could remain in hiding; yet even in the late plays and poems the fugitive soul remains partly concealed. It is only in this last and most ingenuous, the most confessional of Eliot's works, that one can discern no attempt to hide anything: it is as open and clear as a summer day.

It is by human love, not the chivalry of martyrdom that this clarity is reached:

> If a man has one person, just one in his life,
> To whom he is willing to confess everything—
> And that includes, mind you, not only things criminal,
> Not only turpitude, meanness and cowardice,
> But also situations which are simply ridiculous,
> When he has played the fool (as who has not?)—
> Then he loves that person, and his love will save him.
>
> (*CP*, 340)

The greatness of Eliot's major work depends upon its unresolved tensions; in *The Elder Statesman* these are lost. As literature it is very minor; one might say a failure; but perhaps one could say that personally, morally, spiritually, it is his most shining achievement, unexpected in many ways, but most of all, perhaps, in its extraordinary modesty.

'THE FIRE AND THE ROSE'
FOUR QUARTETS

In his 'Notes on Words' Gerard Manley Hopkins distinguishes between two kinds of energy of the mind, 'a transitional kind, when one thought or sensation follows another, which is to reason, whether actively as in deliberation, criticism, or passively, so to call it, as in reading etc; ii) an abiding kind for which I remember no name, in which the mind is absorbed (as far as that may be), taken up by, enjoys, a single thought: we may call it contemplation . . .' The inter-relationship between this 'contemplative' energy and the 'transitional' is at the heart of the problem of Hopkins' magnificent poetry, of almost all poetry; and in the case of Eliot the problem is made more urgent by the fact that the question is the essential theme of much of his verse. As Hopkins puts it: 'Art exacts this energy of contemplation, but also the other one, and in fact they are not incompatible, for even in the successive arts as music, for full enjoyment, the synthesis of the succession should give, unlock, the contemplative enjoyment of the whole.'[1]

> Words, after speech, reach
> Into the silence. Only by the form, the pattern,
> Can words or music reach
> The stillness, as a Chinese jar still
> Moves perpetually in its stillness.

> (*BN*, V)

The comparison with Hopkins is interesting indeed; both poets begin from the contemplative, metaphysical experience; both use, and are partly motivated by, the analogy with music in their structuring of words; both are acutely conscious that the transitional nature of the expression bears a curious and paradoxical relationship to the rapt singleness of attention of the originating experience.

But Hopkins's energy is exclusively the energy of lyrical impulse; it manifests itself in a tense local activity of word and sound generating, interpenetrating and reinforcing each other; transitional forces which rely upon complex accidents of association, memory and sensuous habit, upon time and movement and dynamic mimicry, achieve stability by a strange balance of power in which the multitude of forces support each other in contention. It is by exaltation of 'transitional' energies that Hopkins lays siege to the moment of contemplation; even in the dark horror of the terrible sonnets the loss of vital spiritual energies is expressed through a Herculean athleticism of language.

Eliot, on the other hand, often reaches his greatest points of concentration by a deliberate relaxation of tension in the language. In the *Four Quartets* he repeatedly draws our attention away from the words, undercuts their significance, consciously chooses a graceless or a dull form or word, breaks illusions by commenting on the inadequacy of his own technique:

> That was a way of putting it—not very satisfactory:
> A periphrastic study in a worn-out poetical fashion,
> Leaving one still with the intolerable wrestle
> With words and meanings. The poetry does not matter.
>
> (*EC*, II)

Hopkins's seemingly total involvement in the language of his poetry expresses and serves his even more profound engagement in experience which is beyond words or music. His is fundamentally a poetry of celebration; even the anguished desolation of 'No Worst, there is None' lies in a dark valley between joy and joy, implying the excited and immediate apprehension of the glory of God in its temporary absence. Delight in the word is one aspect of his larger delight for all transitory things as evidence of the inexhaustible creativity of God:

> All things counter, original, spare, strange;
> Whatever is fickle, freckled (who knows how?)
> With swift, slow; sweet, sour; adazzle, dim;
> He fathers forth whose beauty is past change:
>   Praise him.
>
> (*'Pied Beauty'*)

—and Hopkins' verse is praise of God by imitation, by an exalted and passionate making in which both freedom and law (the two are indistinguishable finally in his greatest technical achievements) act out and represent freedom and law in the natural creation. In Hopkins the experience described, both in its transitory and its timeless aspect, is within the poem itself. An experience like the exaltation which he felt when returning from a fishing trip on the Elwy moves into its consummation in a poem like 'Hurrahing in Harvest', and is immediately, spontaneously continuous with that experience.

Eliot moves in a different way. There are points, for instance in Section II of *Ash Wednesday* and some of the Choruses in *Murder in the Cathedral*, where there is a direct expressive absorption in language, but characteristically, in most of his verse, the emotion which he expresses is that of reflection upon emotion; and part of the emotion is a distrust of emotion and of words as part of a distrust of all that is transitory: he shares the exasperation of Sweeney that, 'I gotta use words when I talk to you', and the conviction of St John of the Cross that the only true emotion is reached by a purgation of all that we normally think of as emotion.

The lyrical impulse, though it exists and has magnificent expression in the *Four Quartets* and elsewhere in Eliot, has a peculiarly insecure tenure in his verse. The half-known experience, and the emotion that would go with it are, we are made to understand, *outside* the poetry; the poetry is located in one way or another in time or in space, the experience which motivates it, or towards which the poetry points in different ways and at different moments, is protected from the contamination of time and space, though constantly metaphors of time and space, both negative and positive, are used in the pointing:

> These are only hints and guesses,
> Hints followed by guesses . . .
>
> (*DS, V*)

The kind of experience, then, that releases and empowers the joyful expressive energy of a Hopkins is made into a kind of symbolic language by Eliot; the exact quality of each moment becomes unimportant beside that which they all 'intend'. In the structure of the poetry place becomes important—each quartet borrows its name from a place, and associations of place help to give each quartet its distinctive character. But the place is made to be accidental; one

[225]

which gathers its power to evoke from personal memories or associations, accidents of time or geography:

> There are other places
> Which also are the world's end, some at the sea jaws,
> Or over a dark lake, in a desert or a city—
> But this is the nearest, in place and time,
> Now and in England.
>
> (*LG*, I)

Time becomes important in the structure of the poetry too; but again a particular time, like a particular place, acting as the *locus* of an experience, is made to be not important in itself, important only as part of the expressive pattern, part of a poetry whose subject is what is beyond the poetry. An experience which hints at a more complete and overwhelming experience may be located in personal memory; may therefore be thought of as something past; may be spoken of as 'our first world.' (*BN*, I) Or it may be part of a habit of anticipation, located in a pattern of hope and desire; it may be spoken of not just as 'not here' (*BN*, III) or 'nowhere' (*LG*, II), but also not yet, something which is reserved in assurance for the future:

> And all shall be well and
> All manner of thing shall be well
> When the tongues of flame are in-folded
> Into the crowned knot of fire
> And the fire and the rose are one.
>
> (*LG*, V)

It may, then, be spoken of as beginning or end; and in a poem (as in a piece of music) which is a succession of moments, a time pattern of sound and movement, meaning and association, time past and time future are not to be avoided. Not even time present: the 'uncertain hour before the morning' (*LG*, II), 'Midwinter spring', 'now and in England' (*LG*, I) are precise locations in a present time, somewhere in the scale of time between a beginning and an end, but in terms of the essential experience they are both beginning and end (and neither). So at one point beginning and end are made to loop round and meet each other: 'In my beginning is my end' (*EC*, I); but at another point, the 'end' (in a fetching-out of the non-temporal meaning of 'end') is made to be always now:

> What might have been and what has been
> Point to one end, which is always present.
>
> (*BN*, I)

Hopkins's Windhover is a particular bird, seen, delighted in; its movement enters into the rhythms of Hopkins's mind and into the swing and change of his verse as his mind enters, with the shaping empathy of inscape, into this one bird as evidence of all birds, all nature, all creation. Eliot's thrush is any thrush or no thrush; an ideal thrush, a thrush of memory or imagination; not even a thrush at all, but a way of expressing a movement of the soul:

> Quick, said the bird, find them, find them,
> Round the corner. Through the first gate,
> Into our first world, shall we follow
> The deception of the thrush?
>
> (*BN*, I)

Hopkins's sense of the oneness of the universe urges him to celebrate the concentration of all its glory in a single, living, moving thing, a thing in a world of time and a timeless world equally, and this is his way of apprehending the intersection of time and timeless; in the lyric shout. But in Eliot the lyric impulse, though it is there, and it is real, is for the expression of the unreal: in some sense the experience, or the memory, of 'our first world', and the thrush, the delighted movement of the soul which it expresses, is 'deception'. Whereas Hopkins, like any true romantic, imitates God in the creation, seeking a kind of completeness, richness and energy which mimics reality in its wholeness, Eliot draws back from committing himself to an unqualified creation, preferring the role of cautious suppliant and explorer.

But at the same time Eliot gains an equal universality, not by attacking the emotions of the reader head on, but offering him several patterns of which he may approve (though he is very well aware that his goods are by no means perfect) in the hope that, perhaps, the reader may see in their imperfection some hint or suggestion of something he has known or imagined. The result is that, while in Hopkins we are swept along into a world of Hopkins's own making, in the *Four Quartets* we are constantly directed to our own creative experiences; tentative forms of speech, images which retain an almost heard 'as if' as part of their retinue, ambiguities and careful vaguenesses of expression direct us into our own contemplative world

[227]

rather than the poet's, or into the poet's only as a shadow-play of our own.

'BURNT NORTON'

For these reasons it is entirely appropriate that the whole sequence should begin with so tentative and hesitant a statement, and one so lacking in concreteness of reference. The theory of time it contains has a weighty authority behind it, but Eliot chooses the language of uncertainty, unlike St Augustine:[2]

> It is plain and clear now that neither future nor past nor present exist; nor can we say properly that there are three times, past, present and future; but perhaps we might say there are three times, a present time of past things, a present time of present things, and a present time of future things. Indeed there are three such in the soul, and I cannot see them anywhere else. The present time of past things is memory, the present time of present things perception, and the present time of future things expectation.

Eliot chooses not to speak with authority, merely suggesting the possibility with a carefully placed 'perhaps' and 'if' here and there:

> Time present and time past
> Are both perhaps present in time future,
> And time future contained in time past.
> If all time is eternally present
> All time is unredeemable.

The careful logic of the fourth and fifth lines form a bridge from hesitant suggestion to firm assertion; but the assertion which follows is of a different kind than the tentative suggestions with which he begins. For one thing everything after the fourth line is to be taken in the context of the opening possibility—*if* all time is eternally present, then the rest follows; but follows not in exactly the way that 'All time is unredeemable' follows, by simple logic. The verse moves gradually (imperceptibly for the unwary) from cautious logic to a different kind of statement. The pivot is 'All time is unredeemable', a reference back to *Ash Wednesday*, in which Eliot hopes to:

> Redeem
> The time. Redeem
> The unread vision in the higher dream

and even if the reader does not catch the reference he will catch the emotion that goes with it, the fateful sense of lost opportunities, of the irreversibility of human action, the frustration of hope and desire.

At this point no specific hope or vision or opportunity is mentioned; we merely respond with uneasy half-formed regrets; and when we are reminded that if the proposition we began with is true, *if* all time is eternally present, then both vision and failure are not to be consigned to the comfortable distance of the past, and thus the uneasiness takes a half-turn more:

> What might have been and what has been
> Point to one end, which is always present.

Eliot is busy raising ghosts; ghosts which inhabit possibly every human mind, and which become clamorous particularly when our sense of the distinction between practical present fact and the dream world of memory and imagination becomes blurred. Eliot has achieved this blurring by his modest speculations about time, for the clock and the yardstick are the foundations of the practical world. So the ghosts walk, footfalls echoing in the memory, down a passage and towards a door we never opened.

The images which Eliot employs here—the footsteps, the long corridor, the door into the secret garden, the rose garden itself—are all images which will have their effect immediately on any reader. This is not because they record or describe anything specific—quite the opposite. They are, as it were, skeleton keys which may unlock many doors. In some private worlds they might raise very detailed and well-formed childhood memories; though the memories themselves will doubtlessly not be the accurate record of an event, but the end of a process in which memory elaborates the image. In other worlds, or in the same, they will unlock patterns of fantasy and dream in which half understood fears and longings mingle. In still others, the resonances may include literary memories: of folk tales in which princesses escape through secret doors to dance all night with their

[229]

lovers, of Alice hesitating at the door into wonderland, of Goethe's
memories of his childhood, or a tale about a rose garden by D. H.
Lawrence. A reader who wishes to point to any of these quiet, half-
fulfilled echoes as having an important part to play in the experience
of the poem is doing something perfectly valid: the images have many
possible values, and many of the possible ones will have been consciously present in Eliot's mind as he wrote; others will not have
been, and they will be equally valid within the reader's private world,
and within a public world of critical debate if he argues his point in
such a way that the perception becomes possible for others. But
Eliot's method is carefully withdrawn, and as non-committal as
possible. He is attempting to evoke experiences which are latent in
the reader's mind, not primarily to convey experiences of his own,
and so the images are allowed to have multiple and variable values.

A reader, for instance, who is fresh from reading St Augustine's
Confessions, as Eliot seems to have been as he wrote 'Burnt Norton',
may catch an echo of a turn of phrase, and see in it another evidence
of the kinship between two minds so far apart in time and space:[3]

> Although past things are spoken of as true, they are fetched
> out from the memory, not the things themselves (for they have
> passed) but the words which are conceived from the images of
> things which they have, in passing through our sense, im-
> printed in the mind like footsteps.

So footfalls echo in the memory; and my words echo thus in your
mind. This reader might also catch an echo of an echo in St Augustine: 'I should certainly prefer that . . . I should write . . . so
that my words should echo (*ut . . . mea verba resonarent*) rather
than to set down one true opinion so clearly that I should exclude
all other possibilities.'[4] The reader would be right to recall these,
not just because St Augustine was one of the authors to whom Eliot
returned constantly, but because in his sceptical caution about the
reality of time and his sensitive awareness of the subtle mysteries of
the processes of the human mind he resembles Eliot. He would be
right because St Augustine's refusal to dogmatize, his preference for
touching the sympathetic string rather than the definite note parallels
Eliot's own practice. And finally he would be right, or at the very
least respectful to Eliot's wishes, since he as reader would be doing
something very like what Eliot wished to do as a poet: to read as the
traditional poet would write, with past and future intertwined in a

total experience which goes far beyond the individual's thought and feeling.

We know that the notion of tradition is important in Eliot's interpretation; we can see, too, that in this crucial passage from 'Burnt Norton', he was anxious that the reader should not be circumscribed too much by too definite and precise a reference to a particular element of the tradition, and so he works with variable images which prompt the reader to explore within his own field of references, his own memories and imaginative habit. The key to understanding may be very different indeed if the reader's habit of mind is formed by a culture and tradition other than our own. For instance a Muslim reader may find that the image of the rose garden and other images associated with it recall his experience of Sufi poetry; a Muslim acquaintance of the author's who did not know St Augustine, St John of the Cross, or Lewis Carroll, Goethe or D. H. Lawrence, was able to place 'Burnt Norton' in a frame of reference which was entirely valid for him, and may be for us, if we attend to the echoes without prejudice. Sa'd-uddin Mahmud Shabistari, Jalalud-uddin Rumi, and Shaikh Maslah-uddin Sa'di al Shirazi were all Persian poets who wrote in the thirteenth century. They wrote within a convention which expressed the divine passion of the soul in terms of a pattern of erotic images in which the female soul longs for the embrace of a male God-bearing image.

The Rose Garden was, in the Persian convention, an image of the one-ness of God, and of the consummation of the mystical experience. Rumi wrote: 'Our journey is to the Rose Garden of Union.' *The Secret Rose Garden* (*Gulshan i Raz*) of Shabistari contains a complete exposition of the metaphoric vocabulary of Sufism, in which the image of the Rose Garden itself is crucial: the mole on the cheek of the beloved is the still point of the turning world, the point of intersection of the two worlds:[5]

> The single point of the mole in His cheek
> Is a centre from which circles
> A circumference.
> The two worlds circle round that centre.
> The heart and soul of Adam evolved from there.

The imagery of wheel and point is not exclusively Persian, of course; if we examine the history of the metaphor we can find many versions of it in Hindu, Greek, Christian and Buddhist thought; but for one trained in the Islamic tradition, this would be one of the echoes which Eliot's words create. The Sufi critique of time, too, is very much like that of any mystical thinker, but consider how this sympathetic string would answer to Eliot's words:[6]

> The past has flown away
> The coming month and year do not exist
> Ours only is the present's tiny point.
> Time is but a fancied dot ever moving on
> Which you have called a flowing river-stream.
>
> I am alone in a wide desert
> Listening to the echo of strange noises.

The parallels with the Sufi tradition could easily be multiplied, even to Eliot's thrush, which fulfils something like the rôle played by the bulbul (a member of the thrush family) in many Sufi poems. There is, however, no need to go further: the rose garden image has become naturalized into the European tradition, for instance in Dante's *Paradiso*, XXIII, 70–4, where Beatrice exhorts Dante to turn from looking at her face to see the beautiful garden which flowers under the rays of Christ: 'Quivi è la rosa, in che il Verbo Divino/ Carne si fece.' (Here is the rose in which the Divine Word is made flesh.) Roses grow in the beloved's garden in St John of the Cross's 'Songs between the Soul and the Spouse'; and even a carol like the Dutch seventeenth-century 'Jesus' Bloemhof' will show how much the image has entered into the language of Christian feeling, multiplying the sympathetic strings which Eliot's words can set vibrating. Perhaps, though, before leaving this point, we should mention one of the greatest classics of the Sufi tradition, the *Gulistan* or Rose Garden of Sa'di, which was translated in 1899 by Sir Edwin Arnold, the author of one of the poems which Eliot admired when young, *The Light of the East*. In the introduction to his *Rose Garden*, Sa'di chides a friend for trying to carry away roses and hyacinths, basil and other sweet herbs from a garden, saying that those roses will perish, but Sa'di can give him an imperishable garden of roses—'What use will a bowl of roses be to you? Take a leaf from my rose garden; a flower will last only five or six days, but this rose garden is always delightful.'

> My words echo
> Thus, in your mind
> But to what purpose

[232]

Disturbing the dust on a bowl of rose-leaves
I do not know.

As in parts of 'Prufrock' or 'Gerontion', the pronominal conceit is used with a certain ambiguity—'you' is partly the reader, his mind disturbed with echoes which the poet cannot fully predict or know. At the same time the dialogue is internal, between the 'I' and the 'you' of the mind. In either case the bowl of rose-leaves is an image, not of the reality, but of memory: these are not the living roses of the eternal present, but leaves preserved to gather dust in a corner of the mind until they are disturbed by echoing words.

Other echoes inhabit the garden, apart from all these that have been mentioned and others that cannot be mentioned because they are not part of the public worlds of literary or religious symbolism; and when we follow the eager thrush we can hardly help but associate the garden of 'our first world' with the garden of Adam. But we are prevented from identifying this world simply with the shared myth. Experience is much more variable than this, and though myth to some extent controls our personal feeling, invests the first world with dignity and significance, Eliot is still directing us to the personal response, encouraging us to look back and discover in childhood memory a brightness and meaningfulness which many adults find more easily in their past than in their present. This is a good part of the 'deception' of the thrush: the childhood experience is surely in many ways different from the adult, but the childhood experience which we, as adults, recall with adult minds, is much more to do with what we are now than with what we were then. Its beauty (or its terror, or its boredom, or its joy, or all these together) is second-hand; emotions controlled by the words and images that reverberate after the first experience dies.

And so the experience is described, not in terms of simple sense-experience, as we would think, perhaps, that a childhood experience must be, but in terms of paradoxical ambiguities rather like those of the hyacinth garden passage in *The Waste Land:*

And the bird called, in response to
The unheard music hidden in the shrubbery,
And the unseen eyebeam crossed, for the roses
Had the look of flowers that are looked at.

In *The Waste Land* the hyacinth girl looks, though her eyes have failed; she sees with blind eyes the heart of light, and the heart of light into which she looks is 'the silence'. Here in the rose garden there is music, but unheard music, seeing, but not the seeing of sight. The reference to Donne's 'The Extasie' has been noted by Grover Smith and others, and is important; the trance-like, bodiless state of experience is similar in the two poems (and incidentally, similar to the experience suggested at the opening of 'A Cooking Egg'). But here, in this poem, the reference is complicated by the peculiar adjective: one would not in any case expect to 'see' an eyebeam. The phrase 'unseen eyebeam' conveys, by entirely illogical means (illogical means are the only possible ones here), the continued possibility of a world of experience which lies beyond seeing and hearing, beyond all the senses.

Eliot has moved from cautious logic to an evocative illogic which at first directs us each into our own pattern of memory, allowing the ghosts of our own past to walk; now he directs our imaginations more and more, bidding us to find in that memory, subject as it always is to our present imaginations, the possibility of an experience which seems to us to go beyond the natural, into a world of ecstasy. He takes the reader with him, by the word 'we'; but at the same time he implies something rather more than an invitation. An ecstasy, even a 'partial ecstasy' as yet incomplete (*BN*, II) is a standing outside oneself, a loss of individuality, of personality. In this context, therefore, 'we' means what you or I become if we leave behind, even if only incompletely, our personal selves. And the 'we' of ecstasy, though it is largely described as if it is a memory, in the past tense, is not simply a state belonging to the past but where past, present and future converge into one; the end which is always present. The universality and timelessness of 'we' is enforced by the entry of 'they', 'There they were, dignified, invisible'; inhabitants of a garden which is full of music that is not heard and sights that are not seen, like the spirits which fill Caliban's island, so that an ecstasy of spirit becomes communion with presences that are wonderful beyond understanding, but not beyond acceptance:

> There they were as our guests, accepted and accepting.
> So we moved, and they, in a formal pattern,
> Along the empty alley, into the box circle
> To look down into the drained pool.

> > (*BN*, I)

'We' and 'they', however, are not to be thought of as wholly dis-

[234]

tinct from each other. In one way, 'they' might be thought of as 'we' reflected or in another dimension. In another way we can think of them as figures like the Eumenides in *The Family Reunion*, appearing at first to be vengeful, destructive and terrifying, but, as the protagonist approaches a resolution of self, becoming peaceful, benevolent and entirely accepted. (This would ultimately be the same as the first way, as thinking of 'they' as 'we' in another dimension.) And, as in *The Family Reunion*, Agatha acts out aspects of the reunion by a form of ritual, sometimes in the presence of the Eumenides, sometimes not, so it is of the highest importance that at this moment of unheard music and unseen presences, all should move towards the mystery of the pool in 'a formal pattern'. The formal pattern of art, or ritual, magic, or prayer is a way of indicating the abhuman, the timeless:

> Only by the form, the pattern,
> Can words or music reach
> The stillness . . .
>
> (*BN*, V)

And so the ritual pattern becomes a kind of magical activity, conjuring water out of dryness, light out of darkness, inviting the divine creation to be re-enacted in this ecstasy. Notice, though, how light and water interpenetrate each other, how the water rises 'out of sunlight', how the surface of the water glitters out of that same light which can be seen by the blind, as it was seen by the hyacinth girl, 'out of heart of light.' We have seen elsewhere how water is used by Eliot to suggest the refreshment of spiritual grace; this water is the medium through which the light shines and which is at the same time made by light. St John of the Cross has a passage in which he describes the soul as a window through which light may be seen, but which is not itself the light, describing how the mystical experience of God is yet not union with God; there is a parallel between this and the water and the light here.

Eliot continues, as it were, to direct the reader's experience more and more, to marshal his ghosts into a formal pattern, to persuade the imagination into a special way of seeing. But at the same time he continues to provide points of entry for readers of all kinds. The aridity of contemporary life is suggested by 'dry concrete'—evocative enough for anyone who has lived in a city. And the rose, an image which is immediately valid for one half of the world, is replaced without either explanation or unnatural strain, by an image which is valid for the other half: 'the lotos', which either Buddhist or Hindu would understand without difficulty. The experience is one which transcends all cultural bias, and which can be reached by many routes:

> If you came this way,
> Taking any route, starting from anywhere,
> At any time or at any season,
> It would always be the same.

(LG, I)

So there is no abruptness in the transition when, after the quiet rising of the Buddha's lotos out of the water and out of the light, there is a distant echo of the imagery of Plato, 'And they were behind us, reflected in the pool'. The hint from Plato, the barest suggestion that even this ecstatic approach towards the light is reflection, shadow, illusion, pivots the change of tone from ecstasy to a retreat from joy: 'Go, said the bird.' So we are reminded that in some way the experience itself is not entirely to be trusted; it is an approach towards understanding, but it is still 'the deception of the thrush.' The light which has filled the pool with water is masked by a cloud; 'our first world', from being, briefly, what seems to be a consummation of everything, becomes merely the point of innocence from which we began; a paradise, not a heaven, and a paradise of image and memory only. The bowl of rose-leaves is a bowl of memories; the leaves appear again as 'dead leaves' over which 'they' move, dignified, invisible. Now at last, these leaves of the memory conceal children whose laughter is for simple joy, but at the same time laughter at us for presuming to attempt to 'recover radical innocence'.

Neither this nor the phrase, 'the deception of the thrush' invalidates the experience; it is deception, and it is faintly ridiculous, because we who meet the experience, being human kind, may not meet it face to face, but only through the broken images which are the elements of the kaleidoscope:

> Go, go, go, said the bird: human kind
> Cannot bear very much reality

To use Hopkins's terms, the contemplative energies cannot long be sustained; they decay at a touch into a merely transitional state of being; as the lyrical impulse always awaits a person from Porlock who brings us back into the stream of time.

[236]

The formal study, 'Garlic and sapphires', is a marked contrast to the first section in its form; the deceptively relaxed and informal pattern of the first section is replaced by a rhythmical and rhyming pattern which, though it is by no means classically regular, gives the impression of almost constricting tightness. Garlic and sapphire; hard clear images of sight, touch and smell, representing the moments of sensual clarity which relieve the generally muddy monotony of experience, surround and impede the axle-tree, the prime moving force of the turning world, The circling motion of the world is reflected in the circulatory processes of the body, and both, in an image suggested by astrology, are reflected in the apparent motion of the stars. All this motion is expressed in another way by the rising of the sap in the tree in spring, a reference to the cycle of the seasons. But the tree has its timeless aspect too: it is a familiar Christian image of the Cross. As all this motion converges upon the tree, 'We', while moving with all the complex movement of the natural world, may yet move into the kind of pattern which, in the natural world of change and decay, is a figure of the eternal stillness. As 'We' move 'in light', then, above all the bustling motion, we can look down upon the continuing change and brutality of natural existence, 'the boarhound and the boar', which are yet part of ourselves. But yet, the boarhound and the boar (which suggest, with their mildly antique symbolism, an episode in an Ovidian metamorphosis), while continuing in the blood savagery of natural existence, are 'reconciled', in 'We', because 'We' harmonizes the discord in a new key of being.[7]

This formal exercise is reminiscent of the 'runes' in *The Family Reunion*, a ritual expression of the essence of the drama. It is succeeded by the quasi-philosophical commentary which fetches out its significance. There has been a good deal of commentary on the analogues of the wheel and point symbolism in Aristotle, not so much on the similar images which appear in Buddhist literature and the *Bhagavad Gita*. It is not my purpose to comment in detail upon this except to note that Eliot still gives points of entry from widely varying cultural patterns of symbolism into the experience which he believes to be universal. The *via negativa* which is recommended in this and the third section is not the invention of St John of the Cross but is a way which has always absorbed the attention of Hindu, Buddhist and Muslim mystical writers, as well as Christians.

I would, however, like to comment in some detail on the complex and beautiful devotional exercise of Movement IV. The first

[237]

Movement has explored tenderly and with great delicacy the ecstatic moment, the approach of the soul towards the unheard music and the heart of light through an intent and joyful meditation; but has at the same time discovered the evanescence and deceptiveness of the experience. The third Movement points to the alternative way, the way through darkness and deprivation, through the ascetic withdrawal from all those things which attach the soul to the world. The first Movement ends with the failure of the soul to capture and sustain the light, with the cloud passing across the sun and obscuring its light. The third bids us to see that it is through a willing abstention from joy, even from the ecstatic joy of our first world and its light, that we must approach the ultimately satisfying experience.

We need to appeal to the tradition of asceticism to understand this choice in full. St John of the Cross discusses the theory of it in all his works, and notably in *The Ascent of Mount Carmel*, which Eliot refers to unmistakably at several points in *Four Quartets*, and most notably at the end of Movement III of 'East Coker'. St John describes the great importance in the life of the questing soul of the visionary experience, but warns the spiritual explorer of too great a dependence upon it, bidding him to void the soul of these imaginary forms, however delightful they are, and however important they are in setting the soul on the right path:[8]

> The time and energies which (the soul) would have wasted in dealing with these images and forms can be better employed in another and a more profitable exercise, which is that of the will with respect to God, and in having a care to seek detachment and poverty of spirit and sense, which consists in desiring earnestly to be without any support and consolation that can be apprehended, whether interior or exterior.

He does not underestimate the importance of 'visions, locutions, feelings, or revelations', but encourages the contemplative to 'make no account of the letter or the rind', but to attend only to the love which they contain and represent. Thus:[9]

> When it comes to pass that any soul has such figures formally within itself, it will then do well to recall them to the effect of love to which I have referred, for they will be no hindrance to the union of love in faith, since the soul will not desire to be absorbed in the figure, but only to profit by the love; it will

immediately set aside the figure, which thus will rather be a help to it.

The figure in 'Burnt Norton' is that of the rose-garden; the product of the footfalls in the memory, the bowl of rose leaves ('dry leaves'), and the deception of the thrush, which enables us to be exalted, in this ecstatic moment, to move 'in light upon the figured leaf.'

Now, in Movement IV, Eliot explores the next moment of the soul's passion. In Movement I, a cloud passes, and sunlight, which is an image of the love of God, is obscured. If this image of God, and the images which express the experience, like the rose garden, are to be denied us, what then? How may we apprehend the timeless without joy of imagination, without the symbolic language which is appropriate to time?

Time is all change; light cannot persist in it; night robs us of day, storm clouds rob us of sunlight, death robs us of the senses with which we perceive the earthly light. The passing-bell, in Donne's wonderful Meditation XVII, is not just simply for one man, but for all men, for 'no man is an island, entire of itself. . . . Any man's death diminishes me because I am involved in mankind.' And so for 'us'; and if you or I are destroyed by death, may not perceive light of the sun any more, what is left for us when 'Time and the bell have buried the day?'

> Will the sunflower turn to us, will the clematis
> Stray down, bend to us; tendril and spray
> Clutch and cling?
> Chill
> Fingers of yew be curled
> Down on us?

The life of Nature is shaped by Natural forces; sun, water, the pull of the earth's core, the structure of the living cell. The sunflower yearns towards the light of the sun in its phototropism, or light-shaping; the clematis, too, climbs towards the light, but twists and turns in its climbing—I am told that the force at work here is incompletely understood, but it is called thigmotropism, touch-shaping. And the roots of the yew-tree search into the earth, shaped geotropically, by the earth, by its gravity and the attraction of water, mineral salts and humus.

As natural beings we too are shaped by natural forces; not simply in the way that our bodies take their shapes, but in the way that what Aristotle, and Eliot following him, calls 'appetency' (*BN*, III), shapes our emotions, our desires, our wills. Take away these forces; take away the sun and time, take away the natural forces of attraction, the forces towards which desire and will strive, and what will be the motive force which shapes life? Will it be 'us'? Will it be a new kind of unity?

The verse echoes the pattern of feeling, its movement waning from the sonorous 'Time and the bell have buried the day' to the cold feeling of death in 'Chill', and then rising to a new fullness and joy of movement in:

> After the kingfisher's wing
> Has answered light to light, and is silent, the light is still
> At the still point of the turning world.

The stillness is *after* the moment of joy caught in the swift flight of the bird. The kingfisher (which recalls the fisher king of the Grail myth) answers 'light to light'. Light here is still light of the sun, light of the rose garden, light as a moving image of the still light. The moment of joy is a preliminary to eternity; a necessary one, perhaps, but still a preliminary which must be followed by a descent into the darkness, the 'Chill' of the spiritual night before the still light can be seen.

The poetry itself is like the image of the rose garden; image and memory striving to create a formal pattern which will in a distant way echo the stillness. Movement V of 'Burnt Norton' begins by contemplating the process, the process of art as a whole, and the difficulties which beset the artist who works in words or music, both of which exist in terms of time, whereas the experience to be described is timeless. This leads the poet to the implicit contrast between Word and word, to the contrast between the ultimate and essential human activity and the contingent. The first of the two epigraphs from Herakleitos:

τοῦ λόγου δ'ἐόντος ξυνοῦ ζώουσιν οἱ πολλοί ὡς ἰδίαν ἔχοντες φρόνησιν

can be translated: 'Whereas the Word is universal, most people live as if their thoughts are separate.' Christianity crystallizes the concept of the Word around the mystery of Christ's Incarnation, but Eliot gives us Herakleitos to remind us of the way in which the essential symbolism of Christ's Incarnation is shared by other cultures and other times. 'The Word in the desert' recalls, of course, the temptation of Christ in the wilderness, and at the same time the wanderings of the tribes of Israel through the desert in Exodus, in Eliot's own verse it recalls Movement V of *Ash Wednesday* and the temptation of Thomas in *Murder in the Cathedral*, and a great deal else as well. All these associations bear upon the relationship which occupies Eliot so much in 'Burnt Norton', a relationship which we might once more use the language of Hopkins to describe: the relationship between transition and contemplation. 'The detail of the pattern is movement', or transition, as the figure of the ten stairs in St John of the Cross's *Ascent of Mount Carmel* uses a pattern of movement or transition to point towards stillness; the emotions which accompany the quest are transitional, not the Love which is the end of the quest, the stillness of contemplation. God, Aristotle's unmoved and unmoving mover, may manifest Himself in 'a grace of sense' (*BN*, II) yet this, even in the ecstatic joy of the rose-garden, is:

> Caught in the form of limitation
> Between un-being and being

—as the poetry, the words or the music only catch the Word by the pattern in which the words reach out beyond themselves. And so, in the end of 'Burnt Norton' we return to the beginning, in the cyclical progression which is characteristic of the whole sequence, with the return of the shaft of sunlight, of the dust disturbed on the bowl of rose-leaves, the laughter of the children in the rose garden, and the call of the bird telling us to catch eternity not in a time in which end succeeds beginning, but 'Quick now, here, now, always—'.

Perhaps, in the end, the assertions of Eliot and Hopkins are not so very different, though opposite in their modes; Eliot, telling us to 'Descend lower', seems to be taking the other route from Hopkins, who flies up in sheer joy through the exaltation of natural beauty. But the second epigraph from Herakleitos, after all, tells us that:

ὁδὸς ἄνω κάτω μία καὶ ὠυτή.

—the way up and the way down are one and the same.

'EAST COKER'

The key of 'East Coker' is struck in the opening; 'In my beginning is my end', a reversal of Mary Stuart's motto. 'Burnt Norton' has, of course, pursued this theme, but has stressed a different aspect of it; it is much occupied with the visionary experience and its alternative and successor, the purgatorial discipline of *askesis*. 'In my beginning is my end' suggests not only circularity, but the stability of the experience which is at the centre of, and gives meaning to, the circling succession of change and decay. There is, as there was in 'Burnt Norton', a conscious ambiguity in the word 'end', which, if you do not think of it as a temporal word, means purpose; and if you do not think of 'end' as a temporal word, you may think of 'beginning' in a non-temporal way too, 'beginning' as a movement out of time into a timeless world. Thus 'beginning' is the purpose, or end, of a life, as it is also the ending of an old life. And thus, too, beginning in the sense of being born implies not only the end in death, but the purpose in assuming new life.

Thus, 'In my beginning is my end', while, on one level, it describes the tying of the self to succession and decay, to the cycle of life and death, on another level describes independence of that process. 'In succession'—that is in the processes of time, 'Houses rise and fall, crumble, are extended', and so does the 'house' of the body, to use a metaphor which Eliot has used many times before, and implies here. The process is extended beyond the individual body, as is hinted by the title: Eliot's distant relative, Sir Thomas Elyot, lived in East Coker in the sixteenth century; not only is the house an image of the personal body, but the house as family too.

The place, East Coker, then, is an immediate personal reminder to Eliot of change and decay, of history and family; the association with family history adds another extension of meaning to 'my beginning': the personal self is not something which springs into being at a single point of time; it is part of a historical process, and 'my beginning' is not to be thought of simply as my birth into the world, but the whole process of time and history which converges on me, now, here.

Like 'Burnt Norton', 'East Coker' is a place which contains images; but to be careful we must say that it is not place which contains images, but a state of mind, a 'point of view' which is shaped by the associations of place, and history of place. The associations are made very specific by direct quotation from Sir Thomas Elyot (*The Governour*, I, xxi), describing 'dauncinge' as an image of the sacrament of matrimony; the pattern (as in 'Burnt Norton' words and music are the pattern) which 'betokeneth concorde.' In Elyot this sacrament had profound meaning as a figure of the ordered unity of existence and the ordered unity of the universe within God's supreme will: 'an honourable estate, signifying unto us the mystical union that is betwixt Christ and his Church.'

But Eliot's attitude to the sacrament, to the 'necessarye coniunction' is highly ambivalent; there is a sense in which the repeated, absorbed, preoccupied rituals of ordinary existence are seen as absurd, meaningless, leading nowhere:

> Feet rising and falling,
> Eating and drinking. Dung and death.

There is a sense in which 'the weak pipe and the little drum', the distant, faintly recalled memories of a bucolic past which we all share (Eliot is raising our ghosts again) are insignificant when set within the rolling, circular processes of change and decay. Both our rustic ancestors and ourselves, in the warm hypnotic haze, seem simply to be the slaves of time. But the emotion Eliot expresses is not simply one of arrogant distaste: the ritual, the pattern defines a relationship between the country folk and the fields where they dance and where they labour which has strength and warmth and reality; or which once had these qualities. Now they are memories only to be distantly apprehended, in puzzled wonderment, 'If you do not come too close, if you do not come too close', for the pattern they dance out in their living has a magical order to it quite different from the separation and isolation which we, the visitors (pressing back against a bank while the van passes) must regret: 'coupling of man and woman/And that of beasts' does not have the sniff of disdain about it which a superficial reading would suggest; or at least that disdain is in a complex creative tension with awe and regret for the way 'keeping time' can order the universe so that man, stars and beasts all partake in the one pattern:

> Keeping time
> Keeping the rhythm in their dancing
> As in their living in the living seasons
> The time of the seasons and the constellations
> The time of milking and the time of harvest
> The time of the coupling of man and woman
> And that of beasts.

Eliot implicitly contrasts this lost order, warm, complete though somewhat absurd in its bucolic earthiness, with a contemporary life which lacks a necessary and ordered contact with time. The slide and change of time is given its objective correlative in the wrinkle and slide of wind and sea; in this flux, lacking the old certainties, 'I am here/Or there, or elsewhere'. And the ending truncates the opening paradox: 'In my beginning'. If, now, place ceases to matter and time ceases to matter; if the ancient, imagined simplicity is irrevocably gone, then our purposes are refreshed: we can and must, at every moment, begin at the beginning.

And yet 'East Coker' is in many very important ways about a particular time. It was written and first published during that uneasy period between the beginning of the Second World War and the invasion of Belgium and the Netherlands in May 1940. The 'phoney war', as it was called then, was a time of peculiar uncertainty; the whole of Britain had been taught to expect and fear a war so total that nothing would be left standing: the bombers would fly in and destroy everything in a few catastrophic days or weeks. Families were separated; children were packed off into the country while fathers and elder brothers went for military training. But at first nothing much happened; the Battle of Britain did not begin until July 1940, and while Holland, Belgium and France surrendered one by one the people of Britain sat waiting in a world gone mad, wondering what would happen next.

The formal study 'What is the late November doing' continues the note of time paradox which runs through the first section, but develops it in a different way. The ending of the year bizarrely mimics its beginnings in the spring and its maturity in the summer. This is not simply to be taken as a description of freakish weather conditions; the concurrence of snowdrops, hollyhocks, roses and snow is literally impossible in November or any other month. The transition into the description of strange events in the heavens directs us rather to take the passage as we take, for instance, the Ides of March in *Julius Caesar* (II. ii. 19–23) or the strange events related to the Old Man and Ross in *Macbeth* (II. iv. 6–8). Shakespeare turns upside down the astrological convention that man's fate is governed by the movements of the stars, and makes the heavens reflect a disturbance in the human world. Eliot does the same, but with a wry ironic self consciousness, putting it all in a stylistically antique mode:

> Thunder rolled by the rolling stars
> Simulates triumphal cars
> Deployed in constellated wars

The manner is deliberately unreal, and reflects the feeling of unreality which England felt as it waited for the real engines of war to
deploy in the skies above it; but Eliot isn't only describing the period
he was living through.

In the section parallel to this one in 'Burnt Norton', Eliot imagined
the violence and sensuality of 'the boarhound and the boar' reconciled
among the stars, and spoke of 'we', through formal pattern, translat-
ing the raw disorder of experience into 'light upon the figured leaf.'
But in 'East Coker' the formal study challenges its parallel in 'Burnt
Norton' with a different point of view upon reality. Far from being
reconciled among the stars, the disorder of passion continues, 'the
snowdrops writhing under feet' (notice the violence of 'writhing' in
contrast to the chasteness of snowdrops): and the disorder is not
simply one of the seasons, or simply of the world entering yet again
into a war to end wars. Eliot is not only speaking of the experience of
the world but also of the experience of the individual man; the simple
clear emotion of youth parodied by a monstrous late flowering of
passion in age; the question whether the world will ever conquer its
bloodlust, and the bitter recognition that passion mocks experience,
merge with the violent distortion of the seasons and the constella-
tions into a cosmic vortex (rather like the fracturing whirlwind which
ends 'Gerontion'). The end of the world felt near in November 1939;
wisdom and dispassionate serenity very hard to gain; Robert Frost
enquires whether the world will end in fire or ice; Eliot discovers its
ending not in frigid stagnation but in unseasonably monstrous
passions. But the fire is not the cleansing and refining purgatorial fire
of Dante this time; it is a fire like the Chaos which, in the Greek creation myth, preceded the formation of the universe; the fire of Herakleitos from which everything arises and to which everything returns,
and which symbolizes the constant change and strife of the Universe.
At the same too, it is the fire which all England awaited: 'If we fail',
said Churchill, 'then the whole world . . . will sink into the abyss
of a new dark age.' Eliot's even more sombre fear was that the dark
age had already begun, and that the only possible defence against
chaos was a lonely and continuous struggle for self-discipline and
humility.

It is, then, entirely in keeping with this difficult and almost desperate sense of foreboding that Eliot should be restless with self-
questioning throughout this Quartet; that he should round upon
himself and question his own skills, even his rôle as a poet:

That was a way of putting it—not very satisfactory:
A periphrastic study in a worn-out poetical fashion,
Leaving one still with the intolerable wrestle
With words and meanings. The poetry does not matter.

But the questioning does not stop there: it is a questioning of poetry; it is a questioning of traditional wisdom, the deception of 'the quiet voiced elders': it is even—and this is an insight which, though it in no way contradicts Eliot's commitment to tradition, stresses an unfamiliar aspect of it—a questioning of the value of experience:

There is, it seems to us,
At best, only a limited value
In the knowledge derived from experience.
The knowledge imposes a pattern, and falsifies,
For the pattern is new in every moment
And every moment is a new and shocking
Valuation of all we have been.

The perception becomes central to *Murder in the Cathedral*, in the scene where the fourth tempter outbids the other three; it is implicit in Eliot's acceptance of Bradley's critique of time. But so far, in *The Waste Land*, in *Ash Wednesday*, in his other poems and in his criticism; in his commitment to Anglo-Catholic orthodoxy and ritual; in his Toryism and in his disenchantment with radical feeling of any kind, Eliot has followed a deep instinct for the established pattern; for the virtues, if not of personal experience, at least of the accumulated experience of humanity. And this, of course, is the key to the continuity of feeling which the passage only appears to contradict. It is the personal vision which is the illusion, whether it is of evanescent delight or of horror, not only 'nel mezzo del cammin di nostra vita':

not only in the middle way
But all the way, in a dark wood, in a bramble,
On the edge of a grimpen, where is no secure foothold,
And menaced by monsters, fancy lights,
Risking enchantment.

The blind Samson, in the middle way of his heroic agony, laments his blindness 'amid the blaze of noon'; the blind Milton's pain and isolation in the depraved and godless world of the Restoration speaks through Samson. And Eliot's pain speaks through the parody of Samson in a bitter prophetic declamation, reminiscent of 'Difficulties of a Statesman', upon the waste of human life and energy in encompassing petty material ends.

But it is something more than a grouse about materialism; it is, in the context of this menacing interval between a tawdry bungled peace and a savage bloody war, a lament for lost purpose, or a world which seemed then (and still, sometimes, seems) never to have had any sense of purpose at all:

> And cold the sense and lost the motive of action.
> And we all go with them, into the silent funeral
> Nobody's funeral, for there is no one to bury.

The wry blend of bitter lament and facetious dismissal is characteristic of Eliot: perhaps too characteristic, in a way.

In the parallel sections in 'Burnt Norton' the injunction 'Descend lower' was an invitation to a very purposeful journey; the ascetic's descent into the dark night of the soul to harrow a personal hell; to seek darkness and emptiness as a means of achieving fulness and light. Half-jokingly Eliot once said that he was talking about going down into the London Underground: 'while the world moves/In appetency, on its metalled ways/Of time past and time future.' In 'East Coker' the underground railway image returns; it is characteristic of the way Eliot's viewpoint has shifted that the journey described is no longer the purposeful descent, but the aimless movement of bodies in space and time, and that the horror of hollowness should be so much more acutely felt. Compare:

> Only a flicker
> Over the strained time-ridden faces
> Distracted from distraction by distraction
>
> (BN, III)

with the long complex of similes in 'East Coker' which faintly mimics the Miltonic simile, but stretched into a rambling line:

> As, in a theatre
> The lights are extinguished, for the scene to be changed
> With a hollow rumble of wings, with a movement of darkness
> on darkness,
> And we know that the hills and the trees, the distant panorama
> And the bold imposing facade are all being rolled away—
> Or as, when an underground train, in the tube, stops too
> long between stations

And the conversation rises and slowly fades into silence
And you see behind every face the mental emptiness deepen
Leaving only the growing terror of nothing to think about;
Or when, under ether, the mind is conscious but conscious
of nothing—

The 'Burnt Norton' passage is a fairly predictable piece of rhetoric. The similes in 'East Coker' are not; the simile form suspends the attention, as it were: 'As in, . . . or as when, . . . or when . . .' and we are waiting for a resolution, while travelling through a series of images which bear upon the resolution: we wait for 'So . . .'— but it never comes. And the similes are cast in a lengthened line (the ear, catching the faintly Miltonic note, expects a decasyllable and four stresses to the line; it has to tolerate the excess) which mimics the aimless movement, the 'hollow rumble of wings', the conversation rising and slowly fading. Thus, when the syntactical resolution, the expected 'So . . .' never comes, there is a curious appropriateness; the ordered Miltonic rhetorical structure is far too precise for the world described: our expectaton is defeated and we are firmly shunted on to another line.

But it is a line of retreat. We are led into the statement of the contemplative way, not with the purposefulness of 'Descend lower' nor with the calm decision of 'Little Gidding', but as a retreat from horror. It's a familiar impulse in Eliot; a natural enough impulse, too, for the time when the terror of war, unreal (as it seemed then for so many) as theatrical scenery manipulated noisily on the wings, threatened the end of everything with a ghostly menace. Familiar and natural, yes, but oddly inadequate.

'And now abideth faith, hope and love, these three; but the greatest of these is love.' Eliot does not change Paul's order of preference, not precisely. But there is a strange insecurity in Eliot's retreat into the consolations of the hermit. Paul's magnificent hymn of praise to love admits of no doubt at all of its nature, or of the possibility that, love being real, it could be 'love of the wrong thing.' In Paul's account of the matter love exalts all other virtues, purifies all other virtues, comprehends all other virtues: 'Love never faileth'; but Eliot fears the expansiveness, the generosity of Paul's claim, its joyful enthusiasm.

Eliot's 'classicism' was perhaps always a flimsy and uncertain reaction to the failure of Romanticism; more a matter of keeping the stubborn Romantic impulse, the deceptions of memory and desire, bridled and curbed. But the repressed fantasies chafe, gathering power yet remaining fundamentally unchanged. Expansive emotion may merely be self indulgence, but it may also be the means towards a refining of emotion: there are errors and absurdities on the way, but these are part of the process by which love may become itself. To encapsulate a remembered ecstasy and anticipate a transfiguring fulfilment is to put all the rest of life in brackets, exchange the inevitably repeated errors of maturation for one long grey parenthesis in which faith hope and love dissolve into a thin solution of discontent, and the discontent is called faith.

> Whisper of running streams, and winter lightning,
> The wild thyme unseen and the wild strawberry,
> The laughter in the garden, echoed ecstasy.

The memories are beautiful; that's true. And the beauty is not enough; that's true too. But what might make it enough; what might transfigure it, is not to 'wait without hope' and 'wait without love'; even though hope and love might misdirect again and again. If the value of the remembered garden, ('echoed ecstasy' in the sense that it is no more than a figure of the true ecstasy) is in its pointing, not to Eden but the garden of the agony, in its prefiguration of our sharing in the anguish of Christ at Gethsemane and Golgotha, then it would seem to follow that we must imitate Christ (never a man for being still and waiting without hope or love). I do not think I understand Christianity; much less Christian humility; but this, or something like this should, I would suppose, be at the heart of both.

And I believe that this would have been felt by St John of the Cross too, whom Eliot imitates with little change in the passage beginning: 'In order to arrive there.'[10] As Eliot says, he is 'repeating/ Something I have said before': not just something that he has said before; something which he sees as central to the tradition, and leaves 'some dead master' to say through his own voice. But perhaps the claimed relationship with St John of the Cross is not entirely legitimate.

The next Movement, Section IV, lacks the surprising and delightful compression of its counterpart in 'Burnt Norton'; indeed, it labours the conceit rather heavily, seeking a kind of balance and a kind of wit which is somewhat obsolete, a little frigid for the powerful

emotional significances dissolved in the form. It's a little too portentous, and awkward too; but this is, in a way, appropriate. The whole
Quartet is concerned with the unsatisfactory, and the poetry itself as
unsatisfactory; and this devotional exercise is offered with a half-
concealed shrug of deprecation, a 'that was a way of putting it'.

The meditation is on Good Friday, the day of the Crucifixion; but
the sacrifice of Christ is in more than Crucifixion: it is in the Incarnation itself; a paradox which leads, in a series of daring transformations,
to the successive paradoxes of the Movement. In the acceptance of
Incarnation, Christ accepts a personal death, and thus becomes patient
as well as agent; a sufferer as well as actor. Thus he becomes 'the
wounded surgeon', sharing the distemper which his art cures. The
Son is at one and the same time the Holy Ghost or the Comforter and
the Father, 'the dying nurse' and 'the ruined millionaire' who created
the hospital earth, and whose 'absolute paternal care' brings about
our death. But Christ is not entirely distinct from 'us'—all humanity,
and in particular Christian humanity, is involved in Christ. We may
recall the opening of 'What the Thunder Said':

> He who was living is now dead
> We who were living are now dying
> With a little patience

with its curious, slowly recognized word-play on 'patience' (which
may mean suffering, being the patient); a word which links the poem
distantly, but in a real way, with the themes of action, suffering and
instrumentality in *Murder in the Cathedral* and elsewhere.

The 'enigma of the fever chart' which can only be resolved by the
paradox of the dying God, is given another expression in the fourth
stanza, with its paradoxes of heat and cold:

> The chill ascends from feet to knees
> The fever sings in mental wires.
> If to be warmed, then I must freeze
> And quake in frigid purgatorial fires
> Of which the flame is roses, and the smoke is briars.

One shivers with cold in a fever as one's temperature rises; both the
outer heat and the inner cold, though pain, have a curative function,
cooking the invading organism to destroy it; a paradigm of the purifying pain of spiritual discipline. The stanza recalls *BN* II's physio-

[250]

logical imagery 'The trilling wire in the blood', 'The dance along the artery/The circulation of the lymph', associated as it is with the figure of ascent in the tree. But the image suffers a deliberate reversal; it is the chill which ascends, and the reward is much more ambiguous. The reward is the pain of fire (frigid fire). Fire flowers into roses, into the symbol of divine society; 'the smoke is briars', wild roses, but in their sweetness associated with pain and difficulty; indeed, associated in a faint but recognizable echo with Christ's crown of thorns: spiritual beauty and spiritual pain are necessarily involved with each other.

The last stanza clearly refers to the Eucharist, dwelling on its paradoxical nature, on its overtones of pain and violence, but implying the doctrinal pattern which underlies the pattern of imagery (as it does in so much of Eliot) that when we 'spiritually eat the flesh of Christ, and drink his blood; then we dwell in Christ and Christ in us; we are one with Christ and Christ with us.' Thus our life which is a process of dying involves Christ continually dying; Christ's transcendent life and his healing power is within our dying humanity.

The interesting question is not so much the meaning of the paradoxes as the concentrated and elaborate interest which Eliot shows in them absorbedly delighting in them rather as did the Metaphysical poets of the seventeenth century, but to the extent that the play of paradox holds back the poem, makes it static and word-bound. Again, I believe that the paradoxes are curiously appropriate to the time; word games which hold the passionate problems in a cold, yet curiously desperate and anxious paralysis of attitude much like the paralysis of the world in the months when the poem was written.

The last Movement begins by speaking again of the inadequacy of words and the sense of impotence which goes with it, using the imagery of war and preparation for war to express one's shabby unpreparedness in the face of the enemy:

> And so each venture
> Is a new beginning, a raid on the inarticulate
> With shabby equipment always deteriorating
> In the general mess of imprecision of feeling,
> Undisciplined squads of emotion.

It is this dissatisfaction and the restlessness that arises from it which pivots a change in the emotional tenor of the poem; retrieves its tendency towards a hermetic retreat. 'I said to my soul be still' swings round into another attitude which does not contradict it, but rather comprehends and gives the meditative experience new direction:

> Old men ought to be explorers
> Here and there does not matter
> We must be still and still moving
> Into another intensity
> For a further union, a deeper communion.

The end looks forward to 'The Dry Salvages'; it also looks back to the cancelled parts of 'Death by Water', and the Dantean myth of Ulysses and his aged crew travelling beyond the Pillars of Hercules to an unknown destiny. In the turn of phrasing: 'We must be still and still moving', it anticipates the interest which Eliot shows in 'The Dry Salvages' (and elsewhere) in the Bhagavata doctrine of the yoga of action. But most clear of all is the way it is so deftly explicit about the aim of the journey 'union' and its instrument 'communion', before returning to the home note: 'In my end is my beginning.'

This pivoting is accomplished through a very complex perception which releases the poem from the paralysis which had begun to threaten it. In some sense or other all four of the Quartets are different attempts to find 'home'; 'East Coker' most obviously so of all; and the attempt in 'East Coker' so far is only marginally successful; its memories of the past and associations with history offer no stability, merely an intensification of the sense of change and of exile. And in the unease and instability of the impending war, in the transitory condition of unrest which underlies everything, it is difficult to imagine a 'home' until one realizes, 'Home is where one starts from'; and this releases one from the anxieties, earlier expressed, about the value of experience and the patterns discovered and rejected, deceiving and ineffective, as one accumulates memories. 'In my end is my beginning' may transmute 'Home is where one starts from' into 'Home is where one ends'; and by a further series of imaginative transmutations, home is every moment:

> Not the intense moment
> Isolated, with no before and after,
> But a lifetime burning in every moment
> And not the lifetime of one man only
> But of old stones that cannot be deciphered.

The perception has an intensely humanizing effect; it produces one

[252]

of those rare incidents in which Love, always a difficult matter for Eliot, becomes understood, becomes transfigured into a shining reality in his verse; and when even human, earthly love, and the tranquillity of domestic affection and peace, elsewhere shunned as distracting and inessential, is seen as central to human sanity and peace:

> There is a time for the evening under starlight,
> A time for the evening under lamplight
> (The evening with the photograph album).
> Love is most nearly itself
> When here and now cease to matter.

'THE DRY SALVAGES'

In some ways 'The Dry Salvages' is the least satisfactory of the quartets as poetry, but entirely necessary for 'the complete consort'. 'East Coker' extends the exploration from the individual's vision to a wider field; to the family history of a man and thence to the history of a civilization, and makes individual experience a part of the universal process, the universal process a part of individual experience. 'The Dry Salvages' carries this a stage further. The meditations upon the river and the sea are not entirely, of course, reflections upon the pattern of social and economic geography (though they are this, on one level).

All the commentators on the poem agree that there are memories of the Mississippi here; the title refers to one of the landfalls which might greet a traveller crossing the Atlantic; and it is appropriate that the place which gives the poem so much of its character should be what we call the New World, but was for Eliot himself an old world left behind him long ago.

The Waste Land echoes Conrad's *Heart of Darkness* in its treatment of the river-image; 'The Dry Salvages' echoes both. Conrad's Thames, for all the complex structures of civilization which surrounded it, was a river not very different from the dark primitive river which Marlow followed into the heart of the mystery, shedding all his assurance of civilization until he could see over the edge into the abyss of life's emptiness. In *Heart of Darkness* and *The Waste Land* the river continues to flow through the unreal city, through all the civilization which in terms of the river's time is as brief as summer lightning. The river is thus a time-scale, a measure against which the brevity of man's personal hopes and achievements can be measured; a constant unregarded reminder of the unhurried rhythms of the natural world. It is also, by extension, a reminder of those things which remain continuously valid in man throughout the dramatic alarms and excursions of history, those essentially human patterns of feeling and thought which finally are far more important than the things which seem to be most pressingly urgent at any one moment of time. It is thus a symbol of considerable power and validity for one who writes with the conservative vision of reality, whose assertive Catholic and Tory view of man urges him to see the present concerns of the individual or the immediate concerns of a society as significant only as part of a much wider pattern.

Eliot was such a writer; he was also a writer who believed that poetry depended upon the ritual, magical and religious view of life; and this attitude is logically one with his Conservatism. Thus the image of the river as a god is not an entirely fanciful one; if you attend to the world around you, you may see many gods, though you will not name them so; presences in nature which convince some part of your consciousness that they possess a form of life which you do not understand and do not wish to understand, but which is invested with a dignity and an age which is beyond your comprehension. Wordsworth, Hopkins, Shakespeare, Conrad were conscious of these presences; 'primitive' peoples have always been conscious of them, and there is a primitive in each of us. Eliot, for all his civilized, often prim, often nagging tendency to over-sophistication of manner, was also more than usually attentive to these vestigial patterns of instinctive awe and fear and joy.

The American setting is significant, as I have said, for the American experience is much closer in time to the primitive experience; it is not so very long since the Mississippi and St Louis were the frontier of civilization; the whole process of change which Eliot describes took place within the life-span of many who were still alive when Eliot was growing up in St Louis; *Huckleberry Finn* was written only four years before Eliot's birth, and the world described in it was only recent history. Hawthorne and Fenimore Cooper were not so very much further back in history, and their preoccupation with the meeting point between the civilized and the primitive, with the world of pagan magic never too far away, continues to be a preoccupation of the sensitive American thinker to this day.

The rhythms of the river are paralleled by the rhythms of the seasons; both enter into the consciousness of the growing child, an ever-present reminder of something older, something infinitely slower and more patient than man:

> His rhythm was present in the nursery bedroom,
> In the rank ailanthus of the April dooryard,
> In the smell of grapes on the autumn table,
> And the evening circle in the winter gaslight.

If the river is present within us as a rhythmical pattern of consciousness in which our relationship to a distant past becomes immediate and profoundly significant, so that the magical way of thinking becomes natural and we think of rivers or mountains as gods, we may think of the sea as a vast reservoir of experience much older than a personal experience. If 'no man is an island, entire of itself; every man is a piece of the continent',[11] then the sea about us is that which contains the continent. Since it is not part of us, it remains a mystery which cannot be investigated directly; it is not part of the human world. But it touches upon the human continent, and we can think of the land's edge as part of the sea, just as, at the furthest reaches of our human experience, we may receive intimations of something other than the human, 'hints of earlier and other creation.'

The sea, then, acts as another image of the larger context of man's experience; within this context each individual man's daily concerns become part of a larger pattern in which nothing is ever lost; the sea absorbs everything that has ever happened into its enormous and impassive rhythmical movement, casting up from time to time, without design or purpose, accidental reminders of its vast inclusiveness, images for the mind to work upon. Not only images of a geological past but of the brevity of man's life and endeavour:

> It tosses up our losses, the torn seine,
> The shattered lobsterpot, the broken oar
> And the gear of foreign dead men.

The river is the presence within one of an abhuman consciousness of time and space; the sea the inexplicable and vast abhuman context within which the continent of man lies.

> The salt is on the briar rose.
> The fog is in the fir trees.

Wherever it touches the land the sea reaches into it, affecting every part of its contours, every aspect of its life, and in the same way the experience of man is touched by existence beyond experience. The wild rose, beauty and pain of spiritual experience, is touched by evidences of something older and stronger than man, which flow inland, too, fog seeping into the forests. But whatever the sea is as metaphor, it is also the sea. It has many voices, and these voices are, if we are attentive to the vestigial magical consciousness within us, the voices of gods. However, Eliot's description of the sea would be ineffective if he were merely developing the complex metaphor, and not rendering, with marvellous delicacy of movement, the swell and fall, the many sounds of wind, stone, water, which blend together into a total impression of the endless impassive motion of the Atlantic (for it is distinctively the Atlantic that he evokes, not any other ocean).

It would be interesting to have an extended account of the symbolic uses of the sea in various literatures; the sea of Homer and Plato, and the sea of Renaissance Italian literature is distinctively a Mediterranean, a sea of confined spaces, bright with sunlight and studded with islands; subject to sudden terror with the rising of the tempest as in, for instance, the sudden tempest of Acts 27, but in which storm and terror were sudden unlooked-for visitations. In the literature of the cultures which surround the Atlantic, however, the calm sea and prosperous voyage are unexpected reliefs from the mysterious continuous menace of the vast grey sea, and yet the sea is often seen as something which challenges the consciousness of man, reveals the presence within his mind of great, new, strange tracts of experience quite different from the experiences of human contact and intercourse, tracts of being to be known but never understood. The gods of the Atlantic are hostile, withdrawn and inhuman, their fury not like the crotchety bouts of ill temper of the Olympian Neptune, their quiet moments lacking in the benign complaisance of their Mediterranean counterpart, but full of vast promise of freedom and the joy of release.

The movement of the sea-passage works subtly by a matched

sequence of rhetorical groupings: the emphatic stresses of 'The séa hówl/And the séa yélp' followed by the falling rhythms of 'are different voices' and 'often together heard'—the falling effect, as of the wave receding, would be spoilt entirely if the normal word-order 'often heard together' had been preserved. Then there follows a whole series of phrases, subtly parallel in construction and yet varying in length of rhythmic unit until they partially resolve at 'are all sea voices':

> the whine in the rigging,
> The menace and caress of wave that breaks on water,
> The distant rote in the granite teeth,
> And the wailing warning from the approaching headland
> Are all sea voices,

—but the resolution is only partial. The rhythm picks up again from this point of recession and continues without more significant pause in the ebb and flow of movement until the end of the twenty-three line sentence.

Donne's passing-bell re-appears in a changed form: not a bell rung by man for man warning him of mortality and reminding him of the ultimate unity of all men, but a bell rung by the rise and swell of the sea rocking the warning buoy. 'Burnt Norton' had begun with a critique of time; 'East Coker' turns to grapple with its challenges. Now 'The Dry Salvages' discovers more than one sense for time; it speaks of a kind of time which does not obey human rules and is not amenable to measurement by human standards. Bergson's *le temps* and *la durée*, clock-time and subjective time, are both unreal times when set against the great inhuman rhythms of the natural world; time of rising and weathering of mountain ranges, time of silting of oceans and rising of sea-floors, time of oceans and of rivers. This time is not unlimited in the context of eternity, but it serves to measure the insignificance of other forms of time. It is the nearest thing to the objective reality that time has to offer, and its presence within us, as the river, and around us, as the sea, may help us to stand apart from

> The time counted by anxious worried women
> Lying awake, calculating the future

It may be that this passage refers in a passing way to Penelope and her Joycean counterpart, Molly Bloom; it certainly pleads for a new kind of distancing from the problems of time, not the resting place in the innocent paradisal image of the rose garden, but a stoic withdrawal from suffering which in some ways resembles more the Hindu or Buddhist ways (as we shall see later, the *Bhagavad Gita* is an important point of reference in the Quartet) than the more usual Christian interpretations of the virtues of faith, hope and love. And yet the echo of the Prayer Book, 'As it was in the beginning, is now and ever shall be: world without end', in 'the ground swell, that is and was from the beginning' is entirely appropriate, bringing us back to the long view of life and time and reality in the Christian tradition. This leads in its turn to the reappearance of the bell; not only does Donne's passing bell toll for all mankind because 'I am involved in mankind', but the ancient time of the river and the sea, which are in us and all about us, toll for thee too, because I am involved in the seemingly endless rise and swell of natural time, and it is involved, inescapably, in my whole being.

The second Movement, the formal study, carries these reflections a stage further. The sestina form is interesting, and as Donald Davie has pointed out, seems at times to be desperately forced, most notably in its search for five plausible rhymes for 'motionless'. Perhaps Davie's strictures upon the formal awkwardnesses of the section are a little unjust. The very repetitiveness of rhyme and movement suggest the monotony which is described; the slight note of desperation in repetition of 'motionless', 'emotionless', 'devotionless', 'oceanless', and the return of the sestina to the home rhyme 'motionless', describe the weariness of the cycle, the repeated sense of *déjà vu*, and yet again the massive ineluctable rhythms of 'time not our time' which surround and limit the weariness of 'our time'.

'East Coker' ended by declaring that old men ought to be explorers, hinting at the old myth of Ulysses sailing beyond the pillars of Hercules to discover the unknown; 'The Dry Salvages' II (a late fulfilment of the cancelled lines of 'Death by Water') evokes the difficulties of the journey. 'In my end is my beginning' is a statement confident enough that there is a beginning and an end; 'Dry Salvages' II evokes the despairing soul's fear that there may indeed be no end, no final release from the repetitive cycle, no purpose: 'Where is there an end of it, the soundless wailing . . .?' The section is near to despair; it is the Leaden Echo of the *Four Quartets*, approaching closely to the final horror that, within this endless repetitive pattern of time, even prayer becomes impossible and destructive: where is an end of 'the unprayable/Prayer at the calamitous annunciation?'

'Annunciation' is not capitalized here as it is in the sixth stanza; here it is 'the calamitous annunciation', the disastrous announcement, not the 'one Annunciation.' The syntax is queerly distorted, but the meaning can only be 'when will there be an end to the continuous ever-present announcement of disaster?' This continued prayer is the 'prayer of the bone on the beach', which is 'the bone's prayer to Death its God'. Within the seemingly endless pattern of time it seems the only possible prayer, the prayer which, without our assent, is made continually by our very existence as flesh and bone within a world of time. The rhythms of the river within us, the sea all about us, are the passing bell which announces this continued death; or the counter image to the Angelus bell, which celebrates the God of Death as the Angelus celebrates the God of Life. The sea-journey is slow and inevitable failure, accompanied continually by this reminder of hopelessness and pointlessness, which, it seems, can never be avoided: 'the undeniable/Clamour of the bell of the last annunciation.'

But, as Hopkins, reaching an apparent ending to 'The Leaden Echo' in the tolling of the word 'despair', finds another, a Golden Echo, in 'Spare', so Eliot ends on a tentative, distant, barely recognized hope of an answer: Where is an end of it? There is no end of it, 'Only the hardly, barely prayable/Prayer of the one Annunciation.'

The Annunication, capitalized thus, is the announcement by the angel to Mary that she was to bear Christ; the announcement of the Incarnation, the Word made flesh. This is 'the end of it', both in the sense that it is the ultimate purpose which lies behind the world of time, and in the sense that it offers the Christian the means by which he may achieve a life which is not in the scale of time, by sharing in the resurrection. This is the point of time which organizes the whole of time into a pattern, if we become capable of the prayer (that is, the realization of the Annunciation in our own existences) converting time from mere pointless addition of moment to moment, the prayer of the bone on the beach which is a celebration only of death, to a system, a direction, an end and a beginning which are the same.

The sequence which follows the sestina develops the point. Once again the sudden experience of illumination, the moment in the rose garden, is questioned, seen to be of limited value in itself, though of immense value in that it initiates a search for meaning:

> We had the experience but missed the meaning
> And approach to the meaning restores the experience
> In a different form, beyond any meaning
> We can assign to happiness

—and Eliot repeats the point that a personal experience is not limited to an individual's life, but is a distillation of the life of many generations into one experience. The whole passage is perhaps the most nerveless and slack in the *Four Quartets*, a passage in which Eliot takes the idea that 'the poetry does not matter' a little too far and writes poetry that does not matter.

The question where is an end of it? is one which has occupied many thinkers in many ages; and the thought is bound up with a collective experience: 'the past experience revived in the meaning / Is not the experience of one life only / But of many generations.' But notice that the experience which is shared is not the raw material of experience, but the experience, as it were, when developed by a process which universalizes it. Thus, though in the experience of the Christian, 'the calamitous annunciation', the repeated reminder of mortality which time brings again and again, can be transmuted into the specifically Christian concept of 'the one Annunciation', the announcement of death can be converted into the announcement of life, other cultures may express the meaning in different ways. The rose-leaves which Sa'di's friend gathers must suffer 'the silent withering of autumn flowers', but the decay is arrested in the eternal rose garden. Hindu *advaita* sees the duality of time, 'Time the destroyer and time the preserver', the Gods Rudra and Vishnu reconciled in the singleness of Brahma. The 'agony' is continuous; the Buddhist repeats the grief of the sorrowing Buddha, the Hindu the crisis of doubt which holds back Arjuna from taking part in the battle, the Christian the agony of Christ in the garden at Gethsemane; but the resolution, however differently it is expressed, is essentially the same.

The reference to Krishna at the beginning of Movement III is therefore a way of indicating the one-ness of meaning which may resolve the many-ness of human experience. The setting of the quartet in the New World is a way of stressing the newness of every experience, the nearness of any civilization to the unshaped elements of nature; but the passage to India which the quartet undertakes isn't a geographical journey. The world of India is just as new, the boat just as leaky, the howl and the yelp of the sea just as menacing, and the end of the journey just as much a translation from time and space.

In the *Bhagavad Gita* the god-bearing image is that of Krishna who descends like Christ into the world of humanity. Arjuna, the representative man, comes to the battlefield, which is an image of the strife of the world, convinced of his duty to fight. But at the last moment he is afflicted by a crisis of conscience. Killing is a sin, and to kill those we love is a greater sin: how then can he kill other humans whom he has a duty to love? The problem is a metaphor for a larger problem—how can we act without sin while still within a world of sin? His doubt and horror is a dark night of the soul, and in Hindu mysticism as in Christian mysticism the moment of doubt is a step in the path towards enlightenment.

Krishna, like Buddha, teaches that the essential thing is the unchanging spirit of man, not his mortal body, the changing patterns of the senses. But Krishna advocates that Arjuna should continue to act and fight on the battlefield, but act without passion, without attachment to the world, as it were *impersonally*, so that the essential self is liberated from action: 'Yet these actions bind me not, O Khananjaya; as one impartial I sit not attached to these actions.' Thus, Krishna says to Arjuna: 'Know me, though without action and changeless, as the doer thereof/Actions stain me not; no desire have I for the fruit of actions. He who this understands me is not bound by actions.'[12]

Thus, in terms of Hindu thought, Becket, Harry and Celia follow this 'yoga of action'—they continue in the world, acting in its battlefield, but without attachment to action, or to space or time. In the context of *Bhagavata* thought, this is 'the one Annunciation', and Krishna the Word which releases it. The Word releases man from time, from the rhythm of the sea, and if this release takes place then future and past become indistinct from each other, the future like a keepsake of memory:

a faded song, a Royal Rose or a lavender spray
Of wistful regret for those who are not yet here to regret,
Pressed between yellow leaves of a book that has never been opened.

The second epigraph from Herakleitos is referred to in passing; the recollection confirms the multiplicity of the idea, its independence of culture or time. The curious use of the image of the 'Royal

Rose' must be noticed here. In one way it refers to the moment of illumination in the rose garden, the image preserved in the memory of an experience which in itself seemed to be the truth, but was only a hint of the truth. This, though, is combined with a recollection of English history, the roses of York and Lancaster which became a symbol of civil war and then, at last, when united, of the kingdom of England. These are ancient memories preserved in an image which retains none of the horror, the bloodshed, the vanity, pride and ambition, but still evokes some passing wonder at a strange world which is in some way still part of our experience.

The imagery of movement which has occurred at this point in the quartet in 'Burnt Norton' and 'East Coker' returns, but in a changed way. Herakleitos asserts that you cannot put your foot into the same river twice, since it becomes a different river at every moment. If the river within us is in constant flux then we, too, are different beings at every moment, so 'time is no healer: the patient is no longer here.' The phrase recalls section IV of 'East Coker', but adds something further. If the process of living and dying are one and the same, the process doesn't progress from moment to moment, the whole drama is in each and every moment. Thus the further reference to the doctrine of the *Bhagavad Gita*, 'on whatever sphere of being / The mind of a man may be intent / At the time of death', in that sphere of being he remains after his death. And since 'the time of death is every moment', life becomes a succession of eternal moments, each of which is a whole life.

In 'Burnt Norton' and 'East Coker' the devotional exercise of section IV has drawn together the emotional pattern of the preceding sections and intensified them in a brief, highly organized meditation. In 'The Dry Salvages', Eliot, after having ranged so far through time and space, through cultures other than his own Christian culture, uses the section as a means of bringing the quartet back to 'The nearest place' by a highly conventional prayer which has, however, many overtones which relate it to other parts of the *Four Quartets*. The Lady, Mary, is the intercessor between man and God; her shrine is on a promontory where sea and land, the human and the abhuman, meet. Those who 'Ended their voyage on the sand, in the sea's lips / Or in the dark throat which will not reject them' recall Phlebas the Phoenician to mind. The experience which went into the cancelled parts of 'Death by Water' enters at many points into the whole Quartet, but with many mutations and additions. For instance, 'the dark throat' aptly recalls Jonah swallowed by the whale and his lament to the Lord:

> I am cast out of thy sight; yet I will look again toward thy holy temple. The waters compassed me about, even to the soul: the depth closed me round about, the weeds were wrapped about my head. I went down to the bottoms of the mountains; the earth with her bars was about me for ever: yet hast thou brought up my life from corruption, O LORD my God.
>
> (Jonah 2: 4–6)

Jonah's return to the land of the living fits well with the promise of the resurrection in the Angelus; like Lazarus or Christ, Jonah has been in 'the belly of hell', but has returned. Mary's intercession is sought for those who still remain in that hell, ignorant of the one Annunciation which will release them.

The Annunciation is not an event occurring at a single moment of time; it is the entering of the timeless into time, and the existence of the Holy Ghost is guarantee that this moment occurs at every point of time:

> But to apprehend
> The point of intersection of the timeless
> With time, is an occupation for the saint.

Against this Eliot sets the comedy of ancient and modern witchcraft: science fiction and psychiatry being modish modern versions of old superstitions which seek the excitement of the fantastic in games with time.

Movement I of 'Burnt Norton' is also recalled: 'music heard so deeply/That it is not heard at all, but you are the music/While the music lasts', but recalled in order to stress the imperfection of the image, the incompleteness of the sentiment, and to stress the orthodox doctrine's superiority over the personal revelation. The Annunciation announces Incarnation, and the Incarnation (according to Paul Elmer More the most essential mystery of Christianity) is the resolution of the problem of duality: 'Here the impossible union/ Of spheres of existence is actual,/Here the past and future/Are conquered, and reconciled.' 'The hint half guessed, the gift half understood', is a quiet word-play on the meaning of 'Eucharist', the blessed and willing offering, suggesting the way in which the accustomed ritual of a particular tradition is the means by which such freedom is gained—and this half-caught suggestion is fulfilled in the conclusion to the Movement, which has 'We', the undefeated finding freedom from time and place in a return 'home':

> We, content at the last
> If our temporal reversion nourish
> (Not too far from the yew-tree)
> The life of significant soil.

'LITTLE GIDDING'

It has been pointed out many times that the four quartets are each characterized by one of the four elements; 'Burnt Norton' by air, 'East Coker' by earth, 'The Dry Salvages' by water, and 'Little Gidding' by fire. There is no doubt that this structural system was in Eliot's mind as he wrote the *Four Quartets*, though it is possible that its full potentialities did not occur to him until after 'Burnt Norton' —there is not *very* much more stress on the element of air in this piece than there is, for instance, upon earth, though if one knows the pattern exists, one will, as it were, strengthen it as one reads 'Burnt Norton', by giving particular attention to the symbolism of air.

In adopting a pattern like this, Eliot is taking his cue from Joyce. In his review of *Ulysses*, Eliot had forecast that Joyce's 'mythological' methods would become a most significant mode of expression in the future, and we have seen how, in his own work, Eliot makes use of the philosophic myth both as a structuring device and as a source for the detail of his imagery. The elusive, airy beauty of the rose garden in 'Burnt Norton' is succeeded by the rustic earthiness of the dancers in 'East Coker'; the deceptive insubstantiality and illusion by the heavy gravitational pull of the cycle of change and decay binding the soul to earth. 'The Dry Salvages' replaces the image of death by earth with that of death by water, an image which has been significant in Eliot since 'The Love Song of J. Alfred Prufrock'. But the quartet in which the pattern has its greatest importance is 'Little Gidding'. Fire, in the philosophy of Herakleitos, is an image of the beginning of all and the end of all, the element for which all other elements are exchangeable, and the most powerful image of the constant flux which underlies all natural processes. F. M. Cornford writes of the idea in this way:[13]

Visible flame—fire as a natural object—is only one of many forms in the sense world, and, as such, is on a level with water, air and earth; fire dies into air, just as air dies into water, or water into earth. It is only one embodiment of a substance which must, in some way, be other than it, since that substance persists the same through all embodiments and transformations. Fire is considered primary, only because its mobile nature seems nearest to the moving force of life, and to be its most transparent medium. . . . What is really constant, throughout all the transformations, is *Logos*.

But the way in which Eliot uses the image of fire is composite—he draws from many other sources besides Herakleitos. We have seen now, in *The Waste Land* the Buddha's Fire Sermon with its magnificent rhetorical emphasis on the destructive agony of the senses, merges with the Christian image of the purgatorial fire. The second section of 'East Coker' forecasts the destructive fire which shall end the world; the fourth section of the same quartet speaks of the 'purgatorial fires', the refining fire which cures by burning. So the image of fire is, up to this point, a highly ambiguous one; destructive and yet creative, full of the most terrible pain and distress, but leading to the most exquisite beauty—'Of which the flame is roses, and the smoke is briars.'

'Little Gidding' weaves another thread into this complex fabric of metaphor: the fire of the Pentecost. In order to point the significance of this properly we must look at another structural pattern which can be discerned in the *Four Quartets*. The devotional exercises in the second sections of each quartet (except possibly 'Burnt Norton') all refer to a day which is highly significant in the Church Calendar, and to an incident of great significance in the symbolism of Christianity. In 'East Coker' there is a reference in the last line to Good Friday, the day of the Crucifixion. The last line of the devotional exercise in 'The Dry Salvages', by referring to the angelus, refers also to the celebration of the Annunciation on Lady Day. The day appropriate to 'Little Gidding' is the day of the Pentecost, or Whit Sunday, which celebrates the appearance of the Holy Ghost to the Apostles.

The Pentecost is the fulfilment of Christ's promise that he would intercede with the Father to send the Comforter to be with Christ's disciples after his death: 'And there appeared unto them cloven tongues like as of fire, and it sat upon each of them' (Acts 2 : 3), so that fire becomes at once comfort and fulfilment. 'Little Gidding' is full of the imagery of fire; it is also full of comfort and the promise of fulfilment, enfolding and completing the elusive and deceptive promise of 'Burnt Norton', the painful and difficult exploration of 'East Coker' and 'The Dry Salvages', yet pointing still to further promise and further exploration.

The place, Little Gidding, was the site of a seventeenth-century religious community founded by Nicholas Ferrar and his family. Charles I visited it two or three times, one of the times, perhaps, being after his defeat by Cromwell at Naseby in 1645. Two years later, in 1647, the community was disbanded by Parliament. It was modelled on the ideal of the Christian family; its people sought to live a peaceful, meditative, simple life, and yet, despite their humility and quietness, became unhappily involved in and destroyed by civil strife. It therefore represents the human longing for retreat into contemplation, but not the severe self-denying mortification of the monastic rule.

We can think of each of the place-names which give their titles to the *Four Quartets* as indicating different attempts by Eliot to seek 'home'. 'Burnt Norton' is an attempt to find home in the remembered vision of innocence and unity. 'East Coker' searches into an English family past, 'The Dry Salvages' into memories of a boyhood holiday and the American past. Each of these attempts is, in one way or another, a failure. 'Little Gidding' is most nearly a success because it is a seeking for home in a community of worship; because in Little Gidding all the most essential things—contemplation, worship, human and divine love, blend together with the most quiet and unobtrusive harmony, and lend to accidents of time and place a modest tranquillity of beauty. This 'home' is not a personal home, for neither Eliot nor his family were ever associated with Little Gidding; it is, as it were, an ideal pattern for the home which Eliot discovered in the Anglican Communion. A 'home' of this kind must have seemed especially important in the terror and uncertainty of the Second World War when 'Little Gidding' was written, and the fate of the community destroyed by war must have been particularly poignant when Little Gidding and all that it represented was in danger of total annihilation.

The poem begins with another natural paradox which in certain superficial ways is like the natural paradoxes of 'East Coker' II. But whereas in 'East Coker' the recrudescence of spring in the late autumn becomes something monstrous and disturbing, something totally unnatural, the 'Midwinter spring' of 'Little Gidding' has a rare and evanescent beauty which, though strange, is perfectly at home in nature, and entirely welcome. It is rather like the brief episode of the Little Gidding Community; an ephemeral incident of light in the surrounding darkness of war, an anomaly which stands outside the normal pattern of events, of spring, summer, autumn, winter, of bloodshed and brawling, and in its withdrawn simplicity is a criticism of the more usual pattern of the world. This detachment gives it a peculiar ambiguity in which it is both timeless and in time: 'Sempiternal though sodden towards sundown.' The latinate 'sempiternal' suggests strongly the influence of Dante at this point: it recalls a passage in the 'Paradiso', XII, where Dante and Beatrice are surrounded by two circles of lights like rainbows, a double crown of flames which are described thus:

> Così di quelle sempiterne rose
> volgeansi circa noi le due ghirlande,
> e sì l'estreme all' ultima rispose.
> (*Paradiso*, XII, 19–21)

(so the two garlands of sempiternal roses revolved around us, and so the outer one answered to the inner). This canto of the 'Paradiso' is referred to more than once in 'Little Gidding'; indeed its imagery and tone contribute greatly to the whole mood and pattern of the poem.

In a way the experience is like the filling of the pool and the rising of the lotos in 'Burnt Norton', before the cloud passes and takes the light away; there is a rapt quality, but none of the *visionary* excitement which makes the episode in 'Burnt Norton' finally a deception. This is no longer the soul catching fire from a spark of joy; neither is it the purgatorial agony of 'East Coker' or the near-despair and monotony of the drifting, leaking boat in 'The Dry Salvages'. It is a moment of peace, accepted for its beauty and accepted as a paradoxical hint of something even more beautiful, but it is not the kind of ecstasy which seems to be its own sufficient purpose.

The paradoxes of heat and cold which formed part of the structure of the highly-worked, perhaps over-worked, pattern in 'East Coker' IV return here, but to take their place in the sequence much more naturally:

When the short day is brightest, with frost and fire,
The brief sun flames the ice, on pond and ditches,
In windless cold that is the heart's heat.

But, whereas in 'East Coker' the heat of fever had been the objective
reality and the cold the subject's sensation, here the cold is the
objective fact, and the heat is not heat of fever, but 'the heart's heat',
the warmth of love responding to the stillness. The phrase is somewhat reminiscent of 'the heart of light' in *The Waste Land* and 'Burnt
Norton', but makes no claim to visionary truth, only to the capacity
for love, a more fitting beauty.

In the cycle of the vegetation myth the winter would be the time
of the death of a god, the period before his resurrection in the spring.
In the more ethereal myth of Christianity it might represent the time
of loneliness in which the Apostles waited for the witness that,
though Christ had indeed gone from earth, the Comforter was there
to guide them. Their 'dark time of the year' was lightened by the
Pentecostal fire of the Holy Ghost, and the Christian of any age may
repeat their experience: the Apostles gained the gift of tongues from
the Pentecostal fire; for Eliot it 'stirs the dumb spirit' into a new
eloquence.

The precarious balance of ice and fire, light and darkness, cold
and heat, which catches the elements in a suspension like the
suspension of time, mirrors the delicately poised state of the soul:
in 'Burnt Norton' II, the sap rises in the tree towards the summer of
ecstasy:

> The dance along the artery
> The circulation of the lymph
> Are figured in the drift of stars
> Ascend to summer in the tree.
>
> (*BN*, II)

In 'East Coker' II the ascending motion becomes an over-reaching
in 'hollyhocks that aim too high/Red into grey and tumble down'.
In the fever cure of *EC* IV, in which life is achieved through death,
it is 'the chill' which ascends to 'frigid purgatorial fires'. Here in
'Little Gidding', there is 'neither ascent nor decline' (*BN*, II), but
yet all the life and movement of the sap held in a trembling balance:
'Between melting and freezing/The soul's sap quivers.' The earth
smell of 'East Coker' I, the smell of 'dung and death' is absent, for
this is 'not in time's covenant'—the Covenant of the New Testament

promises a world out of time, of change, of decay. So the bloom is the bloom of snow on the hedgerows, as quick to come as it is to go, an image of the sudden unexpected timeless joy of the soul. It is not, however, the same experience as the experience in the rose garden of 'Burnt Norton'. The rose garden is a vision conjured by ghosts in a private world of the imagination and leaves behind the pain of desire. Here there is no visionary ecstasy: the natural world becomes the alphabet of communication; there is no elaborate piecing together of images of memory, and the emotion which the experience leaves behind is of peace and acceptance, not pain at loss and lingering desire. 'Burnt Norton' resolves discord briefly only to move into the discord of desire again, but this has a far finer and more lasting attunement of feeling.

The journey from the rose garden is motivated by desire; the rose garden and the other 'figures' of that desire are the 'deception of the thrush', and the final and only message of the bird is 'Go, go, go'— the expulsion from Paradise, the injunction to seek, not to *re-discover* the garden (though that is the memory which keeps your hope alive) but to seek that which will fulfil the promise of the garden:

> And what you thought you came for
> Is only a shell, a husk of meaning
> From which the purpose breaks only when it is fulfilled
> If at all.

The recollection of Charles I coming to Little Gidding after being defeated at Naseby is particularly apt here: the humility and love which Eliot describes here are, so often in the Christian tradition, generated in the fall of pride and power. In an even more profound sense the humility Eliot prescribes arises from a loss even more complete, of 'continual self-sacrifice, a continual extinction of personality' (*SE*, 17).

Here Eliot speaks in much the same way as he did of tradition in his early essays, though the dead's assertion of their immortality in the life of the living is much more complete and significant: it is tongued with the Pentecostal fire of the Holy Ghost, it is 'communication' in the etymological sense of binding together or making one, of participating in communion; in the sense of being possessed as the Apostles were, by the holy fire; and this is how tradition lives:

the communication
Of the dead is tongued with fire beyond the language of the
living

The opening of section II, the formal exercise, is a recapitulation of the whole sequence. The formality of the parallel sections in the preceding Movements has been complex and even deliberately complicating, and the various conceits have been developed to the point of over-loading, conveying a certain mild desperation at the insufficiency of words. These three stanzas in 'Little Gidding', however, round off with comparative simplicity and ease the structural metaphor of the four elements. The time of war is subtly present in the background, itself a metaphor for the violence and changeableness of the natural world. Fire, collapsing buildings, rubble, dust and the fireweed which spreads over the debris are familiar memories for anyone who lived in an English city during that war, but the chaos is wider than the war.

The roses of 'Burnt Norton' are destroyed by fire and earth. The 'dust on a bowl of rose-leaves' gathers upon the ephemeral joys of the rose garden. The sudden ecstasy of the spirit is succeeded by the mournful succession of change and decay in 'East Coker', the house of old Sir Thomas Elyot now dust in an open field. The ecstasy of spirit brings hope, and hope entails despair: hope and despair are killed by the sombre awareness of the constant flux of the natural world. But they are also killed by fire; fire as purgatory refines but destroys; by destroying hope it destroys despair too, and fulfils the hope. The 'old man' of 'Ash on an old man's sleeve' has the same doubleness of meaning as it has in 'Gerontion' and *The Waste Land*. The 'burnt roses' are a counter-image to the purgatorial fires 'of, which the flame is roses' (*EC*, IV); burnt roses—one might say Burnt Norton roses—remain as ash on the 'old man's sleeve', while 'the new man' enters into the rose which is born of the flame.

Earth itself is destroyed by water (as 'East Coker' is succeeded by 'The Dry Salvages'), but the water is spoken of in a rather odd way; it brings both 'flood and drouth'; it is 'dead water', just as the earth is 'dead sand'. 'Dead water' suggests its opposite, the waters of life, the waters of baptism; just as in the next stanza it is impossible to read of the deathliness of fire without remembering the Pentecostal fire and the purgatorial fire which are so important to the structure of the imagery. Air, earth, water and fire all play their part in the complete consort; their 'death' is only in one aspect, as part of the world of change which the old man inhabits.

> Water and fire shall rot
> The marred foundations we forgot,
> Of sanctuary and choir.

On one level this describes the ruins of London churches destroyed in the blitz, and many other churches destroyed in old wars; on another level it describes the new barbarism which Eliot felt to be sweeping across Europe and the world, destroying the ancient traditions, destroying the ritual, magical and religious view of life upon which civilization depends. But it would be quite wrong to regard this as simply historical commentary. Air, earth, water, fire are forces in the world of nature, but by metaphor they are the forces which attack and deprave the soul; the death of air, earth, water are fire are aspects of the death which afflicts the 'old man'. This kind of fire and water will destroy the forgotten foundations; but the subtle hint remains that the four elements, and particularly fire, may be in another manifestation the instruments of salvation:

> The only hope, or else despair
> Lies in the choice of pyre or pyre—
> To be redeemed from fire by fire.
>
> (LG, IV)

The ancient alchemists, in their search for the quintessence, the fifth essence, or the principle of life which lies beyond and behind the changing balance of the four material elements, discovered distillation and laid the foundations of modern chemistry. The *Four Quartets* themselves are a pattern of unity in diversity; the elements of which this unity is constructed, like air, earth, fire and water, are living poetry, 'but that which is only living can only die', unless they all assume and point to a quintessential reality. The chemistry of these three stanzas is, as it were, a distillation, a negative process by which each of the elements destroys its predecessor, until we are left with nothing which can be expressed by the material alphabet of the elements; what is left must either be nothing or everything. It was only by faith that the alchemists assumed their quintessence despite their repeated failure to isolate it; a similar faith is implied by the destructive process of the poetry here.

[271]

In the other quartets the compact formal study has been succeeded by a comparatively relaxed, sometimes almost spinelessly slack, commentary in a quasi-philosophical tone. There is no place for this in 'Little Gidding'—the formal study is a preparation for the greater compactness and organization of the second half of the Movement.

In its form, the passage is an imitation of Dante, though Eliot found that the English language did not adapt itself to the rhyming pattern of *terza rima*, and contented himself with an occasional and irregular chime of half-rhyme. Yet the technical problems he had to solve in this magnificent passage remained considerable, and he has declared that he took more trouble over it than over any other passage he had ever written. As 'Ash on an old man's sleeve' is a kind of recapitulation of *Four Quartets*, so the Dantesque passage is a kind of recapitulation of a whole life, and a whole view of life.

The titular symbolism of Little Gidding, a place tenuously and briefly out of war, is replaced by another place symbol—wartime London in a brief respite from bombing; the time-paradox of 'Midwinter spring' by another time-paradox, the ambiguous period between night and day—'the uncertain hour before the morning.' In clock time it is much the same as the time between midnight and dawn in 'The Dry Salvages' I, when anxious women worry about past and future; but in the time of the soul it is a very different kind of moment; a moment like that in which the Apostles awaited the midwinter spring of the Pentecost in the dark time after the Crucifixion. It is 'at the recurrent end of the unending', not simply because the dawn, which seems to end the night, only 'points' to another night, but because the ending of horror and death as the bombers depart is not a real conclusion—the horror and the death are still there, in all time. The outrageous comparison of the German bomber with the dove as icon of the Holy Ghost, makes the destructive world of time mimic darkly the visitation of life in the Holy Ghost. The 'flickering tongue' of the machine-guns mimics Pentecostal fire, identifies the dove, too, as the serpent of Genesis in a different guise. The 'dead leaves', which appeared in 'Burnt Norton' as the images of memory from which the mind constructs the ecstatic vision, continue to blow about the streets of the mind, disturbing its quiet stillness with their tinny unreal sounds; but it is as near to stillness as time can possibly be.

In the London metaphor the 'three districts' might be almost anywhere, the point is that this place is not in any one of the three, an ambiguous nowhere of the mind; and it is impossible to escape the suggestion that on another level the three districts are the three times—time past, time present and time future. This no-place of the mind in a temporary cessation of war, is also in no-time. Smoke rises from burning London; but the image recalls a usage which goes back as far as 'Burbank with a Baedeker'—*nil nisi divinum stabile est; caetera fumus,* and 'the smoky candle end of time', and has reappeared in 'East Coker' as the smoke of the purgatorial fires which becomes 'briars', the mixed image of sweetness and pain in the cure of death. London's burning; time's burning: the smoke is part of the shift and change of the Heraclitean flux; but the fire, though of death, can flower ephemerally into a reminder of something half-forgotten.

The whole passage so far prepares for a meeting; a meeting whose significance is partly created by the way in which it is prepared for. London, the place, recedes, together with all time and place, following the 'dark dove' in its homing. The meeting is only on a city street in an accidental and metaphorical sense; the meeting happens in a state of mind: it *is* the state of mind.

But it is one of the most abiding habits of the human mind to dramatize its moments of crisis, of enlightenment, of despair, of realization. 'I met one' is a dramatization of such a critical moment; as indeed was: 'I would meet you upon this honestly' in 'Gerontion' or the denials of 'one, settling a pillow by her head' in 'Prufrock'.

Perhaps the experience nearest to this one in Eliot's earlier verse is the episode of 'the third who walks always beside you' in the last section of *The Waste Land.* The 'one' is 'blown towards me like the metal leaves'; that is, like a memory returning to the mind; its appearance is unexpected, seemingly accidental, at first unrecognized, as was the appearance of Christ to the apostles on the road to Emmaus when 'their eyes were holden that they should not know him' (Luke 24: 16). Possibly, indeed, a Christian, from his point of view, may validly see a kind of identification between the 'one' of 'I met one' and Christ, or the Christian community. Both intimate and unidentifiable; for the Christian community Christ is necessarily an intimate presence; unidentifiable because all those who have entered the community have thus far surrendered their identity, becoming part of a composite family of the spirit: 'a familiar compound ghost'.

This experience of 'one and many' may be recognizable in

Christian terms. We may also understand it in other terms. Just as in some contexts, 'the Word' may be understood as the second person of the Trinity, in other contexts as the complex inheritance of tradition; so here the 'one' who is met in this no-place no-time of the mind can be thought of as the human tradition. And this would, in Eliot's way of thinking, approach the Christian interpretation; since Christ, or the Church, would be the embodiment of the whole community's culture; the centre upon which the tradition concentrates.

We may remember Gilbert Murray here, and think of the relationship between 'I' and the 'dead master' as like the relationship between the *Homeridae* and 'Homer'. The 'familiar compound ghost/Both intimate and unidentifiable' is thus the whole composite pattern of tradition; in its literary manifestations, Homer and Dante and Milton and Shakespeare and Donne and Flaubert and Conrad (and yet Eliot); in its theological manifestations Paul and Augustine and Aquinas and John of the Cross (and yet Eliot); in its philosophical manifestations Herakleitos and Plato and Aristotle and Bradley (and yet Eliot); in its ecclesiastical manifestations every Christian from Simeon onwards (and Eliot including them); there are innumerable other manifestations—altogether 'Both one and many'.

> So I assumed a double part, and cried
> And heard another's voice cry: 'What! are *you* here?'
> Although we were not. I was still the same,
> Knowing myself yet being someone other—
> And he a face still forming.

Here Eliot explores the outrageous paradox of identity which his attitudes towards past and present force upon him, with a calm and joyful wit. The paradoxes are by now absorbed and digested: one does not feel, as one might in 'Prufrock' or 'Gerontion', that the maker cannot fully understand his own puzzles. 'So I assumed a double part': in approaching the meeting with 'one', 'I' employs a dramatic fiction, knowing that it is a fiction. 'And cried/And heard another's voice cry': even as the dramatic division of the self occurs, there is a paradoxical recognition that 'I' no longer exists as 'I', but as something 'other'. '"What! are *you* here?"/Although we were not': 'I' no longer has any separate identity; by the same token, neither has 'you'; now 'I' and 'you' are both 'we', an identity which comprehends more than the single self, or that self doubled; but not 'here', for 'we' can only be in no-place, no-time: for the moment the war of place and time is suspended.

Even in this new kind of ecstasy, so much less unreal in its joy than the formal pattern of movement in the rose garden (perhaps *because* it is more real), there remains the paradox that 'I was still the same', though its sameness is in 'another's' aspect. We can use one of Eliot's favourite words for unfolding the paradox a little: the experience is an 'intersection' in which the 'I', the 'myself' may be known as continuing on one plane, but on another plane of the intersection there is something quite different, 'someone other'; and that 'someone other' is never the same, but always developing: 'And he a face still forming.' The 'he', or 'someone', which intersects 'I' at a moment of meeting continues to form as 'Homer' did with each of the *Homeridae*, as the community of Christ does with each new communicant, as 'the mind of Europe' does with every human experience within the European continuum of thought and feeling:

> yet the words sufficed
> To compel the recognition they preceded.
> And so, compliant to the common wind
> Too strange to each other for misunderstanding,
> In concord at this intersection time
> Of meeting nowhere, no before and after,
> We trod the pavement in a dead patrol.

The words 'strain,/Crack and sometimes break' under the burden of the paradox; and it is inevitable that the attempt to 'explain' them will cause difficulties. It will be sufficient for the moment to say that the 'recognition', or 'meeting' is an intense experience which is forced upon the mind by the hallucinatory fiction of dissociation: the sudden awareness that one is not simply an isolated being, but simultaneously a focus for a collective human identity, solves the division which the hallucinatory experience momentarily creates.

'And so, compliant to the common wind'; an echo of the 'Paradiso' re-inforces the newly won harmony:

> Poichè il tripudio e l'alta festa grande,
> sì del cantare e sì del fiammegiarsi
> luce con luce gaudiose e blande,
> insieme a punto ed a voler quetarsi
>
> (*Paradiso*, XII, 22–5)

(as soon as the spirited dancing and high great festival, both of singing and sparkling light with light, joyful and benign, accordant at a point of time and act of will, had stilled them.) The 'common wind' impels, not 'I' and 'you', but the new singleness which 'I' and 'you' merge into: the wind is a familiar image for the spirit which informs that common identity. It has appeared in 'Gerontion', where Mr Silvero and the rest, though 'vacant shuttles' in themselves, 'weave the wind'; in *The Waste Land* where, though the dead men rule, 'The wind/Crosses the brown land, unheard', and in this section of 'Little Gidding', where it is 'the urban dawn wind' which blows 'one' towards me, like the metal leaves of the memory.

The passage gains its intensity, in the first place, from the knotted tenseness of the experience communicated, from the difficulties which language places in the way of the communication; but it is neither the difficulty, nor the *precise* nature of the experience, which first holds the attention of the reader. In a passage such as the opening of *Ash Wednesday* V, Eliot deliberately draws attention to the insufficiencies of language, and to his own desperation with language as a tool. Here, where the problem of language is every bit as difficult, he seeks a slightly more oblique way into the problem. Again, as in the opening of 'Burnt Norton', he begins by raising ghosts; describing a situation which, even though we may not have experienced it with this kind of intensity, is known, whether as a fear or as strangely wonderful, as part of our imaginative life, or as part of our dreams. In *Ash Wednesday* V we are made to run head on into problems of language and meaning; here we are made to suspend our disbelief, and with it our anxious concern with language, our demand for a workaday precision, and to co-operate imaginatively in discovering and exploring a deeply felt need—a need which cannot easily be satisfied by a use of language which obeys the usual rules and seeks to protect itself against logical analysis.

To put it another way: Eliot is acting an essentially magical rôle, the rôle of the medium or the oracle at the mouth of the Underworld, reporting upon a dream which comes to him through 'the hornèd gate' of Virgil. In primitive societies this function is essential to the well-being and to the cohesion of the group. For instance, the Shamans of Malayan aborigine tribes still practice ritual oracular ceremonies in which they sing of their meetings with the strange and terrible spirits of their very complex otherworld. The practice is an essential one for the whole group: take it away and the group would die, the young, perhaps, migrating into another culture, the old hanging on to memories for a few years in a broken half-life. The oracular experience is as essential to the community as that other, central, definitive pattern which gives the tribe its coherence and identity, the language of the tribe.

As cultures move away from closely integrated magical structures such as these, other rituals take their place, but poetry is among the most conservative factors of cohesiveness, returning most easily to primitive ways of perceiving and organizing perception, and winning the greatest tolerance from its audience in doing so. We talk about the 'licence' of the poet, and part of what we mean is that we allow, even expect the poet to relate experiences and emotions which in other contexts would be dismissed as madness: we have learned how to allow certain sceptical and critical reactions to lie fallow while the poet speaks, if he speaks well. At the same time other kinds of critical activity are at their most lively as the poet persuades us of the power of his dream to discover areas of our experience which we commonly ignore, suppress or fear. We become more than normally aware of the extraordinary ways in which the organization of meaning, sound, rhythmical intonation and syntactical pattern may break an experience apart and re-build it in a new way.

Let us take the opening of the Dantesque passage. The first eight lines are devoted, apparently, to an elaborate definition of time and place, each clause beginning with a preposition of time and place: 'In', 'Near', 'At', 'After', 'While', 'Over', 'Between'; all suspending the reader's attention, as it were, with questions of where and when, before at last we are allowed to come to the question what; what happened? 'I met one' thus achieves a peculiar force. But even though the first eight lines are *formally* a definition of time and place, the internal paradoxes of the statements about time and place throw doubt upon time and place and subvert the forms of language in which they are cast. It is, for a start, an 'uncertain' hour. It is 'near the ending' of 'interminable' night. The paradox is repeated and extended; it is 'the recurrent end of the unending': the time is 'In', 'Near' and 'At' nothing remotely like the kind of time which we are used to ordering our lives by. Time is collapsed into an infinitely repeated series of approaches to an end which never comes. The paradox is partially expressed by the circularity and repetitiveness of sound—not an easy matter to analyse, but something to do with the awkward polysyllables, the recurrent negative prefix: 'un', 'in', 'un', and the changeable forms taken by 'end', one after the other: 'ending', 'end', 'unending', varied, but not relieved, by the intervening 'interminable':

> In the uncertain hour before the morning
> Near the ending of interminable night
> At the recurrent end of the unending

The total effect of this, and what follows, is to create a context for 'I met one, loitering and hurried', (with its air of formality and its trailing paradox) which makes of the meeting something much more than an accident of time; an inevitable happening, though unexpected; something implied by the dissolving of all the expected structures and relations of time and space.

The conversation between the poet and the master is most strongly reminiscent of Dante: one cannot help supplying the translations 'Io dissi' and 'ed egli a me' for 'I said' and 'And he'; and the reminiscence contributes a great deal to the tone and mood. With his guides, Virgil, Statius, Matilda, Beatrice, Dante is always attentive, quiet, full of wondering humility in his questioning; Virgil, particularly, becomes an embodiment of the poetic tradition, and Dante's humility that of a poet fully aware of his debt to the past. In his adaptation of Dante's tone Eliot has preserved the courteous formality even, or especially, when he speaks of the *ease* of the relationship: the rightness, and the strangeness, are those of an often repeated ritual relationship which constantly yields something new, while it is at the same time something always known:

> I said: 'The wonder that I feel is easy
> Yet ease is cause of wonder. Therefore speak:

—it is for this reason that any rehearsal of 'thoughts and theory' is inappropriate, except for the quiet hint that their best embodiment is in liturgy, the echo of the Lord's Prayer in:

> and pray they be forgiven
> By others, as I pray you to forgive
> Both bad and good.

There are few places in Eliot, indeed in any poet, where there is so natural and convincing a harmony between the earthy image, rich in suggestion and in energy of language and the neatly generalized epigrammatic statement as in the passage which follows:

> Last season's fruit is eaten
> And the fullfed beast shall kick the empty pail.
> For last year's words belong to last year's language
> And next year's words await another voice.

and part of their ease, and their authority, lies in the way they follow on from the adaptation of a familiar ritual. The Lord's Prayer is the only piece of ritual which most speakers of the English language know; it is associated in a profound way with our whole experience, with growing up, with our first experiences of authority and education, with our first encounters with traditional wisdom and institutional folly; it is the first magical formula we learn, and it is the last we forget. When it is alluded to in this way it transfers some of its authority to the words it is associated with.

But the images and ideas which follow have a less direct relationship to our accustomed experience:

> But, as the passage now presents no hindrance
> To the spirit unappeased and peregrine
> Between two worlds become much like each other,
> So I find words I never thought to speak
> In streets I never thought I should revisit
> When I left my body on a distant shore.

A less *direct* relationship, but one which we can imaginatively perceive without difficulty. Even if we suppress memories of literature in which similar visitations occur; Odysseus conjuring Tiresias, Hamlet's father returning to Elsinore, Yeats invoking the sages of Byzantium; even if we can manage to forget the vestigial remains of magical belief, the superstitious doubts which mediums, astrologers and palmists feed upon, there is no-one, I suppose, who has not become uneasy for a moment when listening to a ghost story, or who has not, for a moment, fancied the presence of the dead at his side, or behind him. Eliot's conjuration is not meant simply to produce a pleasurable *frisson* of anxiety, nor simply to fulfil and comfort our primitive need for assurance that there is a life after death, another world in which we shall continue to live, in some way more real than we are in this. It is rather to assure us that the past re-asserts itself

[279]

in our present, especially in those moments when we are most fully *aware*. And these moments are, precisely, the moments of poetry:

> Since our concern was speech, and speech impelled us
> To purify the dialect of the tribe.

Eliot borrows and adapts from Mallarmé: 'Donner un sens plus pur aux mots de la tribu', but his own usage has a much more comprehensive import. 'Speech', in the context of the whole of *Four Quartets*, expands in meaning to refer, not only to the accidental forms of human language, but to all those complex and related significances which cluster around *logos* or 'the Word': the interpenetration of the human and the divine, the one truth which the visible world half conceals and half reveals, the curious mysteries which human language stubbornly insists upon despite the consistent critical effort of reason. 'To purify the dialect of the tribe' is thus to refresh the language of humans continually, as poets must do; but to do it in such a way that language is brought more closely into contact with these resilient assumptions (irrational though they may be) which control our behaviour in ways so subtle that we cannot always determine them.

The bitter prophecy of 'the gifts reserved for age', pursued with such pressing rhetorical urgency (the power of the rhetoric and the assumed authority of prophetic utterance make it difficult for us to protest at the half-truth) is redeemed, at least in part, by the 'unless', so carefully delayed until the conclusion of the prophetic statement

> 'unless restored by that refining fire
> Where you must move in measure, like a dancer.'

There is no need at this point to comment again on the significance of 'that refining fire' or the measured pattern of the dancer (with its memories of Sir John Davies, Sir Thomas Elyot, 'East Coker', Yeats). The form of words, or something like it, is made inevitable by the whole developing pattern of *Four Quartets*, and its inevitability, our sense that we can trust to the resolution of doubt and pain in this or some such way, is part of the success of the poem. From here onwards the 'complete consort' moves with a firm and natural step towards resolution in a perfect cadence.

Meanwhile, however, there is a return to the time and place of war. The quiet word-play of 'disfigured' recalls the usage of 'figured' in 'Burnt Norton' and elsewhere, suggesting the swift, distorting

[280]

change from enchanted design to the uncertainties of time: and yet the baffled paradoxes of 'the recurrent end of the unending' are broken by the dawn:

> The day was breaking. In the disfigured street
> He left me, with a kind of valediction,
> And faded on the blowing of the horn.

The last line suggests, at first, many romantic or magical memories; but in a world of fact it is a very unromantic thing that is referred to, the signal 'All clear' which announced the return to 'normality' in the war years, if you can describe the continued state of abnormal tension and unease endured by Londoners during the early part of the war, a 'normal' state.

The third movement of 'Little Gidding' is concerned with the problems of personal salvation, certainly; but the quality of Eliot's concern here is deeply affected by the time at which he wrote. The strength or depth of his early commitment to an ascetic ideal has, I believe, always been faintly suspect; a means of justifying a peevish distaste, a boredom and a horror which is not so much born of a shrewd understanding as of a moral failure; there is at times too much facility in the anguish of 'Preludes', 'Rhapsody on a Windy Night', *The Waste Land* and 'The Hollow Men'; Tiresias is a shadow far more than that other revenant, the Marlow of *Heart of Darkness*. But in 'Little Gidding' Eliot approaches the problems of humanity with greater dignity. It is true that the prophecy of the 'dead master' gives a dark account of the terrors of age ('unless . . .'); but part of its terror, the greatest part, is the discovery of one's human failures; arrogance, lack of understanding, ignorance both of one's own motives and other people's needs:

> Of motives late revealed, and the awareness
> Of things ill done and done to others' harm
> Which once you took for exercise of virtue.

The third movement consolidates this move away from ascetic discipline as *escape* from emotion; it is no longer 'wait without love/ For love would be love of the wrong thing', that chill heresy of a twilight war; it is *indifference* which is the enemy now. There is at least a new emphasis here, a contention that divine love and human love share something, that each enforces the other. The emphasis, in 'Gerontion', upon the deceptiveness of history has mutated into

'History may be servitude,/History may be freedom', an aphorism which, by itself, might be merely facile, but is given depth by the very sensitive reflections upon history and patriotism which precede and follow it.

Dame Julian of Norwich had written in *Revelations of Divine Love* of Christ's words to her in a vision: 'Synne is behovabil, but al shal be wel & al manner of thying shal be wel'; 'behovabil', and Eliot's nonce-word 'behovely' mean useful or necessary: thus Julian's prophecy discovers comfort in the necessity of the *felix culpa*, the happy fall of Adam which lost man the earthly paradise, but gained Christ and the promise of heaven for man. The traditional emotion, cast as it is in the warm, but distant words of a woman long dead, prompt the effort to revalue the past, not in terms of ideas or actions, wars or policies, parties or principles, but in terms of people, made familiar by an urgent sense of their nearness in this time, which could well have been, as Eliot was writing, the end of English history. Love of country becomes transfigured through love of people, an imaginative re-living of history issues in a new awareness of the present.

Eliot is careful to avoid identifying the people he remembers too precisely. For good reason: the people of 'this place' are clearly enough the Community of Little Gidding; but their plight and their strength is at the same time a kind of ideal model for England at war 'not wholly commendable . . . some of peculiar genius,/All touched by a common genius,/United in the strife which divided them.' The king at nightfall certainly suggests Charles I escaping from Naseby, 'three men, and more, on the scaffold' might suggest many sufferers in the turbulent England of the Civil Wars, 'one who died blind and quiet' aptly recalls the blind Milton. But at the same time each phrase, in its careful lack of definition, recalls Christ, 'the common genius' which achieves the 'constitution of silence.' Eliot is, certainly, reflecting upon history. At the same time he is transforming history into something which is useful in a particular way to a turbulent present: 'We have taken from the defeated/What they had to leave us—a symbol:/A symbol perfected in death.' Over and above this he is shaping both history and symbol as metaphor for a Christian ideal; what gives power to the symbol as consolation is the way in which all these men imperfectly imitate Christ, and perspective may fulfil the imitation more perfectly. What Eliot is doing, above all, is enabling himself to return to Julian's words with a more achieved sense of the interpenetration of the human and the divine, a sense of the necessity of sin, but yet its ultimate defeat by an attentive self-knowledge; a self knowledge which is bound in with a sense of history; a sense of history and a self-knowledge only achieved through love.

The formal exercise, section IV, is one of the few lyrics in which Eliot was ever able to be convincing in an entirely formal stanzaic pattern. One is reminded strongly of the devotional poems of George Herbert; and fittingly, not only because Herbert knew the Little Gidding Community well, but because Herbert's peculiar blend of verbal ingenuity and quiet humility, of passionate emotion and calm acceptance, of terror and doubt resolving into complete acquiescence, strikes precisely the kind of religious note which Eliot himself seeks to strike in 'Little Gidding'.

And yet the relationship between the mode of parable, the use of emblem, the strict form, and the emotions they carry, is radically different from Herbert's practice in a significant and subtle way. The only line which could have found a natural place in a poem by Herbert is 'Who then devised the torment? Love'; a consonance between the two poets remarkable enough in itself. But the whole world of feeling differs by just the same degree as England before the Civil Wars differs from England after the Battle of Britain. The blend of consonance and dissonance is sought deliberately; no kind of imaginative sympathy can reproduce the world of Nicholas Ferrar and George Herbert; but it may bring the two worlds, separated by so much time, into a contact which enriches our experience of both.

Perhaps the most striking difference between the two poets is in Herbert's confidence; a confidence which allows him to re-affirm by understatement, by quiet speech which in its simplicity acts out humility and recovered innocence:

> You must sit down, sayes Love, and taste my meat:
> So I did sit and eat.

whereas the pressure of anguish and doubt in Eliot expresses itself in an abnormal artifice of form, and in a deliberate seeking after words and phrases whose relative unfamiliarity arrests the attention: 'incandescent terror', 'the choice of pyre or pyre', 'suspire'. In 'The Collar' or 'Affliction' the point at which Herbert convinces us most is the point at which he stops insisting upon anguish and frustration of will and desire; Eliot, on the other hand, presses the point by a heightening of anguish, and a tightening formalization of language:

> The dove descending breaks the air
> With flame of incandescent terror
> Of which the tongues declare
> The one discharge from sin and error.
> The only hope, or else despair
>> Lies in the choice of pyre or pyre—
>> To be redeemed from fire by fire.

The assertive urgency is bound up with, and partly justified by, the war metaphor: the images of the dove and the fire have ambiguous and simultaneous reference to the eternal and the temporal, to an ideal beauty and a destructive horror. The 'dark dove', the enemy plane of Movement II, was the carrier of death; the dove of the Holy Ghost is the bearer of life. The dark dove brought incendiary bombs, and, since its flickering tongue makes it a kind of serpent, the fire of Hell. The light dove brings the flames of Pentecostal fire, the fire of inspiration and purification. The composite image, the dove both light and dark, brings with it the whole dilemma of man: choice; and each possibility that can be chosen is terrible, like a fire.

The shirt of Nessus killed Hercules; that hero chose to escape from the 'intolerable shirt of flame' by burning himself on a funeral pyre, and became a god. Once more the theme of death and resurrection returns; but the paradox that Nessus (who hated Hercules) is replaced by Love, intensifies the paradox of insurrection—that life lies in death to oneself. There's an odd word-play here: 'suspire' appears to mean 'live'; but it really means to sigh or yearn; a subsidiary meaning is to breathe. Thus the process of living is made to be a continual process of longing, whether it is the light dove or the dark which brings the fires of torment.

> Who then devised the torment? Love.
> Love is the unfamiliar Name
> Behind the hands that wove
> The intolerable shirt of flame
> Which human power cannot remove
>> We only live, only suspire
>> Consumed by either fire or fire.

Compare 'The dove descending' with a characteristic piece of Herbert, no less complex than Eliot, though its vocabulary is simple and its syntax that of everyday speech. The complexity of the Herbert arises from the subtle difficulty of the moral problems it describes, and from the delicate awareness of a mind sensitive to those problems.

> He that is weary, let him sit.
>> My soul would stirre
> And trade in courtesies and wit,
>> Quitting the furre
> To cold complexions needing it.
>
> Man is no starre, but a quick coal
>> Of mortall fire:
> Who blows it not, nor doth controll
>> A faint desire,
> Lets his own ashes choke his soul.
>
> ('Employment')

The reason why 'The dove descending' is so very much more laborious in its poise is, perhaps, because the civilization within which Eliot works is so much less ordered in its structures, more tolerant, indeed encouraging, of headlong change, and shyness of stasis shows itself in a flight away from elaborate doctrinal structures. In a critical and subversive age poets like Eliot and Pound were forced towards ellipsis and discontinuity as a kind of formal mirror to doubt and disorder; there is no doubt that they echoed a feeling of excited disorientation in their audience. The *Four Quartets* is, in large part, an attempt to reverse the flight; but the effort to establish the form is sometimes too constricting, just as the effort to assert a doctrinal view occasionally comes too near the surface.

The first twelve lines of the fifth Movement, then, describe a harmony, a beauty of order, which in one sense is better achieved by Herbert (among other poets) than it is by Eliot in *Four Quartets*, but Eliot knew this:

> And what there is to conquer
> By strength and submission, has already been discovered
> Once or twice, or several times, by men one cannot hope
> To emulate—but there is no competition—
> There is only the fight to recover what has been lost
> And found and lost again and again.
>
> (*EC*, V)

This sense of the instability of achievement in poetry is still present in *Little Gidding*: 'Every phrase and every sentence is an end and a beginning/Every poem an epitaph'. Poetry is part of transition, and has all the insecurity of transitory effort, particularly in an age of war; but like all human effort, it is reconciled in something more important; we each contribute to a human tradition, a human unity.

> We die with the dying
> See, they depart, and we go with them.
> We are born with the dead:
> See, they return, and bring us with them.

Once we are aware of this, history ceases to be anything to do with time, 'a pattern/of timeless moments . . . /History is now and England.'

If this is true, the instability of achievement does not matter: it does not matter that the ecstasy we remember has gone, never to return, just as it no longer matters that the man who wrote the poem is dead, the poem his epitaph. The exploration continues in every moment; the re-discovery is there in every moment.

And so it is appropriate that images from 'Burnt Norton' should re-appear: 'the unknown, remembered gate'; 'the children', now in an apple tree borrowed from the popular tradition of Paradise; and the song of the bird: 'Quick now here, here, now, always.'

Four Quartets begins with a memory (and Eliot doesn't hope to give us the memory as his, but as our own); a memory which is full of affirmation, but which disappears as you turn to look at it. It goes on to speak of the search to fulfil that memory through destroying it, and destroying all the joy and longing and desire and sorrow which goes with such memories. At last it returns to the memory, to the affirmation, but now bound in with the negation, each as part of the other; despite the paradox, not a complex state:

> A condition of complete simplicity
> (Costing not less than everything)

The comforting words of Dame Julian, 'And al shal be wel', follow the moral paradox 'Synne is behovabil', and point to the resolution of the paradox. The *Four Quartets*, too, ends by pointing to such a resolution, a resolution which goes beyond affirmation and negation. The metaphor of resolution draws together many memories (though it sings perfectly well on its own):

[286]

And all shall be well and
All manner of thing shall be well
When the tongues of flame are in-folded
Into the crowned knot of fire
And the fire and the rose are one.

The tongues of flame recall the Pentecostal fire; they recall, too, the way in which Eliot has spoken of the 'dead masters' of the human tradition, those whose language, after their death, is 'tongued with fire'. And it recalls Dante's request that he might remember something of Heaven:

> e fa la lingua mia tanto possente,
> ch'una favilla sol della tua gloria
> possa lasciare alla futura gente.
> *(Paradiso*, XXXIII, 70–2)

(and give my tongue such power that it can leave behind for the people of the future just a single spark of flame of Thy glory.)

Later on in the same Canto Dante speaks of the eternal light of heaven enfolding all the accidental detail of experience, fusing all into one reality:

> Nel suo profondo vidi che s'interna
> legato con amore in un volume,
> ciò che per l'universo si squaderna;
> sustanzia ed accidenti, e lor costume
> quasi conflati insieme per tal modo,
> che ciò ch'io dico è un semplice lume
> *(Paradiso*, XXXIII, 85–90)

(In its depths I saw gathered in, bound by love into one volume, all that is read throughout the universe; substance and accidents and their relations, as if fused together in such a way that what I speak of is one simple flame.)

The image chosen by Dante to describe that unity is the image of a rose; the image he chooses to describe the purifying process which is necessary before he may see the rose is the image of the fire. Eliot combines the two images in his concluding lines. But the relationship with Dante is far more complex than a mere borrowing. There are points in Eliot's verse where Eliot's imagery has become almost parasitic upon Dante; where, as in 'The Hollow Men', the 'multifoliate Rose' has little meaning in itself, and one must resort to Dante for explanation. In *Four Quartets*, however, rose and flame have appeared in so many mutations, gathering meaning on each occasion, acquiring evocative resonances and subtleties of tone, that here at the end the images act as summation of the complex experience of the poem. Eliot does not presume, like Dante, to speak of this 'one' which fire and rose create, as something which has been known: the tense is future (but the poem's critique of time alters the way we think of the future tense by now); the journey is incomplete (but 'In my end is my beginning' alters our sense of direction); the experience remains, as it was in 'Burnt Norton', elusive and at the same time ever-present: 'Quick now, here, now, always'; but at last we have been shown how here and now and always, are (if we are quick to see it) infolded into one.

NOTES

CHAPTER ONE

1 F. H. Bradley, *Essays on Truth and Reality*, Oxford, 1914, p. 277.
2 F. H. Bradley, *Appearance and Reality*, 2nd edn, 9th imp. (corrected) Oxford, 1930, p. 148.
3 *Ibid.*, p. 306.
4 P. E. More, *The Greek Tradition*, vol. III, *The Christ in the New Testament*, Princeton, 1924, p. 2.
5 Irving Babbitt, *Democracy and Leadership*, Boston and New York, 1924, p. 161.
6 Irving Babbitt, *The New Laokoon*, London, 1910, p. 226.
7 P. E. More, *The Greek Tradition*, introductory volume, *Platonism*, Princeton, 1917, p. 181.
8 P. E. More, in a letter to T. S. Eliot, quoted by A. H. Dakin in *Paul Elmer More*, Princeton, 1960, p. 290.
9 F. H. Bradley, *Appearance and Reality*, p. 151.
10 F. H. Bradley, *Essays on Truth and Reality*, p. 175. Quoted by Eliot in *KE*, 21.
11 Irving Babbitt, *Rousseau and Romanticism*, Boston and New York, 1919, pp. 220–39. (Though this book was published in 1919, it seems to be based on lectures delivered at an earlier date.)
12 St Augustine, *Confessions*, III, i.
13 T. S. Eliot, 'Beyle and Balzac', *Athenaeum*, 30 May 1919, p. 393.
14 F. H. Bradley, *Appearance and Reality*, p. 150.
15 *Ibid.*, p. 158.

CHAPTER THREE

1 Irving Babbitt, *Democracy and Leadership*, p. 34.
2 *Ibid.*, p. 35.

3 W. B. Yeats, 'Discoveries' (1906) reprinted in *Essays and Introductions*, London, 1961, p. 284.

4 Gilbert Murray, *The Rise of the Greek Epic*, 4th edn, 1934, p. 178.

5 *Ibid.*, p. 94.

6 *Ibid.*, pp. 255–6.

7 James Joyce, *A Portrait of the Artist as a Young Man*, (Penguin edn), Harmondsworth, 1960, p. 214.

8 From *Promenades Philosophiques* (1905–8). I have no access to this work at the time of writing, but Ezra Pound quotes it in the original French in his essay 'Rémy de Gourmont', reprinted in *Literary Essays of Ezra Pound*, London, 1960, p. 353.

9 Rémy de Gourmont, *Le Problème du Style*, 14th edn, Paris, 1924, p. 107 quoted in *SE*, 217–18.

10 T. S. Eliot, 'Literature, Science and Dogma', *Dial*, Vol. lxxxii, no. 3, March 1927, p. 243.

11 F. M. Cornford, *From Religion to Philosophy*, (Harper Torchbook edn), New York and Evanston, 1957, p. 187. Originally published in 1912.

12 Lancelot Andrewes, *XCVI Sermons*, 1629, p. 112.

CHAPTER FOUR

1 G. K. L. Morris in *Partisan Review*, vol. xxi, no. 2, 1954, and Mrs Eliot in *FT*, p. 125–6.

2 Leonard Unger, 'The Rose Garden', in *T. S. Eliot, Moments and Patterns*, Minneapolis, 1966, pp. 69–91.

3 Origen, *The Song of Songs, Commentary and Homilies*, tr. R. P. Lawson, London, 1957, p. 21.

4 Arthur Edward Waite, *The Pictorial Key to the Tarot*, New York, 1960, p. 116. (Originally published 1910.)

5 St John of the Cross, *The Complete Works*, tr. and ed. E. Allison Peers, new edn, London, 1953, vol. I, p. 34.

6 John Webster, *The Duchess of Malfi*, III. 2.

7 Irving Berlin and Ted Snyder, *That Mysterious Rag*, London, n.d. First copyrighted in 1911.

8 *Theologia Germanica*, tr. Susanna Winkworth, New York, 1949, p. 328.

9 Joseph Conrad, *Heart of Darkness*, collected edition, London, 1946, p. 162.

10 *Ibid.*, pp. 93–6.

11 Bernard Bergonzi, 'Maps of the Waste Land', *Encounter*, vol. xxxviii, no. 4, April 1972, p. 81.

12 Sir James G. Frazer, *The Golden Bough*, 3rd edn, London, 1963, vol. IV, ii, p. 5.

13 Fyodor Dostoevski, *The Brothers Karamazov*, tr. Constance Garnett, London, 1912, XI, 8.

14 St John of the Cross, op. cit., vol. II, p. 307.
15 *Pervigilium Veneris*, 85–90.
16 Thomas Kyd, *The Spanish Tragedy*, IV, i.

CHAPTER FIVE

1 T. S. Eliot (a review of), *The Growth of Civilisation*, and *The Origin of Magic and Religion*, by W. J. Perry, *Criterion* vol. ii, no. 8, July, 1924, pp. 489–91.
2 Jane Ellen Harrison, *Epilegomena to the Study of Greek Religion and Themis*, 2nd edn, New York, 1962, p. xliii.
3 Harrison, *op. cit.*, p. xliv.
4 Harrison, *op. cit.*, p. xlviii.
5 T. S. Eliot, 'War Paint and Feathers', *Athenaeum*, no. 4669, 17 October 1919, p. 1036.
6 Harrison, *op. cit.* p. 43.
7 Lancelot Andrewes, *Sermons*, selected and ed. G. M. Storey, Oxford, 1962, p. 120.
8 St John of the Cross, *The Complete Works*, tr. and ed. E. Allison Peers, new edn, London, 1953, vol. I, p. 104.
9 St John of the Cross, *op. cit.*, vol. I, p. 105–6.
10 F. M. Cornford, *From Religion to Philosophy*, New York and Evanston, 1957, p. 187. (Originally published in 1912).

CHAPTER SIX

1 T. S. Eliot, 'The Possibility of a Poetic Drama', *Dial*, vol. lxix, November 1920, p. 442. (Reprinted in *The Sacred Wood*.)
2 T. S. Eliot, 'The Poetic Drama', *Athenaeum*, No. 4692, 2 April 1920, pp. 441–2.
3 F. M. Cornford, *The Origin of Attic Comedy*, ed. Theodore H. Gaster, New York, 1961, pp. 4–5. (Originally published in 1914.)
4 E. Martin Browne, *The Making of T. S. Eliot's Plays*, Cambridge, 1969.
5 *The Times*, 29 May 1934, quoted by Browne, *op. cit.*, p. 32.
6 Jane Harrison, *Themis*, Cleveland, Ohio, 1962, pp. 340–63.
7 Gilbert Murray, 'Excursus on the Ritual Forms Preserved in Greek Tragedy' in Jane Harrison, *Themis*, pp. 343–4.
8 Richard Hooker, *The Laws of Ecclesiastical Polity*, Vol. I, iii, pp. 1–2.
9 E. Martin Browne, *op. cit.*, p. 76.
10 *The Song of the Lord*, tr. Edward J. Thomas, London, 1931, IV, 18–20, pp. 49–50.
11 E. Martin Browne, *op. cit.*, p. 154.
12 Sir Thomas Browne, *Religio Medici*, LI.

13 E. Martin Browne, *op. cit.*, p. 233.

14 T. S. Eliot, 'Religious Drama: Ancient and Modern', *University of Edinburgh Journal*, vol. ix, Autumn 1937, p. 13.

15 E. Martin Browne, *op. cit.*, p. 107.

16 E. Martin Browne, *op. cit.*, p. 107.

17 Gilbert Murray, 'Excursus', in Jane Harrison, *Themis*, p. 344.

18 J. P. Hodin, 'The Condition of Man Today. An Interview with T. S. Eliot', *Horizon* vol. xii, no. 68, August 1945, p. 88.

19 E. Martin Browne, *op. cit.*, pp. 184 and 200.

20 E. Martin Browne, *op. cit.*, p. 186.

21 E. Martin Browne, *op. cit.*, p. 311.

CHAPTER SEVEN

1 Gerard Manley Hopkins, *The Journals and Papers of Gerard Manley Hopkins*, ed. Humphrey House, completed by Graham Storey, London, 1959, pp. 125–6.

2 St Augustine, *Confessions*, XI, 20.

3 *Ibid.*, XI, 18.

4 *Ibid.*, XII, 31.

5 Sa'd-uddin Mahmud Shabistari, *The Secret Rose Garden*, tr. Florence Lederer, London, 1920, p. 29.

6 Shabistari, *op. cit.*, p. 46.

7   The enthusiasm that has marked the modern movement has plainly not been sufficiently critical. Perhaps the first discovery that any one will make who wishes to be at once critical and enthusiastic is that in a genuine spiritual enthusiasm the inner light and the inner check are practically identical. He will find that if he is to rise above the naturalistic level he must curb constantly his expansive desires with reference to some centre that is set above the flux. Here let me repeat is the supreme rôle of the imagination. The man who has ceased to lean on outer standards can perceive his new standards or centre of control only through its aid. I have tried to show that to aim at such a centre is not to be stagnant and stationary but on the contrary at once purposeful and progressive. . . . Life is at best a series of illusions; the whole office of philosophy is to keep it from degenerating into a series of delusions. If we are to keep it from thus degenerating we need to grasp above all the difference between the eccentric and the concentric imagination.
    Irving Babbit, *Rousseau and Romanticism*, Boston and New York, 1919, p. 258.

8 St John of the Cross, *The Complete Works*, tr. and ed. E. Allison Peers, new edn, London, 1953, vol I, p. 234.

9 *Ibid.*, p. 238.

10 *Ibid.*, p. 59.

11 John Donne, Meditation XVII, in *Devotions upon Emergent Occasions.*

12 *The Bhagavad Gita*, IX, 9 (tr. Edward J. Thomas).

13 Francis Maurice Cornford, *From Religion to Philosophy*, New York and Evanston, 1957, p. 188. (Originally published in 1912.)

INDEX OF WORKS BY ELIOT

(The principal references are in *italic* type)

[295]

GENERAL INDEX